GUARDIANS OF THE LIGHTS

GUARDIANS OF THE LIGHTS

The Men and Women of the U.S. Lighthouse Service

Elinor DeWire

PINEAPPLE PRESS, INC.
SARASOTA, FLORIDA

For my mother, Ruth R., and my father, Richard H.

Inquiries should be addressed to:
    Pineapple Press, Inc.
    P.O. Drawer 16008
    Southside Station
    Sarasota, Florida 34239

LIBRARY OF CONGRESS CATALOGING IN PUBLICATION DATA

De Wire, Elinor, 1953-
    Guardians of the Lights: The Men and Women of the U.S. Lighthouse Service / Elinor De Wire. — 1st ed.
        p.   cm.
    Includes index.
    ISBN 1-56164-077-8 (alk. paper)
    1. Lighthouse keepers—United States—History. 2. Lighthouse keepers—United States—Family relationships. 3. Lighthouses—United States—History. 4. United States. Bureau of Light-Houses.
    I. Title.
    VK1023.D4   1995
    387.1'55'092273—dc20   94-42571
    [B]   CIP

First Edition
10 9 8 7 6 5 4 3 2 1

Design by Cynthia Keenan
Printed and bound by Edwards Brothers, Ann Arbor, Michigan

CONTENTS

ACKNOWLEDGMENTS

The diversity of stories and personalities in this book is the culmination of 20 years of research and interviews. Weaving together all that I have read, heard, and seen was a joyful but sometimes challenging experience that would not have been possible without the help and encouragement of many people.

Thanks go to Ken Black, director of the Shore Village Museum in Rockland, Maine, who has been a constant friend and compatriot in my pursuit of this story; Wayne Wheeler and the staff of the U.S. Lighthouse Society in San Francisco for holding up a beacon to light my way on this journey; the Coast Guard Public Affairs Officers for generously sending photos and other materials and lending me the keys to many lighthouses; Valarie Kinkaid and the helpful staff of the U.S. Coast Guard Academy Library and U.S. Coast Guard Museum; my good friend Richard DeAngelis for his reproduction of archival photos and his unflagging friendship and devotion to my work; Lloyd Treworgy and Larry Anderson for loaning me their words and Don Treworgy for his sensitivity to my need to write; Brae Rafferty and the crew at Project Oceanology for a memorable trip to Ledge Light; Barbara Gaspar and Marjorie Pendleton for their warm remembrances and visits; Susan Peters and Connecticut Public Television for preserving conversations with New England lightkeepers; Connie Small for hours of good conversation and great apple pie; Willie Emerson and Georgia Norwood Emerson for sharing their memories and taking photos; Philmore Wass and Harold Jennings for pictures and stories from their youth; Sarah Gleason for kindly providing interview material; Linda King for her many letters and materials on St. Simons Light; Stephen Jones for encouragement and his candid memories and pictures; Jack Hettinger and Harry Blackdeer for pictures of lighthouses; Nadine and Jerry Tugel for their letters from Battery Point; Raymond "Skip" Empey for a memorable trip to Boston Light; June and David Cussen and the crew at Pineapple Press for getting me through the publication process and making my work available to readers; and to many more friends who have encouraged, sometimes prodded, but always applauded my work.

Special thanks go to my husband, Jonathan, and my children, Jessica and Scott, who always indulge my "bright" preoccupations with patience and love and have traveled many miles with me to visit lighthouses and their keepers.

PROLOGUE

Everybody loves lighthouses.
—Wayne Wheeler
President, U.S. Lighthouse Society

The lighthouse stood on an island a mile off the mouth of the Kennebec River, Maine, an alabaster tower showing a beacon 186 feet above the Atlantic. Its brilliant, cyclopean eye rolled around in its head as if scanning the sea for a ship in distress, or at the very least a small fishing boat headed back to the sleepy town of Bath after a day of lobstering. There was no sun in the late afternoon sky on that January day in 1972, and the wind coming in from the sea cut my face, rubbing salt into my skin until it stung almost intolerably. I had heard somewhere that lighthouse keepers' wives thought the briny sea air was good for their complexions. I'd also been told that long ago, in this lighthouse on Sequin Island, a lightkeeper had murdered his wife in a fit of anger because she could play only one song on the piano.

Sequin Lighthouse, one of the oldest in Maine and the most elevated of the lights Down East, took its name from an Abnaki word meaning "to spit into the sea." This was the first authentic, working lighthouse I had ever seen, a nostalgic image like one in a storybook I loved as a child, except that Sequin Lighthouse had no mermaid reposing on its rocks, combing her emerald hair with a sprig of coral. I listened to the solemn moan of the foghorn, which came at regular intervals to help mariners distinguish it from the other horns along this part of the coast. The drone and flash were so hypnotic I failed to notice a rogue wave creeping up the rock ledge at my feet. It sprang high and hurled itself over my head. Drenched and shivering, I retreated, but not before the image of the lighthouse, probing the purple twilight with its dazzling beam, had burned itself into my soul.

A decade later and 3000 miles from Maine, I watched from a cliff at Point Bonita as a bank of dense fog approached the Golden Gate. Its gray, cinereous vapors clutched the shore within min-

Though clear and sunny in this photo, the Golden Gate's Point Bonita Lighthouse sees its share of fog. The sentinel shines through the murk about 20% of the year. Fogbanks roll in from sea rapidly, setting off the station's clamorous foghorns and causing rocks to loosen from its cliffs. (U.S. Coast Guard)

utes, gliding over the rocks, the scrub pines and footbridge, snuffing out what had been a bright, pleasant August afternoon. From the misty pall came the hoarse groans of the foghorns, the wildcat screeching of fog sirens, the clang and bang and bong of fogbells — the symphony of San Francisco Bay in poor visibility. With a mechanized hum, the beacon inside Point Bonita Lighthouse awoke, spilling its amber light over the Golden Gate and the seemingly endless waters beyond.

Behind me, the headlights of cars leaving the dirt parking area flashed on, their halogen rays bouncing off the minuscule droplets of fog. As I readjusted my stance against the railing along the cliff, some rocks loosened under my feet, tumbled downward with a clatter, and disappeared into the unseen chasm below. The end of their journey was confirmed seconds later by a faraway "splash."

It wasn't always a foot that set off these miniature avalanches of rock. The deafening concussion of the Point Bonita fog signal could also cause them. The cliff here has rumbled and shuddered from numerous earthquakes, including the devastating 1906 San Francisco earthquake; but mostly it has eroded from the scouring of wind and water, aided by the intense vibrations of cannons, bells, horns, and whistles. Little by little, pebble and cobble, the cliff has been crumbled away by the interminable din. Lightkeepers learned to sleep with the noise, to pause in their conversations whenever the signal sounded, even to live with pictures hanging awry on the walls and flatware dancing about on the kitchen table — all because of the Golden Gate's recalcitrant fog.

It was all very romantic, I thought — a lighthouse standing by the sea to guide home the weary sailor, and the lighthouse keeper in the lantern, trimming the wicks and keeping a solitary watch for a ship in trouble. Fog, storms, shipwrecks, rescues — what an adventure lighthouse keeping seemed to be! I wanted to travel back in time, climb the spiral stairs, wind up the clockworks of the lens mechanism, polish the brass and clean the glass, watch the seabirds winging through the beams of light, sip coffee in the late hours of the night with a book in my hand and the hum of the beacon turning on its pedestal above me. I wanted to live that kind of life . . . . until December 1985, when I met the keepers of New London Ledge Lighthouse.

The glamour and intrigue of lighthouses dimmed a bit with that visit. The Coast Guard crew at New London Ledge Lighthouse, a mile out in Connecticut's Thames River Estuary, did not exemplify the romantic image of lighthouse keeping I had found in books and articles and visits to old lighthouses in parks and museums. Even so, like the "wickies" (keepers) of old, the men seemed grateful for the company of myself and a marine scientist named Brae Rafferty from Project Oceanology in Groton. Rafferty had a special interest in lighthouses and wanted Ledge Light to continue to serve the public as an educational facility after it was automated and its keepers removed.

We landed at the lighthouse in the early afternoon. It was a square, caisson structure with an Empire-style house and lantern rising from it. Rafferty helped me jump from the pitching boat to the lower platform of the lighthouse, then kept hold of my arm as we climbed the long, steep staircase up to the square house and tower. Two of the three keepers on duty were waiting at the top of the stairs, one with his hand outstretched:

"Slippery, ma'am; watch your step," he warned, pointing at the wet, brown slime on the platform and the lower part of the stairway. I was grateful not only for his firm arm but also for the warmth coming from the open door as we reached the top of the stairs. It was cold out on Long Island Sound, about 6 degrees with the wind chill factored in. I wore several layers of clothes, heavy boots and a rain slicker, and had a wool cap jammed down over my ears. As I stepped into the lighthouse and began to remove those bulky outer layers, three sets of hands came to my assistance. It reminded me of a story Alaskan lightkeeper Ted Pedersen had often told about a woman arriving at one of the remote, frigid light stations in the Aleutian Islands to sell magazine subscriptions. Pedersen was so beguiled by the sight of a representative of the female gender, however unfeminine she may have appeared in her arctic gear, that he bought about a dozen magazines.

Everyone gathered in the kitchen of Ledge Lighthouse, where it was obvious the men had been awaiting our arrival with coffee and conversation. A paperback book lay face down on one end of the table, next to a plate containing a half-eaten piece of toast. On the counter was a microwave oven, a blender, and several cartons of cigarettes. In the window facing south, a set of binoculars was propped, looking toward land:

"We keep the biggest set in that west window," said one of the crew, pointing into the next room. "That window in there faces Ocean Beach, and in the summer we can see the girls in bikinis. This time of year we just watch the shore; maybe we'll see something interesting, maybe we won't. It doesn't matter all that much, because there's nothing else to do out here."

In the adjoining room — the one with the largest set of binoculars — was a TV turned on with no one watching it. I was told the

Arriving and departing from a light station wasn't always easy. Here, the keeper of Tree Point Light Station is lowered from a tender's derrick into the murky shallows of Alaska's Inside Passage, where he will row himself home to the light. Photo was taken about 1930. (U.S. Coast Guard)

TV was rarely off; it was like an umbilical cord connecting the men with civilization: "We like game shows and soap operas. Ask us what's going on with any of the soap operas!"

I didn't ask, but continued my surreptitious inspection of the place. It didn't seem as clean as I had expected. Lighthouses were supposed to be immaculate, but there were crumbs on the countertops of this one, and half-full cups of coffee sitting around in brown stained cups. While we talked, the keeper in charge made a peanut butter and jelly sandwich:

"Out here I find myself eating all the time; bored, I guess. I've put on a few pounds since I came here."

There was no spiral stairway up to the light and no round rooms to make it difficult to hang pictures and arrange furniture. Only the lantern itself was round. "Watch out for Ernie," said one of the men as Rafferty and I started up the stairs to look at the beacon. Ernie was, and remains, the station ghost. He is probably the most famous resident of Ledge Light, since his legend far outshines anything else about the sentinel, including its keepers.

It was uncomfortably hot up in the lantern — surprising on a day so cold outside. The beacon was an aero-marine type, not at all beautiful, and certainly not the antique of shimmering prisms and brass I had expected. We scanned the panorama of sea and shore and tried to identify landmarks in Groton and New London, each about a mile away. "It's bad enough when you can see and hear things going on ashore," said the youngest man, who had followed us to the top of the tower, "but when you can smell it too, that's the worst! Some Sundays I can smell barbeque grills going and mowed grass. Makes me really want to get off this light."

As we looked toward the mainland from the cramped lantern room, the thought of living on Ledge Light wasn't appealing. Rafferty grinned, seeing my disappointment. "No grass to mow; no door-to-door salesmen!" he quipped.

Back down on the lower deck, I strolled through the rooms with the youngest crewman tagging at my heels, captivated, I decided, by the presence of a 32-year-old woman who seemed totally fascinated with this home on the sea. In the TV room was a large wall mural of the lighthouse and a bookshelf full of paperbacks and magazines, mostly adult material and well worn. I scanned the titles, to the embarassment of the young keeper, and commented that the collection in no way resembled the portable government libraries that once circulated among the offshore and remote lighthouses. He gave me a blameless shrug, then hastily pointed out a book on weather forecasting, as if to redeem my

The lighthouse at Charleston's Sullivans Island, built in 1962, is the epitome of modern lightkeeping. Its beacon is completely automatic, the porcelain exterior never needs painting, and an elevator makes trips to the lantern a breeze. (U.S. Coast Guard)

faith in the lighthouse bookshelf.

The boat from Project Oceanology returned to fetch Rafferty and me. The water had gotten rougher, and I was given ample advice as to the best way to step off the dock onto the pitching boat. Once aboard, I turned to wave good-bye and express my gratitude to the men; it came out more like a benediction. Everyone was on the outside platform to see us off except the officer-in-charge; he preferred to attend to duties inside the lighthouse rather than watch people get in boats and go back to shore. Perhaps he was having another peanut butter sandwich to pass the time.

"Not the kind of life I'd want," Rafferty said as the boat pulled away. I nodded, watching Ledge Lighthouse grow smaller. Within two years its keepers would be removed, and it would be automated and sealed up tight to prevent vandalism. No one would ever again experience a visit with the working keepers of the square, brick light at the mouth of the Thames River.

Lest We Forget . . .
There are few people today who remember what it was like to live at a lighthouse, and fewer still who remember what it was like to keep one. In an age when even the small boat can navigate by satellite fix, traditional lighthouses have lost some of their impor-

Most of us have a picture postcard idea of lighthouse life — white picket fence, curtains at the windows, children romping on the lawn. This family at Maryland's Greenburg Point Lighthouse in 1885 is among the few that fits such a fanciful portrait. (Nautical Research Center)

tance as navigational aids. We now have space-age lighthouses in the sky, metallic giants adrift in space silently receiving and sending signals to the counterpane of ships and sea below. No one needs to light their lamps or trim their wicks; they can even see through the clouds.

Only a small number of the near 1500 lighthouses built in this country remain on duty, and those that do are operated by a cadre of sophisticated robotic mechanisms. Light sensors turn the beacons on and off, humidity sensors activate and deactivate the foghorns, automatic bulb changers rotate new lightbulbs into position when old ones burn out, solar panels collect energy to power the lights. Remote computerized monitoring systems keep watch over dozens of lighthouses at once and sound the alarm if something goes wrong. There are no matches, no oil lamps, no boots tramping up the spiral stairs each night, no human hands to trim the wicks and polish up the brass. Spiders weave their tenuous webs on stairs and windows and walls undisturbed.

Lighthouse keeping has officially become obsolete in this country, and will soon be gone in other parts of the world as well. Practically speaking, it makes no sense to pay a human to do the work a machine can do for less expense and with less risk — at least that is the justification given for automating lighthouses. Some people argue, however, that having no keeper at a lighthouse carries its own risks, in addition to being a disappointment to the romantics among us. Can a light sensor respond to a ship in distress? Will a foghorn frighten away vandals? Who will clean the windows, sweep the walk, dust away the cobwebs, and fly the flag? How will we preserve the rituals and traditions of three centuries of lighthouse keeping in America?

Most of us have a picture-postcard idea of lighthouse life. Even with modern advancements in navigation, we still like to imagine the lighthouse kept like a home. There ought to be curtains at the windows and wash on the line, a big happy dog romping on the lawn and children playing in the tidepools. At sunset, someone's hand should turn on the beacon, and warm yellow light should fill the rooms inside the keeper's house. We think it ought to be this way, but it isn't anymore. And it won't be ever again.

In the 1960s, the Coast Guard, under whose aegis all light-

houses are operated and maintained, began a massive automation program for its navigational aids. Lighthouses have always
been expensive to run, and with many of them growing old and in
need of repairs, budgets were strained. In addition, there were,
and still are, lighthouses so isolated and dangerous as to be unfit
for human habitation.

Imagine living in a stone tower on a stump of rock surrounded
by water on all sides, with only one or two companions and no
communication with the mainland save an occasional passing ship.
Many lighthouses were like this years ago, before there were radios and telephones, motorboats and helicopters. At the
Saddleback Ledge and Mount Desert lights in Maine, months sometimes went by without visitors or a delivery from the supply tender. In early winter, the sea thrashed so violently against Lake
Superior's Stannard Rock Light, it sealed the keepers inside the
tower as if it were an icy tomb, forcing maintenance crews to hack
away the ice around the door in order to reach the men. Stannard
Rock was fittingly nicknamed "The Loneliest Place in the World."
If something went wrong on such a station — an illness, an accident, a fire — it was sometimes days or even weeks before the
keepers obtained assistance.

Tending an island lighthouse was little better: Not a blade of
grass grows at Boon Island off the Maine coast; the ambience of
this desolate light station has always been decidedly gray — gray
rocks, gray sea, gray sky, gray tower. Sailing ships gave it a wide
berth, keeping far enough away that a distress signal was not readily
seen. When a keeper died here in the early 19th century, leaving
his wife alone on the island, it was more than a week before help
arrived, and only then because a ship had reported the light out.
The cruelty of life on Boon Island was blatantly revealed to the
crew of the vessel sent to investigate. They found the keeper's
young wife wandering about the island in tattered clothes, wild-
eyed and babbling to herself. Her dead husband still lay in his
sickbed.

Until this century there was no freshwater at Loggerhead Key
Light, except what was caught on the roof during a passing thunderstorm and stored in a cistern that was often more putrid than
pure. This station seemed to float tranquilly in the Gulf of Mexico,

kissed by clement breezes and collared by tawny sand and opaline waters, 65 miles northwest of Key West. It seemed an Arcadian assignment, yet it was hot, humid, blistered by the sun, and plagued by hordes of hungry mosquitoes who feasted on the island's two human inhabitants. The soil was too sandy for gardening or keeping livestock, and provisions spoiled quickly. The first keeper's wife thought she and her husband were Robinson Crusoe and his companion, Friday, so sequestered were they from civilization. In desperation, she wrote to First Lady Mrs. John Quincy Adams, plaintively outlining the circumstances of her husband's job, the lack of social life, and the hardships she was forced to endure. The First Lady must have been moved by the woman's plight, for shortly thereafter the keeper was given a transfer to a mainland lighthouse.

Hawaii's Molokai Lighthouse seemed to stand watch at the end of the world when it first flashed on about the turn of the century. It was situated on a narrow finger of land at the edge of the Kalaupapa leper colony where the victims of Hansen's Disease lived an existence of shame and misery. Supply vessels often refused to dock at Molokai Light, for fear of the crew contracting the disease. Provisions for the lighthouse were wrapped in heavy brown paper, piled onto a raft, and given a hefty shove toward shore where the keeper retrieved them. A note attached to the raft cautioned the keeper to remove all packaging from the supplies and burn it, then wash his hands thoroughly with soap and hot water, lest he contract leprosy. The nearby colony's wretched inhabitants called the sentinel "The Lepers' Light," as symbol of hope. For the Lighthouse Service, however, it was a warning to "keep away" and dreaded duty for the men assigned there.

The most unfortunate keepers may have been those assigned to seaswept lighthouses or the watch towers in the Aleutian Islands of Alaska. Minots Ledge, Spectacle Reef, Carysfort Reef, Cape Spenser, Scotch Cap, Cape St. Elias — these names meant nothing short of a prison sentence for their keepers. The Coast Guard automated these lighthouses first, since they were not only dangerous places to live and work, but very costly to maintain as attended stations. No one complained much; these were not the scenic lighthouses sought out by summer vacationers. Scotch Cap

Dismally called "The Leper's Light," Hawaii's Molokai Lighthouse was a dreaded assignment. Its keepers shunned the residents of the nearby Kalaupapa Leper Colony until after World War II, when sulfa drugs ended the fear of Hansen's Disease. Photo taken in July 1941. (U.S. Coast Guard Archives)

and Cape Sarichef, better known as the "Tombstone Twins," were almost 1400 miles from Ketchikan, where the supply tender was homeported. At Christmas, the tender brought the keepers a scraggly evergreen tree to decorate; no trees grew on Unimak Island, evergreen or otherwise.

Keeping the Lights Symbolically Burning
At this writing only one lighthouse in the United States still has resident keepers. The Boston Light, the first to be officially established in this country, is manned (only men serve there) as a gesture of respect for a very old and venerable occupation. Boston Light keeps the tradition of the lightkeeper. Three Coast Guardsmen have the honor of being the only active-duty lighthouse keepers in the country. But even they admit their lives are much different from the old "wickies," a moniker from the days when oil lamps lit the waterways and keepers had to trim the wicks to show

The last three civilian keepers of the Boston Light pose together at the base of the historic tower in 1941. They were succeeded by a string of Coast Guard keepers who still tend the light at this writing. From left to right: Charles Jennings, Maurice Babcock, and Mr. Hart. (Courtesy of Harold Jennings)

a clean and clear light. There are no matches or lamp wicks at Boston Light today, nor at any other lighthouses in this country. The Boston "wickies" are now "switchies," switching the beacon on and off with the flick of a finger. And even that is soon to change, with the installation of a light sensor.

Still, it isn't as impersonal and robotic as we might think. My faith in the romantic image of lightkeeping was rekindled during a visit to Boston Light in May 1991. There was a definite feeling of family life among the men and a call to duty; and there was pride in their work. They talked about cooking and painting and mowing the lawn, about having to clean and polish the lens and turn on the old air-driven fog signal if the new laser signal failed. "All the dandelions in the universe grow on this island," said the youngest man, who kept the lawn groomed in summer. "Dandelions must thrive in moist, salty air." He shot some basketball with me and talked about wanting to be a history teacher someday. I reminded him that he was living a chapter of history that would soon end and that he would have some incredible stories to share with his future students.

As the boat pulled away from the dock at Boston Light near sunset that evening, the silhouette of the old stone tower and the men standing on the dock waving good-bye aroused memories from the past, tales of the wickies and their devotion to the lights, of storms and shipwrecks and rescues, of fog and ice; but also of evenings like that one, when the water was like glass and the first bright stars were sparkling overhead like sequins on violet-tinted silk. Moments after the boat eased away from the dock, the youngest Coast Guard keeper shouted for the crew to "hold up a second!" He reached in a shirt pocket and pulled out a folded envelope, addressed and stamped. Leaning out over the water, he handed the letter to a passenger at the stern of the boat. It was homework he had done for a correspondence course.

Before the stories of lighthouse keeping are lost or discarded, we should tell them. To record all of them would be an impossible task, since more than a thousand lighthouses have stood watch on American shores, and their keepers number thousands more. The memories are adrift in diaries and logbooks, family Bibles and musty attic trunks. A few of the keepers have recorded their

A few of the old civilian lightkeepers left detailed records of their lives. Ted Pedersen, who died a short time before this book was completed, was an inexhaustible source of information and pictures. In his scrapbook was this candid 1930 snapshot of a haircut he received after returning from leave from Cape Sarichef Light. Keepers at these remote outposts were given a full year of paid leave for every two years of duty. The barber is lightkeeper Ed Moore. (U.S. Coast Guard)

remembrances on tape, with the benefit of their voices preserved; some have written their own biographies. Stories have been recorded firsthand by family members, by personnel who served the lights in offices or on tenders at the various lighthouse districts around the country, or by authors like me, who want to share their passion for the history and lore of lighthouses. Indeed, most of the recollections preserved here have traveled through many hands.

Regardless of the source, we should keep alive these memories and stories so that future generations can know what it meant to be a lighthouse keeper in America. Former Coast Guard historian Robert Scheina has said that lighthouse keepers — like cowboys and pirates — continue to fascinate us though their time has passed. The likeness of the old lightkeeper — leather faced and sea-legged, with a grizzled beard and stump of a pipe — lives on, and a cult of sorts surrounds the preservation of that memory.

I can't guarantee that every tale told in this book is absolutely true, for all stories lose or gain something in the telling, and a few have probably spontaneously materialized in the froth of a tankard of ale or in someone's fertile imagination. What I can promise, though, is a slice of lighthouse life the way it was lived at various times and places in American history. Through this gathering of memories, stories, and legends — some very old and from unknown sources and some directly from the mouths of those who lived them — I've tried to sketch a portrait of the lighthouse keeper in America. A few misconceptions might be cleared up, and perhaps a few treasured, sentimental ideas will be dashed to pieces, too. There will be surprises — things you never imagined about lighthouse keepers — but also the familiar fare we've grown to expect from those intrepid souls who sat up nights watching for ships in trouble and polishing the brass out of boredom.

Most of all, I hope an appreciation for lighthouse keeping will emerge in these pages. In many ways, lighthouse keepers were pioneers living in remote areas of the country and keeping a beacon to guide those who dared to follow, standing watch in the deep hours of the night when others slept, braving the surf to rescue some foundering soul when others took to their storm cellars. Lighthouse keeping was often lonely, sometimes dangerous,

The old, leather-faced, whiskered keeper of the light — a romantic symbol of
deliverance from a sea of trouble — is depicted in this U.S. Coast Guard Archive
photo of a 19th century light station and its uniformed attendant. The sentinel is
thought to be the original Point Bonita Lighthouse. (U.S. Coast Guard Museum)

occasionally courageous, seldom thankless. Along with the surfmen
of the U.S. Lifesaving Service, who patrolled shipwreck-prone
beaches and assisted vessels in distress, lighthouse keepers were
bound by a moral code that put the lives and welfare of others
above their own. People have always admired this aspect of
lightkeeping, the call to duty that was almost biblical in its symbol-

ism of keeping a light burning for those in darkness. It still char-
acterizes the U.S. Coast Guard today, a benevolent arm of the
U.S. Department of Commerce that was born from the amalgam-
ation of the U.S. Lifesaving Service and the U.S. Revenue Cutter
Service in 1915, and merged with the U.S. Lighthouse Service in
1939.

I've been gathering the pieces of this large and diverse story
for years. I've traveled to lighthouses on many coasts, taken photographs, interviewed the keepers and their descendents, poked
around in local libraries and historical societies, read numberless
books and articles, amassed binders full of notes, and drawn crude
sketches of things I saw or had described to me. Here is where
they all fit together. Every story worth telling about lighthouse
keepers is not here, but there are many. Some have been told
before; some have not; some have been asleep in musty places for
a very long time.

Pull up a chair, kick off your shoes. I'll tell you some tales
about keeping lighthouses.

Elinor De Wire

June 1994

The Keepers of the Light

We are the keepers of that steadfast light
That guides a people's course and destiny;
Not ours the skill directing over the sea
The mighty beams that blaze the path aright:
Ours but the hands that, serving, keep it bright.
The bringers of the oil, the workers we
Who day long, without pause and faithfully,
Toil that its radiance may pierce the night.
Above us are the wills that guide and turn:
It is not ours to watch nor question these:
Ours but to see each wick is trimmed and fit.
Lest on a night of storm it fails to burn
And a Great Ship goes down in awful seas.
O, Keepers of the light, keep faith with it!

Theodosia Garrison

CHAPTER 1

Up The Spiral Stairs

Into solitude went I,
and wisdom was revealed to me.
—Winnebago Holy Song

Mount Desert Rock, Maine, circa 1858

The keeper's wife shaded her eyes from the afternoon sun and scanned the flat horizon to the west. It was the fifth time she had climbed the lighthouse since noon, five arduous trips up the winding stairs to look for the dory that would bring her husband and two small sons safely home. It had been nearly two weeks since the keeper had left for the mainland to get supplies and buy new shoes for the boys. Shoes wore out quickly on Mount Desert Rock, what with the boys scampering about like little mountain goats among the jagged rocks and ledges. The keeper had planned to buy his provisions and return home in two days time, but a gale blew in unexpectedly and transformed the 23-mile void between the lighthouse and the mainland into a bubbling, blue-gray soup.

Alone on Mount Desert, which was little more than a chunk of rock rising out of the sea with a tower on its summit, and with only her infant daughter and a gray cat for company, the keeper's wife had kept watch over the lamps and the horizon. Her vigil was a safeguard against the madness that could easily have overtaken her. The hours were measured by the lighting and extinguishing of the lamps, the days compressed into one long watch of hope for her family's safe return. She dared not think that they had not made it to shore; for who would know if they were drowned until their boat washed up on a beach somewhere and was identified as that of the keeper of the Mount Desert Light? There was nothing to do but tend to the lighthouse and wait.

She sighted the dory on the very afternoon she had resolved to hail a passing ship for help, for her food stores were running desperately low. At first it was merely a glint of metal oarlocks and

An 1839 engraving of Mount Desert Rock Lighthouse portrays the drama and excitement of the lightkeeping life. In reality, the station was a lone stump of rock with a cold, damp tower and house on its summit, miles from civilization. (U.S. Coast Guard Archives)

a dark spot rising and falling on the distant horizon, bobbing like a lonely buoy; but as the dory drew nearer and took shape, the keeper's wife could discern the wool-capped heads of her sons and her husband's arms moving rhythmically at the oars. The breeze carried his song, murmured as cadence for his weary arms and to soothe the children huddled together in the bottom of the boat with the barrels of provisions.

It was more than an hour until the dory was maneuvered into the slip and safely stowed in the boathouse. The keeper lifted his sons onto the ramp, and they ran to their mother shouting of the things they had seen on the mainland — horses pulling carriages, stores with jars of rainbow-colored candies, church spires and bells, bridges drawn up and down by oxen, trees with swings on their limbs, and flowerbeds bursting with blooms. Tugging at her skirt affectionately, they pointed to a large barrel the keeper was hoisting onto the ramp. It contained a gift from the mainland, they said, something she would treasure above all the other gifts that had been carried over the sea during her 12 years on Mount Desert.

The keeper always brought his wife a gift when he returned from the mainland, usually some small trifle to brighten her gray existence. Once it had been a roll of yellow oilpaper that covered only one wall of the kitchen, the one that caught the morning sun. Before that it had been a jar of pungent cloves to mask the damp, salty smell of the pantry. Once he had even returned from South-west Harbor with an old man in the dory who carried a tuning fork and some rachets to fix her sea-soured piano. The piano was fixed within hours, but the old man stayed ten days, his return home delayed by foul weather.

When the keeper finished unloading the dory he ambled up the ramp, stretching his sore arms, then opened them wide to greet his wife. Sweat glistened on his forehead, though the spring air was cool, and his expression was stern. But it melted into a boyish smile when his wife brushed her lips over his moustache and fished in his shirt pocket for mail. Letters were her lifeline to the shore, and she would read and re-read them until their edges grew dog-eared and the ink faded in the humid salt air. Perhaps the fishermen who passed the rock, or some vessel headed down the Gulf of Maine, would bring a letter now and then; but the biggest haul of mail came on her husband's return from the main-land.

The keeper knew that his wife would cry, as she always did when his dory returned. It was a safety valve in her heart that always opened after the ordeal of her time alone on the light was done. She would not have cried aloud in his absence. Odd, gulpy sounds escaped from her as they embraced, anguish mixed with joy. Tears gave way to laughter as the boys implored their father to open the barrel containing the gift. "When the the meal is done and the lamps are lit," he assured them, rolling the large cask into the house and parking it by his chair.

At dusk, the keeper wound his way to the top of the light-house and checked the oil pans of the lamps. They were filled, and the wicks were trimmed. The reflectors were polished and the delicate prisms cleaned. Even the clockworks were prepared for the night. His wife had made everything ready for the evening lightup; he needed only to turn up the wicks and touch a match to them. The feeble glow that appeared in the lantern was caught in the silvered reflectors, twisted through the prisms, and cast out into the twilight in eight bright beams visible miles at sea. The beauty of it, and the wizardry, still amazed him. He sat with his light for a while to be sure it burned well, then descended the stairs to the house where his wife was clearing away the meal and restocking her pantry with the much-needed provisions.

It was the first night in weeks that the lighthouse beams comforted her, sweeping by the kitchen windows like brilliant spokes on a lighted wheel. She made coffee for her husband, and set out his tobacco and pipe. He settled into his chair by the south window, where he could see the light reflecting off the oilhouse door. She did not speak to him, knowing he was counting the seconds between flashes to be certain the light characteristic was accurate. "Dark . . . one, two, three, four . . . dim, flash, dim . . . one, two, three, four . . . dark . . ." She knew its timing exactly. She had slept in his chair enough nights, one eye shut and the other on the oilhouse door.

When he finally leaned back and removed his boots, she brought him a mug of steaming coffee and placed their sleeping baby daughter in the crook of his arm. The boys waited quietly at their father's feet, eyes flitting back and forth from each other to the barrel standing beside the keeper's chair. When he nodded, grinning, they raced to fetch a claw hammer, which they placed in their mother's hand while guiding her to the barrel. She chided them softly for spending the family's pittance of a salary on trinkets: "I have need of nothing fancy," she said, as she pried loose the lid of the barrel. "Nothing!"

It was true; she had all the necessities in life, albeit simple ones. But the keeper could think of a hundred things she had given up to live with him on this forlorn rock, intangible things like church bells ringing, elms shivering in the breeze, April mornings on the mainland when pink apple blossoms sent their perfume riding on the air, when tulips yawned and opened their eyes, and jonquils cried tears of dew. Mount Desert Rock contained none of these things. It was bleak and barren and cold; nothing green grew upon it, nor was there a particle of earth on its face — only rock, gray and dismal.

The barrel lid opened with a screech of nails bending against oak, and an earthy smell touched everyone's nose. The cat pricked up his whiskers and sniffed with curiosity. The keeper's wife closed her eyes for a moment and allowed the odor to seep into her brain. It was a familiar smell, one that stirred memories of her youth and the family garden with its dirt freshly turned and neat little rows of flowers just beginning to sprout.

"We couldn't take you with us to the mainland," said her husband, "so we brought the mainland to you."

The soil was cool and moist, and it smelled of roots and earthworms. She let it sift through her fingers, crumbled its little clumps, measured its weight in handfuls. It felt familiar, yet at the same time strange. She allowed her fingers to nuzzle it in an emotional reunion of flesh and earth and memory. The keeper withdrew a small envelope from his pocket, being careful not to wake his baby daughter, and inverted it over the table beside his chair. Hundreds of tiny seeds spilled out and rolled in all directions. Her favorites were there: zinnias, marigolds, nasturiums, along with parsely and chives.

The lighthouse family at Mount Desert Rock poses on their rocky lawn about 1880. Soil packed in the rock crevices and planted with flowers added bits of color to the gray and dismal station. Several generations of families planted these unusual rock gardens. (U.S. Coast Guard Museum)

When the first rays of sunlight shot up on the eastern horizon, the keeper extinguished the lamps and began to polish their sooty globes. Far below, on the barren pinnacles of their rocky home, his wife carried buckets of the earth and packed it into the rock crevices. Her skirt was soiled and her hair hung scraggly about her dewy face, but the keeper saw a renewed youth and radiance in her, as if by some miracle of reverse time. The tiny seeds were nestled in their stony flowerpots and soaked with rainwater from the cistern. By late June they would burst forth in a riot of color, leaving every sailor who passed spellbound to see flowers blooming on the bleak, pelagic stump known as Mount Desert Rock. Autumn storms would tear away every last fragment of earth, and it would all have to be replaced and replanted the following spring; but the effort seemed small to those who drank in the meaning. Sailors began calling it "God's Rock Garden." Every spring thereafter, they brought boxes of soil to the family at Mount Desert Rock and watched in awe as the barren landscape was remarkably transformed.

Egg Rock Lighthouse, Massachusetts, circa 1850
The new keeper of the Egg Rock Lighthouse took charge of the small offshore station early in October, accepting the keys and the logbook from the departing keeper, who offered an admonition to "lay in supplies and fuel, heavy and deep, before the winter seas mount." The new keeper carried his bride ashore to the lighthouse and lifted her effortlessly across the stone threshold. She was a petite girl half his age whom he had married with the good blessing of her parents, who like many people of their day considered it an honor to add a lightkeeper to their family. She was not a hardy woman, but Egg Rock was only a mile from shore. He could take her home often, he thought, to visit with family or to shop in the small stores of Swampscott and Nahant. If she needed a doctor there was a sturdy rowboat in which to convey her to shore or to bring the doctor out to Egg Rock.

The October sunlight sparkled on the mile-stretch of sea between the lighthouse and shore as the keepers exchanged good wishes. The departing keeper and his wife stepped in the boat that had come for them and rowed away, waving a hesitant good-

The lightkeeper's existence was centered on the beacon, which could not be abandoned, even in the most adverse situations. Keepers who were assigned to places like Egg Rock accepted the possible tragic consequences of living on a lonely island at sea. (U.S. Coast Guard Museum)

bye. They could not imagine such a frail girl as the new keeper's wife on Egg Rock. She more closely resembled a delicate china doll than a lighthouse keeper's wife, and her languid eyes and weak little cough gave them serious concern. "See that you stock enough wood," cautioned the departing keeper's wife, remembering the horrid cold of the house in winter. "And burn it wisely." Her words were lost on the freshening breeze, however, and carried away before the new keeper and his wife could hear.

Their concern was genuine and tenable: The new keeper's wife was not well. Her cough lingered from an illness she had not quite recovered from before her wedding a month before, and she was entirely too thin for her frame, however small and dainty. In fact, on the very night of her arrival on Egg Rock, the new keeper was compelled to tend both the lighthouse and his spouse. The cold and dampness of the place caused her to wheeze miserably, until she became so choked with phlegm she could not cook the evening meal or help with the lighthouse chores. The keeper bundled her warmly in a chair by the stove and put a pan of water on to boil, in hopes the steam would pacify her rattling lungs.

The couple were unprepared for the harsh conditions on Egg Rock, and the new keeper, who may have feared loneliness most of all, deluded himself in thinking his ailing wife could adjust and enjoy her captivity among the billows. Surrounded on all sides by the sea, with the house and light tower on the island's highest point, Egg Rock received the fury of 3000 miles of sodden Atlantic wind. The house was never dry, drafts seeped in every crack, a chill crept up through the floors, and worst of all, the water between Egg Rock and the mainland, though barely a mile across, became a churning, frigid expanse in winter. And winter here was a protracted ordeal, long and gloomy and tedious, able to be endured by only the strongest constitution and the toughest hide.

Within days, the keeper's wife began an irreversible decline. Her hands and face became chafed from the cold, and her feet grew splotchy from poor circulation. Her hair dulled and hung in limp tendrils framing her colorless cheeks; her voice dwindled to a faint rasp. She spent her days huddled by the stove sipping warm liquids and struggling to breathe. By November, her barely audible cough had become a croaking, suffocating pneumonia.

The keeper despaired, trying to do the work alone and care for his ailing wife as well. What little medicines he had to treat her did nothing. Worst of all, the water between Egg Rock and the shore had become an unwelcome gray immensity. No vessels passed near the rock, and the shore lay too far away for a distress signal to be seen. The keeper dared not attempt the rough crossing with his wife so ill, nor could he chance leaving her alone on the rock while he went for help. In this quandary he continued for weeks, until it seemed he went about the dreadful business of tending the beacon, and the sick woman, in a daze. After a time he ceased speaking to his wife, who lay in a stupor on her makeshift bed by the stove. Sometimes he lay beside her, listening to her labored breathing and overcome by his own lassitude.

One morning in December the keeper returned from extinguishing the light and found his wife dead, relieved at last from her torment and with an expression of peace on her face. There were no tears from the keeper. He merely sat beside her, holding her small hand until it grew cold and stiff, and wondering what he should do with her body. There was no one to relieve him of his duties if he took her ashore, which was impossible anyway, with the sea still too rough to risk a crossing. There was no place to bury her on the island either, since what little soil existed was frozen solid and did not afford enough depth to hold a casket. As the embers died down in the stove, he thought of the long winter ahead and the misery that lay before him alone on the light.

Tenderly, he dressed his wife in her best clothes and carried her to the oilhouse, where he fashioned a coffin from pieces of

Egg Rock appears more hospitable in this turn-of-the-century postcard view than in earlier years when a keeper's wife died there because the mile of sea between the island and the mainland was too rough to permit safe crossing for a doctor. (Elinor De Wire Collection)

crates and scrap wood that had been stowed in the rafters. The box was not large, for his wife was hardly bigger than a child, and in her illness had withered even smaller. He wrapped her in a blanket, said some reverent words over her departed soul, and nailed shut the improvised coffin. Resignedly, he stood it upright in a corner of the oilhouse and shoved some boxes against it.

Weeks passed without relief. If anything, the situation worsened, with the sea unrelenting, the temperature plummeting, and no vessel hoving near enough to be hailed for help. Sea spray had left the rock and lighthouse looking like an ice castle, and every morning brought the challenge of breaking open the door to the outside and chipping away the ice from the windows of the house and the tower; otherwise, the entire place might have imprisoned the keeper until spring. With robotic efficiency, he lighted and extinguished the lamps, polished and dusted, made entries in his logbook, chipped ice, and when the necessity arose, trekked to the oilhouse mortuary to replenish his oilcans, careful to avoid looking at the wooden box standing upright in the corner. He had concluded that it would be many weeks before he could make a crossing to Nahant to hold a proper funeral for his wife.

In late March there came a warm spell that melted the entire station and sent a soothing air over the sea. As the eaves dripped and icicles let go of their anchorages along the roof and lighthouse railing, the keeper thought of his wife and the need to get her ashore, for she also was certainly thawing. He spent two days freeing the dory from its frozen mantle and preparing it for the perilous trip ashore. Then, on a warm equinoctial morning that seemed right for travel, he put out the lamps and trimmed and polished for his return that evening, then went to the oilhouse to fetch his deceased wife.

The coffin, though small and light, was a ponderous affair to load into the dory. It was still solid from its months in the deep freeze of the oilhouse, but once in the sunlight it began to creak and contort, and to exude a fetid odor of decay that multiplied with each hour. The keeper knew that he should not delay in getting it ashore, so he trussed it with ropes on an improvised hoist and dropped it down into the boat with a nail-loosening thud which a hammer quickly repaired. He regretted that his diminutive wife

The pleasant life in a lighthouse, as portrayed in this 1880s sketch from *St. Nicholas Magazine*, was not the case for every lighthouse family. (U.S. Coast Guard Archives)

could not repose undisturbed during this requisite trip through lighthouse purgatory; rather, she was irreverently bounced about inside her coffin as it found a seat in the dory and rode the swells toward shore.

The row was exhausting in the choppy gut between Egg Rock and the mainland, but once within sight of shore, the keeper was greeted by a swarm of curious landlubbers who had spied the box in the dory and had rowed out to help. He made a brief explanation of his dire situation and implored the townsfolk to fetch a minister and conduct a funeral with haste. This they did, never once questioning the reason for the woman's death or the keeper's inability to summon help for her. The lighthouse keeper was well-respected in Nahant, and everyone knew that Egg Rock often exacted a terrible price from its caretakers. The funeral was conducted promptly and was attended by many local residents, who dropped their day's work and paid their respects to the family of one who had died in service to the lights. For people along the shore, the beacons were almost biblical in symbolism and their keepers the apostles of light. The parents of the dead girl, though grieving, bore no malice toward their son-in-law. They knew it was demanded of him to stand by his light, regardless of personal peril or tragedy. Their daughter had died honorably.

With his departed wife properly interred and the early afternoon sun canting westward, the keeper, nearly starved from the morning's exertion, lost no time in accepting an invitation to dinner at the home of an old friend. The gesture was especially appealing because his friend had a widowed sister who might best be described as mature and capable, and perhaps even a little desperate to escape her current situation of obedience to her brother. When she realized the keeper was her ticket to freedom, she tightened her corset, rouged her cheeks to convey the best state of health, and put on her loveliest dress. The designing brother made sure the lighthouse keeper and the widow were left alone in the parlor to chat after dinner, and by mid-afternoon a proposal had been made and accepted. The widow hastily filled a trunk with a practical island trousseau and stepped in front of the parlor mantle to be wed to the keeper by the same minister who only hours before had performed the funeral for the keeper's first wife.

By late afternoon, the two were in the dory headed for Egg Rock, with the entire town standing on shore to wish them well. No one seemed the least bothered by the fact that the keeper had buried one wife and married another on the same day. To be asked to live alone on the lighthouse at Egg Rock was unthinkable, a prison sentence. The lightkeeper was regarded with a level of admiration and awe that transcended the social customs of mainlanders; his hasty remarriage was not only accepted but also expected, so long as he was back out on the lighthouse at dusk to kindle the wicks and keep the watch.

Fable or Fact?

The families who lived at Mount Desert Rock and Egg Rock are gone now. Toward the end of the 19th century, the Lighthouse Board passed a regulation forbidding women and children to live on isolated, offshore light stations. Such remote lights as Mount Desert, Saddleback Ledge, Tillamook, Minots, and St. George Reef were made "stag stations" — only men allowed. Somehow, those rugged lighthouse families, tested by a life of hardship and misery which we can only imagine, became almost mythical in character, performing deeds that seem above human ability and enduring adversity and misfortune well beyond that of ordinary humans. The preceding tales of Mount Desert and Egg Rock are typical of the quixotic image that has shaped our modern definition of the title "lighthouse keeper." The stories themselves are certainly based in truth, but how much is fable and how much is fact cannot be ascertained after so many years. And perhaps no attempt should be made to rectify that, for it might rob the lightkeeping story of much of its color — those marvelous tints and hues that cause the flame of the lighthouse lamp to burn all the more vibrant.

> *Where goes the switched off light,*
> *Last moment lord of sight;*
> *Vanished now — one with night?*
> Lloyd Treworgy

"The Light-Keeper"
Robert Louis Stevenson

II
As the steady lenses circle
With frosty gleam of glass;
And the clear bell chimes,
And the oil brims over the lip
        of the burner,
Quiet and still at his desk,
The lonely Light-Keeper
Holds his vigil.

Lured from far,
The bewildered seagull beats
Dully against the lantern;
Yet he stirs not, lifts not his head
From the desk where he reads,
Lifts not his eyes to see
The chill blind circle of night
Watching him through the panes.
This is his country's guardian,
The outmost sentry of peace,
This is the man
Who gives up what is lovely
        in living
For the means to live.

Poetry cunningly guilds
The life of the Light-Keeper,
Held on high in the blackness
In the burning kernal of night,
The seaman sees and blesses him,
The Poet, deep in a sonnet,
Numbers his inky fingers
Fitly to praise him.
Only we behold him,
Sitting, patient and stolid,
Martyr to a salary.

Cigarette in hand, Alaskan lightkeeper Ted Pedersen anxiously waits in uniform outside Cape St. Elias Light Station in 1927 for the district's white-gloved inspector to arrive. On the whole, lightkeepers were exceptionally fastidious in their work and ardently devoted to their stations. (U.S. Coast Guard)

CHAPTER 2

ALL IN A DAY'S WORK

All rising to great place is by winding stair.
–Francis Bacon

November 30, 1886: "Killed two mosquitoes
this day."
–Keeper J.W. Ingalls
Billingsgate Lighthouse, Cape Cod

Most of us imagine that keeping a lighthouse was easy work, a place where relaxation, hobbies, reading, and beachcombing were routine. Albert Einstein once suggested that the cultivation of a great mind might be more readily accomplished if the genius-elect were sent to the peace and solitude of a lighthouse. "I notice how the monotony of a quiet life stimulates the creative mind," he said. "Certain callings . . . entail such an isolated life. I think of such occupations as the service in the lighthouses." Likewise, Pablo Casals was in favor of shipping gifted musicians off to the shore, with a cello case in one hand and scissors to trim the wicks of the lighthouse lamp in the other. Many a novelist has mistakenly assumed the lighthouse keeper is on a permanent, littoral vacation, or at least an extended one. There was, and still exists, the misbegotten notion that keeping a light was a strike of the match at sunset and a puff of dousing breath at dawn, interspersed with a little dusting and polishing and a few trips up and down the stairs.

Depending on where a keeper was stationed, duties varied from mildy dangerous to outright death-defying. The trials of storms and other catastrophes are discussed elsewhere, but here should be mentioned the everyday perils to which the keeper was exposed — those tasks that required both skill and fortitude, as well as ingenuity.

Many lighthouses were tall, and situated on windy and precarious points of land or on islands and rocks at sea. Keeping the lantern panes clean and polished to assure the clarity of the light was an acrophobic's nightmare. Bird droppings, salt spray, ice buildup, and smoky film from the oil lamps had to be cleaned away daily, if not several times a day. The gallery, or catwalk as it was more appropriately called, was a narrow, unprotected platform encircling the lantern and buffeted by wind. In order to reach the highest lantern windows, a keeper had to stand on the gallery railing or on a small ladder. If the gallery was wet or iced over, there was considerable risk of a fall. For this reason, most lighthouses had handholds built into the iron framework of the lantern windows.

There were occasional falls and a few fatalities. In 1859, at St. Augustine Lighthouse in Florida, keeper Joseph Andreau had rigged a makeshift scaffold in order to paint the tall tower. The contraption held firm, but Andreau slipped and plummeted some 150 feet to his death. Perhaps as a small measure of propitiation, the government appointed Mrs. Andreau the new lightkeeper.

At most stations, and all smaller ones, keeping the tower painted was the job of the lighthouse keeper. A ladder was used to reach the bottom sections, but the top was usually done with some sort of homemade scaffold, usually a chair suspended from the catwalk by ropes or a barrel that a man could stand in and be hoisted up and down the sides of the tower. Upkeep of the paint was important not only for the preservation of the stonework, woodwork, and metalwork, but also because it served as the tower's daymark, distinguishing it from neighboring lighthouses during the daylight hours. Some stations had elaborate daymarks and a considerable amount of ornamentation. Keeping a station like Cape Disappointment or West Quoddy Head properly painted required constant attention. After 1873, when its now-famous barber pole daymark was first painted, Cape Hatteras Light wore down dozens of brushes and drank hundreds of gallons of paint whenever its cosmetics had to be renewed.

At times, and at certain stations, there were unusual challenges in the daily routine. At "Ann's Eyes," the nickname for the twin lights on Thachers Island off Cape Ann, Massachusetts, keepers had to traverse 300 yards of boulders to get from one light tower to the other. The risk of injury was enormous, and almost always there were twisted ankles and bruises during the first few weeks after a new keeper arrived at the station. Most learned the route over the rocks quickly and could find their way on the darkest night or in the thickest blizzard.

When Aaron Wheeler came to Thacher's Island in 1814, he decided the trek between the two lighthouses had to be made safer. In the summer of 1825 he began clearing a path by hauling away the boulders. Larger ones had to be broken into pieces, and when the rocky route was finally cleared Wheeler chiseled down the remaining stones to make the walkway relatively smooth. The work was completed in about five months. For his effort, the government paid him $100.

At North Carolina's Currituck Beach Lighthouse in the years 1900-1903, lightkeeper W.J. Tate spent his spare time working on a project as unique as Aaron Wheeler's stony path. Tate's wife, who ran the post office in Kitty Hawk, received a letter early in 1900 from a Mr. Wilbur Wright, who was interested in the weather conditions of the area and the topography of the hills around Kitty Hawk. The Tates were very excited about Wright's plans to test a flying machine. They sent him a full report, and a few months later Wilbur Wright arrived on a schooner to survey the area. While in Kitty Hawk, he was hosted in the Tates' home.

Of course, everyone knows the ending to this story: Wilbur Wright went back to Ohio, got his brother Orville, and the two proceeded to make history on the dunes at Kill Devil Hills. What most people don't know is that without the help and encouragement of the Tates, the Wright brothers might have given up their experiments in flight. W. J. Tate recalled: "The mental attitude of the natives toward the Wrights was that they were a simple pair of harmless cranks that were wasting their time at a fool attempt to do something that was impossible. The chief argument against their success could be heard at the stores and post office, and ran something like this: 'God didn't intend man to fly. If He had, He would have given him a set of wings on his shoulders. No, siree, nobody need not try to do what God didn't intend him to do.' I recall not once, but many times, that when I cited the fact that other things as wonderful had been accomplished, I was quickly told I was a darned sight crazier than the Wrights were.'"

The Wrights' first experimental glider was built in the Tates' yard at Kitty Hawk from pieces prefabricated in Dayton, Ohio. Mrs. Tate's treadle sewing machine was used to sew the sateen wing coverings. Keeper Tate assisted the Wrights in launching their experimental gliders; he lent them tools and offered what physical labor and advice he could. His wife made sure the two determined inventors did not go hungry and were furnished with all the domestic help and personal encouragement needed to keep them focused on their goal. The Tates probably believed in the Wright's dream as much, if not more, than the brothers themselves.

Long after the historic day when human flight became reality, the Tates and Wrights were still close friends. W.J. Tate took an avid interest in aviation and made an inspection of lighthouses in an airplane in 1920 with his aviator son-in-law. In 1928, on the silver anniversary of the first flight, W.J. Tate was given the honor of unveiling a plaque to the Wright Brothers in his front yard on the spot where the first glider was assembled. He also assisted historians in locating the exact place where the first flight took place. No one doubted his word; he had been there when it happened.

Simple Needs, Complicated Solutions
Things we take for granted on the mainland often presented immense challenge at lighthouses, particularly those situated offshore in places difficult to access. Something as simple as mail service could become an arduous chore. A popular story told on the West Coast relates how the keeper of an offshore lighthouse ordered a turkey for Thanksgiving dinner. The freshly killed bird was wrapped in butcher's paper and delivered by a rural route carrier to the keeper's mainland mailbox on a lonely stretch of road that looked across to the isle lighthouse. Bad weather prevented the keeper from getting ashore to pick up the turkey, and when he did finally manage to make the trip and opened his secluded mailbox, a revolting stench greeted his nose. The foul fowl had been sitting inside the metal mailbox, baking in the sun for five days.

On Tatoosh Island off Puget Sound, the keepers of the Cape Flattery Lighthouse depended upon "Old Doctor" for delivery of their mail. As an 1898 article in *Overland Journal* explained: "The regular means of communication with the outside world is the canoe of the Indian mail-carrier. He makes the seventeen mile trip from Neah Bay (weather permitting) twice a week and also transports passengers to and fro for a consideration. As they are paid by the trip, these carriers take some tremendous risks. Old Doctor, a veteran carrier, has had three canoes smashed to kindling wood at various times in endeavoring to make a landing in the surf. Often the only way to get the mail sack ashore is to throw it from the bobbing canoe to a rock, where the keeper stands ready to catch it."

Drinking water and food storage also presented problems at remote lighthouses. In recent years, water for offshore lighthouses was usually taken out by a supply vessel and pumped into a holding tank. At older stations, keepers caught water from roof runoff during rains and stored it in casks or in a cistern. The difficulties attendant with collecting water in this way were numerous. Not only was the water supply regulated by the weather, but such things

Avery Rock Lighthouse in Maine's Machias Bay was typical of the offshore lighthouses of New England. There was little or no soil for grass to grow, and fog signaling was an important part of the work, evidenced by the bellhouse to the left of the light tower in this 1892 photo. (U.S. Coast Guard Archives)

as salt buildup, bird droppings, particles of roofing material, and dirt could be carried into the water tanks. When the supply got low, many a crew kept watch for an approaching raincloud, then scurried onto the roof with scrub brushes and buckets of soapy water to wash it clean.

At least one station was reported by the Lighthouse Board as having problems with lead in the drinking water, caused by the water passing over lead paint on its way to the cistern.

The solution to this problem was twofold: First the government installed "cocks," or vents, on the pipes leading into the tanks so that when a rain shower began the entire structure could experience a freshwater washdown and the water would vent off into the sea. After the initial cleansing was accomplished, the vents would be closed so that the water would then run into the holding tank. A distilling device was also planned as part of the solution; however, it was not needed. The "cocks" worked so well that concentrations of lead in the water were reduced to well below the safe minimum. The Lighthouse Service eventually developed nontoxic paint that had the same or better durability than lead-based paint.

Cisterns were troublesome, too, particularly in the more tropical regions where bacteria thrived and all sorts of small creatures were attracted to the dark and cool interior of the tanks. The cistern at Loggerhead Key Lighthouse in the Gulf of Mexico remained putrid no matter what measures were taken to cleanse it. Even today, the cistern at the Boston Light requires a healthy dose of chlorine to keep the interior free of algae and bacteria and the water potable.

Fresh food storage was a trial at hot, humid lighthouses, especially those offshore. The table fare was often no better than on a ship at sea where salt beef and wormy hardtack reigned supreme. Some keepers cleverly took advantage of the cooler sea water by rigging theft-proof, tightly sealed storage cans for meat and other perishables; these were lowered into the sea on sturdy lines to which small bells were attached to alert the keeper should a hungry fish attempt a robbery. Bottles of milk were also sometimes kept cool this way.

Retired Sailors and Soldiers Encouraged to Apply

Like most government ventures, lighthouse keeping was a complicated profession, and it became more so as time went by. Prior to about 1850, before the government began to strictly regulate the daily work of lighthouse keepers, the only qualifications for the job were that the applicant be able to read and write. (This was a rule loosely followed, however.) Knowing how to swim was not considered important, nor was the ability to handle a boat, but most people who applied for the job had some experience on the water. Many were retired sailors and sea captains whose "long habit of keeping watches on shipboard renders them more reliable than landsmen," wrote F.A. Talbot.

There was no age limit for a lightkeeper until after 1850, and elderly men and women were sometimes appointed and served until their deaths. Even after a maximum age for employment was instituted, some keepers served well past retirement age.

A keeper's marital status was of little consequence, though records indicate most lightkeepers were married with families, and that a wife and children were considered a benefit, with all the work there was to be done at a lighthouse. In 1875, an unmarried applicant for the job of keeper of Lake Superior's Isle Royale Lighthouse was told the position would probably go to a married man, since the inspector making the appointment felt Isle Royale was no place to live alone. The resolute applicant immediately located a willing woman, was hastily wed, and got the job. He was so grateful for the appointment that he named his first child after the inspector who had hired him.

The exception to this unwritten preference for married keepers was offshore rock lighthouses such as Tillamook, St. George Reef, Mount Desert, Saddleback, Spectacle Reef, Stannard Rock, and Minots Ledge. Though families did live at some of these remote stations early on, by the latter half of the 19th century the Lighthouse Service was reluctant to allow wives and children at such sequestered and dangerous sites. The rock lighthouses were designated as "stag stations" where only bachelors or married men willing to live apart from their families could serve. However, some of the remote island stations still had families in residence. Anacapa Island, Southeast Farallon, Little Gull, Dry Tortugas, and Matinicus

WESTS AND WALTENBERGS

Though government regulations said nothing about a keeper's marital status, most of those hired were married. The contributions of spouses and children were considered beneficial, not only for the sake of a keeper's happiness but also because of the enormous amount of work that had to be done. In this photo taken about 1925, two keepers from Alaska's Guard Island Light join their wives for a pleasant meal in the station dining room. (U.S. Coast Guard)

Rock were among these. In the opinion of those who administered lighthouses, an island didn't seem as harsh a place for a family, since a boat could be anchored, and there was solid ground underfoot for a garden, and grass for pasturing a cow.

In Colonial days, the position of lightkeeper was often obtained by virtue of owning the land on which the colony desired to build a lighthouse. This was the case with the Thomas family of Plymouth, Massachusetts, where two beacons — the Gurnet Twin Lights — were established in 1768. The berms on which these little towers were built are still visible today, though a single tower now does the job that two once did. Most of the lighthouses established before the Revolution were operated on family-owned land on the condition that the family be appointed to keep the lighthouse. Pay was miserably low for these early lightkeepers, but in many cases it provided income on poor sandy soil that otherwise would have been useless.

A number of lighthouse keepers were war veterans, some of whom had lost a leg or an arm and had been given a lighthouse job as a reward for heroic service or because the injuries prevented them from returning to their pre-war jobs. Widows and grown children were also sometimes given a deceased husband's or father's position as lightkeeper, provided the government was satisfied with the family's work. While the job was never hereditary, some stations boasted generations of keepers all from the same family. The Garratys of Lake Huron were typical, with a collective service of 184 years among them. It was also not unusual for lighthouse families to intermarry. Children raised at lighthouses often grew up feeling ill at ease with anyone who had not experienced their lifestyle; hence "beacon brats" were usually ideal matches in matrimony.

On the Florida Panhandle about 1888, lighthouse families were among the few residents. This family at St. Marks Light can be seen on their porch through the high grass. The station privy is to the left of the house, standing on stilts. (U.S. Coast Guard Archives)

Having good connections in government was a plus for any-one applying for a lightkeeping position, along with loyalty to the party in office. San Francisco author and philosopher Ambrose Bierce sardonically defined the word lighthouse as "... a tall build-ing on the seashore in which the government maintains a lamp and a friend of a politician." This fact is amply substantiated in government records, and though many of those same friends of politicians were capable lighthouse keepers, some were not. Charles K. Hyde, in his research on Great Lakes lighthouses, uncovered a typical case of political favoritism. Colonel George McDougall Jr. was not only the son of a wealthy Detroit family but a lawyer as well, and one much reviled in the courts for his foul temper, shady legal practices, and bouts of drunkenness.

But he had a friend in government — the collector of customs in Detroit — and after his law career bombed, he managed to se-cure the job of keeper of Fort Gratiot Lighthouse. This lawyer-turned-lightkeeper was apparently unfit for duty for a multitude of reasons, including his immense girth, acquired through excesses of food and drink. He was forced to climb the lighthouse stairs sideways and could barely squeeze through the opening into the lantern. Howard Goshorn might have been thinking of McDougall when he humorously penned: "A lighthouse is no place for a fat man. Space is at a minimum!"

Not until after the formation of the Lighthouse Board in 1852 did the government gain a firm and fair hand in the appointment of lighthouse keepers, and even then it took some 30 years to purge the system of its long-standing vices. Corruption and scan-dal in the administration of lighthouses in the early 1800s, along with numerous complaints about keepers, resulted in an inten-sive investigation of the service in the 1840s. It revealed poor management by the Treasury Department and an overall lack of regulation of the many men and women who tended the lights. Additionally, the U.S. was found lagging far behind Europe in terms of lighthouse technology, with many of the light towers deteriorated and some near collapse.

What followed was a massive reconstruction of the entire light-house establishment. Districts were set up and managed by me-ticulous and, at times, unforgiving superintendents and inspec-

Lightkeeper Al Pecor cleans the lantern glazing at Los Angeles Harbor Light in 1938. Daily work at a lighthouse meant cleaning glass and polishing brass, necessary to assure a clear and bright light. During bad weather a keeper might clean the windows several times a night. Special handholds were built into the window frames at some lighthouses to give the keeper something to grasp when attending to this dangerous task. (Nautical Research Center)

tors who visited the lights and evaluated their condition and the performance of the keepers. Requirements for applicants for the job of "Lighthouse Keeper" were clearly outlined: They had to know how to read and write, do basic arithmetic, handle a boat, and file accurate reports and paperwork with the government. They also had to be between the ages of 18 and 50, though once appointed lightkeepers, they could serve until the infirmities of old age left them unable to work.

The diversity of applicants was enormous, as was their approach to getting the job. A typical letter of application read:

September 16, 1859
Jacksonville, Florida
Sir,
    Understanding that a person is required to take charge of the Light

House at Jupiter Inlet, I would most respectfully offer my services as keeper.
My intimate knowledge of the whole of that section of the county,
owning lands there, and earnest desire to get that portion of our state
settled, induces me to make the application.

L.H. Dunlop

A letter to the Commissioner of Lighthouses around 1912 read:

I am writing to you for a position as keeper in a lighthouse anywhere
from New York to Portland, Maine. I am the daughter of a barge captain
and know much about the Sound and I also have a pal and we are both
willing to do hard work and I know I would enjoy that lonesome life
keeping a light burning.

I know how to row and run an engine and steer a boat. I am afraid
we will not get this position on account of us being girls but we shall wear
trousers instead of skirts.

Some applicants were very specific in their requests for work, such
as this one received by the Lighthouse Board shortly after the
Civil War:

I don't want it [a lighthouse] in southern California where it is hot,
or where it is fierce storms or bitter cold, but where it is liveable with some
advantages; a well paying lighthouse where I could let my youngest girl
go to school, where there are certain refinements and nice families for her
to know as a growing child. If you had a bit of grass and some chickens
and a cow I feel we would give you the most help; hope there are lobsters
and good fishing, but please no sharks!

Certain applicants arranged to have recommendations sent on
their behalf:

Understanding that the present keeper of Fire Island Lighthouse,
Mr. Charles Fordham, has tendered his resignation, I take the liberty of
addressing you in favor of the appointment of Ira Oakley of Babylon for
that position.

Mr. Oakley is a firm friend of the Administration, a strong Union
man, very active, energetic, perfectly temperate, about 45 years old, with
a small family of grown up children who possess the activity and industry
of their father. I have known him for 15 years and my knowledge of his
qualifications induces one to believe him well fitted mentally and physi-

cally for the situation and that by his appointment a faithful, competent, and reliable keeper would be procured.

A. Thompson
November 27, 1863

Once a keeper received an appointment, he or she took an oath promising to carry out the assigned duties with energy and enthusiasm and to serve loyally and honorably.

No formal training was conducted for the early lightkeepers in this country, but beginning about 1820, they were given written materials explaining the operation and care of the reflectors and lamps; later, a booklet called *Directions to Lighthouse Keepers* was distributed and served as a training manual and the first source consulted if there were questions or problems. It contained detailed directions on the duties of the lightkeeper and the operation of the station. Like many government publications, it was mired in its own contents, and was probably not consulted as frequently or as open-mindedly as the Lighthouse Service intended, but it was an early attempt to bring some semblance of conformity to the job and establish standards for performance.

Following the reorganization of the Lighthouse Service in the 1850s, an apprentice-type system was officially adopted. Keepers entered the service as assistants and learned their responsibilities under the watchful eye of a veteran head keeper. Salary, of course, was commensurate with experience and rank, plus the nature of the station to which a keeper was assigned. Offshore keepers earned more money, as did keepers of the larger stations or twin lights or stations where ancillary duties were needed, such as tending a buoy or post beacon.

Most lightkeepers were also required to keep daily weather journals as well as records of the number and types of vessels that passed. The station logbook — a standard at lighthouses after about 1820 — became mandatory after 1850 and was checked by the district inspector on a regular basis. It contained a summary of the daily activities of a station, along with any events of importance, such as a wreck or rescue, visitors at the station, or local happenings of note. Many logbooks colorfully chronicled the life and tenor of a particular place and time.

Logbooks frequently mention visitors at lighthouses, usually family or friends of the keeper. A group gathers at Maine's Winter Harbor Light about 1870, most likely on a Sunday, the only day keepers were permitted leisure time. One lightkeeper stands on the lantern gallery while the other appears at right in front of the house. (U.S. Coast Guard Archives)

From Copper Harbor Lighthouse logbook, Lake Superior:

June 24, 1900: I opened this journal today after having used the old one for nearly fifteen years. Our two children [are] grown from infants to a young man and woman and this little house is the place they have learned to call home. What an uncertain world this is. Who can look into the future? I made the first entry in this journal on a quiet Sabboth afternoon. Who will write the closing one?

September 30, 1930: Am retiring from the Lighthouse Service today, leaving Mr. Haven in charge of the station. Have spent the most of my life in the service and am leaving it with best wishes and not much regret.

From Grand Island Lighthouse logbook, Lake Superior:

April 20, 1874: Maple sugar making has begun at last, and as usual it is accompanied with plenty of tooth ache. I consider hot maple candy the Dentist's Best Friend.

From Currituck Beach Lighthouse logbook, North Carolina:
March 1, 1876: The Italian Bark Ottarina *struck this beach and went to pieces the next day. The crew of the L.S.S. [Lifesaving Station] lost their lives attempting to rescue the crew . . .*
February 15, 1888: During the past week we have been on the beach picking up bodies from the wreck [of the steamer Metropolis*], trying to identify them and take them home for burial.*
December 19, 1888: Snow, very cold fresh breeze. Snow frozen on the storm panes.

From Calumet Harbor Entrance Lighthouse logbook, Lake Michigan:
November 13, 1880: The sunset [is] behind a bank of dark clouds, yet it is not gloomy for the poets and our good sense teaches us there is a Silver Lining beyond.
May 18, 1882: I am often told that I cannot grow trees here . . . . My trees are doing well and not many years hence will shade the entire yard. The woodbine and ivy planted around the house and running up the walls proves a nuisance on account of it's festering so many worms.

From Rock Island Lighthouse logbook, St. Lawrence River:
July 25, 1872: A small fishing skiff with a man and wife came to this light for shelter during the storm; they had to spend the night.
August 6, 1872: President Grant is having and receiving a great crowd of people at Pullman Island.
July 12, 1873: River flies very many and very troublesome about the lantern nights.
October 20, 1873: Keeper built a flight of stairs, starting near the wood house door and landing on top of the rock, towards the pump, at his own expense.

If an appointment to a lighthouse were obtained, there was no guarantee of keeping it, even after years of faithful and commendable service. One error in judgment, minor or significant, was sufficient cause for discharge. Thomas Jefferson took a firm stand during his administration, saying: ". . . the keepers of lighthouses should be dismissed for small degrees of remissness, because of the calamities which even these produce."

One of the first lighthouses ordered built by the new Federal Government in 1789, the Montauk Point Light was given special attention by President George Washington. His Secretary of State, Thomas Jefferson, felt lightkeepers should be discharged for the smallest measures of "remissness." (National Archives)

Keepers were suspended for letting their lights go out, sometimes even when it was beyond their control. They were removed for drunkenness and insubordination, for being absent from their stations without good reason or falsifying statements in their logbooks, for indulging in certain types of sideline businesses or taking in boarders, and for generally being derelict in their duties. Until the passage of the Civil Service Act in 1883, they were also dismissed for being affiliated with an unpopular political party.

In 1854, the *Sandwich Register* carried these lines concerning the removal of the keeper of Wings Neck Lighthouse in Massachusetts: "Mr. Lawrence was a faithful, capable man and was appointed at the time the lighthouse was built. His crime consisted in having been appointed by the Whigs."

Cape Cod fisherman Collins Howes received an appointment to the Chatham Twin Lights because he had lost a leg in a fishing accident and could not go to sea. This practice of giving lightkeeping positions to disabled seamen and war veterans was commonplace in the 19th century; however, it did not protect them from political abuse. With the election of James Polk in 1845, Howes was removed from the Chatham Twin Lights in favor of a patron of the new administration. This he accepted without argument, but when the new keeper died suddenly, and the widow was appointed keeper, an embittered Howes began a slanderous campaign to have her ousted. Neighbors of the widow rallied in her defense, writing letters to the President and praising her abilities, not to mention her lamentable predicament of raising several children without a husband. Her lighthouse duties aside, she was a typical woman for her day and had no real political power to influence a decision about her suitability as a lightkeeper, but likely her deceased husband's friendship with the Polk administration worked in her favor. Howes lost his bid for the job.

The political reins that so strongly dictated keepers' appointments prior to the Civil Service Act, as well as preferences given to disabled veterans, were illustrated in the following letter, mailed to a Wisconsin senator in 1872 concerning the hiring of a keeper for a lighthouse in Racine:

"He has no bad habits — is faithful and true — was a soldier in the war of the rebellion — is a cripple for life by reason of freezing in the prison farm at Saulsbury — and it need hardly be added is an ardent friend and supporter of the current adminstration."

Formal inspections of stations and their personnel were instituted in the 1850s by the new governing board of the Lighthouse Service. These surprise visits were intended to keep the keepers on their toes and to assure that the stations were maintained in good condition and properly attended year-round. A competitive atmosphere began to permeate the service, since inspectors had the power to nominate individual stations and keepers for awards, including the coveted "Superintendent's Star" given for exemplary performance.

Inspectors supposedly arrived unannounced on government vessels called lighthouse tenders. The smaller of these ponderous, round-hulled work ships were named for flowers and shrubs, while the larger tenders were given the names of trees. It's difficult to imagine the rough-cut crewmen of these vessels sitting around in smoky bars on the shorefront boasting about their jobs aboard

the *Hyacinth, Geranium, Arbutus,* or the *Dandelion*; but such feminine names belied the hard work and durability of the tenders.
Not only did they build lighthouses and maintain them with supplies, repairs, and personnel, but they also brought the lighthouse
inspector on his rounds.

Inspectors were held in high regard. They were always respected, sometimes feared, and occasionally hated. It's said they
came wearing white gloves, looked in every corner and in every
closet and cupboard. Even bureau drawers were inspected in bed-
rooms to see that their contents were clean and neatly folded.
The lighthouse itself was scrutinized for dirt, tarnished brass, and
fingerprints on the lens. Tools and supplies were inventoried and
records reviewed to see that items such as coal and oil were frugally used. Keepers had to account for every gill of oil and every
wick in the lamp. They could be dismissed if the figures didn't
compute to the inspector's satisfaction or if there was any suspicion that government materials were being wasted or sold for
personal profit.

A keeper was required to be in uniform when the inspector
arrived and to willingly pause in the daily routine to accompany
the inspector on his rounds. Assistants, including wives who held

The sidewheel lighthouse tender *Holly* delivers supplies to Point No Point Lighthouse in Chesapeake Bay. A fleet of government-built tenders serviced lighthouses from about 1840 until the Lighthouse Service was absorbed by the Coast
Guard in 1939. Beginning in 1869, lighthouse tenders were christened with bo-
tanical names, a tradition the Coast Guard has continued in the naming of its
buoy tenders. (U.S. Coast Guard Museum)

It's likely the keepers of the "sparkplug" lighthouse at Mile Rocks in San Francisco Bay were never surprised by the tender's arrival. They spent a lot of time
on the gallery walkways jogging around and around, or hitting a golf ball tied to
a rope. This 1960 photo shows a launch conveying fuel lines to the lighthouse while
the tender *Magnolia* anchors away from the rocks. (Nautical Research Center)

official positions, were also expected to present themselves in
uniform or, in the case of the women, for whom no uniform was
prescribed, neatly attired. To allay any complaints concerning
surprise visits, inspectors made a practice of flying their ensign

while aboard a tender and having the whistle sounded as they approached — a warning intended to give the lighthouse keeper just enough time to wash up and put on the uniform.

Most families were not taken by surprise, however. A variety of clever means were employed to find out just when an inspector would arrive. A communications network with the neighbors was a popular method. One keeper at Saugerties Lighthouse on the Hudson River had an agreement with his neighbors that they would hang a white bedsheet out the upper floor window of their house when they sighted the tender approaching. Since they were situated at a curve in the river, and were able to see the inspector's vessel when it was about a half-hour away, they could give the Saugerties lightkeeper advance notice with an emergency airing of the bedclothes. This allowed the keeper just enough time to do some quick dusting and polishing.

After phone service became available at lighthouses, there might have been a call from a friend at the district offices who knew the date and time of an inspector's arrival at a particular station. More often, an inspector's approach was discovered by less sophisticated means. Lighthouse tenders were noisy vessels each with its own characteristic engine sounds. Stephen Jones, who served at Delaware's Harbor of Refuge Lighthouse, remembered being able to discern the inspector's tender from all other vessels by the sound of its diesels. Since inspectors were also supposed to fly their personal flag when they were aboard a supply tender, a good set of binoculars or a small telescope was useful.

Sometimes it was helpful to have a work horse or mule on hand. A mule named Jerry at Southeast Farallon Lighthouse off California always sounded the alarm when he spotted the supply tender on the horizon. He knew its arrival meant work: He would be caught, harnessed to the little cart that brought coal up the tramway, and forced to labor for hours. Hence he reacted to the sight of the tender with hysterical brays and a wild stampede to the opposite end of the island.

Spouses and children were included in the inspections, if only through the tension and worry of the keepers. Marie Carr remembered inspection day at Long Island Sound's Little Gull Light in the 1920s. The tender was usually spotted pulling out of New

London just after daylight. She would get the children out of bed and dressed, for no one could be lounging about during an inspection, except in the case of sickness. Carr's kitchen was spotless and her youngsters were shiny-faced and sated with pancakes by the time the inspector stepped through her door for coffee. She always made sure she wore a clean apron and that some tantalizing smell of pie or muffins or bread was wafting through the house. Every little detail mattered, even the smells, which if friendly enough might melt a harsh inspector's heart.

Lighthouse children sensed that inspectors held some sort of power over their parents and were awed by the appearance of these men. Even discussion of inspections could arouse apprehension, if not dread, in a child. Philmore Wass, who as a boy lived at Libby Islands Light in Maine, remembered an inspector named Luther who became confused in Wass' mind with God. "I thought they were the same, the only difference being that Luther occasionally appeared in uniform." Joe St. Andre had similar memories, having spent his youth at several Great Lakes lighthouses and experienced many grueling inspections: "He [the inspector] was like probably the second coming of the Lord."

Glimpses of Daily Life

In 1912, under the competent leadership of George Putnam, the Bureau of Lighthouses began issuing the monthly *Lighthouse Service Bulletin*. It was the first official newsletter for lighthouse keepers and contained a smorgasbord of interesting copy, from stories of heroism and exceptional performance of duty to informational work-related topics, to articles of interest to lightkeepers but also sometimes written by them. For example, the February 1917 issue had a formula for fly poison, while January 1918's issue offered a recipe for "Baked Hominy and Cheese." Statistics on the number of hours of annual fog at various lighthouses were offered in the December 1918 issue; the August 1926 edition featured an article on "Sport," the canine mascot of a Great Lakes lighthouse tender.

A more detailed sampling from the *Lighthouse Service Bulletin* follows:

December 1912: The keeper of the Wadmelaw River lights, South Carolina, reports the following incident: "On Thursday afternoon, May

29, when the man who assists in this work was ascending the Beacon No. 3, and while nearly at the top, he heard just above his head a terrific buzzing sound that caused him to hurriedly descend. Peering around for the cause, he was amazed to discover a huge rattlesnake that had coiled itself just under the light box; arming himself with an oar he succeeded in making it plunge overboard by thrusts of the oar; when to his amazement, as well as discomfiture, the now thoroughly angered reptile, instead of making off, swam back to the beacon, and proceeded to ascend, weaving its body in and out between the steps. Fortunately he managed to give it another well-directed blow with the oar, which caused it to drop back into the water and float off apparently dying."

May 1921: After more than 38 years in the Lighthouse Service, during which period he has not been ill a single day, L.D. Marchant, of Hudgins, Va., now permanently ashore, attributes his good health to the fact that he has been where doctors could not get to him....

While trips ashore were infrequent, Mr. Marchant did not complain much of the loneliness of the life [at lighthouses on the Chesapeake Bay]. His wife and family lived with him while he was keeper of Watts Island Lighthouse, but they tired of the life, and when Mr. Marchant was transferred to Stingray Point they lived nearby on the mainland.

"During the 32 years I remained at Stingray Point," Mr. Marchant added, "the life was somewhat lonesome, but the light station is furnished with a library of about 60 books. After the work of the day was over I spent the rest of the day in reading. The libraries are exchanged from station to station about every three months, so I did not have to read the same books over."

April 1912: Method is the very hinge of business, and there is no method without punctuality. Punctuality is important because it subserves the peace and good temper of a family; the want of it not only infringes on necessary duty, but sometimes excludes this duty. The calmness of mind which it produces is another advantage of punctuality; a disorderly man is always in a hurry; he has no time to speak to you because he is going elsewhere, and when he gets there, he is too late for his business, or he must hurry away to another before he can finish it. Punctuality gives weight to character. . . .

September 1928: The President and Mrs. Coolidge visited Devils Island Light Station, in the western end of Lake Superior, on August 22 and inspected the station, according to a report received from the keeper,

Hans F. Christensen.

The presidential party arrived at noon on the yacht Nellwood from Bayfield, Wis., with a party of about 50 on board, the yacht being convoyed by the Coast Guard cutter Crawford, the steamer Madeline, and two speed boats. Lunch was served on the east dock at the light station, and the Nellwood left at 2 p.m. for Madeline Island.

The light keeper states that the President and Mrs. Coolidge expressed themselves as well pleased with the visit to the lighthouse and hoped they would be able to make another visit next year.

It is believed that this is the first time in a long while that a light station had been honored by a visit from the President.

January 1918: Cottage cheese and nut loaf (serves 8): 1 cup cottage cheese, 1 cup walnut meats (or other nuts), 1 cup bread crumbs, juice of a half lemon, 1 tsp. salt, 1/4 tsp. pepper, 2 tablespoons chopped onions, 1 tablespoon oleomargarine, vegetable oil, or meat drippings.

Mix the cheese, nuts, crumbs, lemon, salt, and pepper. Cook the onion in the fat and a little water until tender. Add the onion and sufficient water or meat stick to moisten. Mix well, pour into a baking dish, and brown in the oven. One pound of beans cooked and put through a seive may be substituted for the nuts. In this case pimento is good for

Landing supplies at Cape Sarichef Light in the Aleutian Islands was risky business due to dangerous seas. A June 1915 notice in the *Lighthouse Service Bulletin* mentions the purchase of line-throwing guns to land mail, supplies, and the keepers themselves. (U.S. Coast Guard)

seasoning. The cooked beans and cheese are both moist, so that usually no additional liquid is necessary.

June 1915: Great difficulty has been experienced in the past in landing supplies and mail at the Scotch Cap and Cape Sarichef Light Stations, Alaska. Owing to the situation of the stations, the condition of the sea is very often unfavorable to making landings through the surf for days at a time. Measures have therefore been taken recently for the purchase of line-throwing guns for these stations and also for the Cape St. Elias Light Station, Alaska, now in the course of construction, which, it is believed, will be very useful in landing mail and in connection with landing supplies and transferring the keepers to and from the stations during unfavorable weather.

July 1932: An instance of resourcefulness on the part of a keeper that will result in some economy, has been reported by the superintendent of the sixth district. The keeper J.H. Carlin, of Brunswick, Ga., wrote the superintendent as follows:

"Visited the old dump grounds and salvaged bolts and clamps from old bumpers, ample to make repairs to St. Andrews Sound Beacon ladder. Had to do a little blacksmithing, about an hour, to bend up angle irons, make good ones, too, out of steel, some were three-fourths inch thick, and will last some time. The bolts I got proved to be excellent material, something we can hardly get in the market. The blacksmith job cost nothing. I had my own forge, and the coal was salvaged from the waste coal along the railroad track, so we will be out nothing but the little time taken to get the parts together.

Working in the Public View

While the Lighthouse Service was adamant that lighthouses not become tourist attractions, a certain amount of public relations work was expected of the keepers. On Sundays in particular, even into the last years of the profession in the 1980s, the public was permitted to visit lighthouses and were given guided tours by the uniformed keepers. Some lighthouses were more popular tourist destinations than others. During the post-Civil War era, so many visitors came to Sankaty Head Lighthouse on Nantucket that the keeper was obliged to widen the opening leading from the watch room to the lantern to accomodate ladies in fashionable hoop skirts. Peter Richards, who served as assistant keeper at Michigan's

Tourism at lighthouses boomed after the Civil War and continues today. Among the nation's most visited sentinels is rustic Bass Harbor Head in Maine's Acadia National Park. (Courtesy Richard DeAngelis)

Pointe Aux Barques Lighthouse in the 1890s, had a more difficult problem: The sheer height of the lighthouse sometimes frightened visitors so much they had to be carried down the stairs on Richards' back.

Split Rock Lighthouse, built in 1910 north of Duluth, Minnesota, received thousands of visitors in the summer, due to its spectacular lake vistas and the grandeur of the tower itself, 178 feet above Lake Superior on a cloven precipice of brindled gray-brown rock. Travelers were drawn to this and other picturesque sentinels where they could enjoy a Sunday picnic or walk the beach, or simply take in the supposed healthful vapors of the lakes and sea. The romance of it all was enlarged by the unrealistic portrayal of lighthouse life on the covers of magazines, such as the *Saturday Evening Post*, in paintings by artists like Edward Hopper and Sir Edwin Henry Landseer, and by authors like Daphne DuMaurier and Eugenia Price.

Maine's Portland Head Light was popular with 19th-century

Probing the night with its benevolent beam, Portland Head Lighthouse has appeared on countless postcards, calendars, and greeting cards. Throughout its long career it has assisted not only the mariner but also clever advertisers. In recent years a Portland jewelry store promoted its wares with an image of two huge watches strapped around the lighthouse as if it were a giant's wrist. (Elinor De Wire Collection)

postcard companies, due to its accessibility to visitors, its rockbound shoreline and old stone tower, its Victorian keepers' house, and the sweeping panorama of the busy harbor and slate-colored seas. Poet Henry Wadsworth Longfellow drew inspiration from this site, sitting on the rocks just offshore of the lighthouse. It is said that his poem "The Lighthouse" was written under the benevolent beam of Portland Head Light, though some historians believe the poem actually refers to Minots Ledge Light off Cohasset, Massachusetts. Longfellow's often-recited sea ballad "The Wreck of the Hesperus," about the horrible loss of a ship on a ledge off Gloucester, Massachusetts, probably gained much of its intensity and realism from watching the seas break over the crags below Portland Head Lighthouse.

Equally inspiring was Point Pinos Lighthouse at Monterey, California, with its cypress trees hunched over in the wind and the little Cape Cod-style house with a lantern jutting up from its roof spewing friendly golden rays over the Pacific. Keeper Allen

Luce, who tended the beacon in the 1870s, extended his hospitality to a thin, gaunt traveler of Scottish blood who later wrote: ". . . you will find the lighthouse keeper playing at the piano, making ship models and bows and arrows, studying dawn and sunrise in amateur painting, and with a dozen other elegant pursuits and interests to surprise his brave, old-country rival." He signed the keeper's guestbook in the familiar RLS scrawl — Robert Louis Stevenson.

Such glamorous images of the lighthouse keeper as painter, poet, and musician prompted many people to plan a vacation at the shore near a lighthouse, where it was believed life's most restful and edifying experiences could be had. The lighthouse was thought to be a tonic for the body and the soul. But not all lighthouses were as quaint as Point Pinos and not all keepers as fortunate as Mr. Allen Luce. Point Pinos remained a pleasant assignment year-round, save an occasional blustery storm. But Minnesota's Split Rock had another side to its personality: No one came to visit after October unless he or she planned to stay for six months. Winter was serious business along Lake Superior before the advent of electricity, telephone service, snow plows, VCRs and a cabinet full of old movies.

Portland Head, though not as miserable as Split Rock in the thick of winter, was still damp and cold until modern heating was installed. Like many aging masonry towers, its stone walls drew moisture on the inside. Keepers said the tower would "sweat," and when it was cold enough, the moisture turned to ice, making the entire column of stone like a huge refrigerator. Sometimes a blizzard obscured all vision, or the wind was so powerful a rope had to be stretched between the house and the outbuildings and around the base of the tower. The keepers, looking like marionettes, pulled themselves along this ropewalk of sorts to get from one place to another without being lost or blown over the cliffs. The tourists of summer saw none of this. In their minds, the life of the keeper was all sunshine and gentle breezes, wildflowers peeking up from fissures in the rocks, fish jumping, and picnics spread on the green lawn.

Living in a fishbowl with fairweather friends coming to visit was not without its consequences. Some lightkeepers grew bored

The urge to amuse themselves at the expense of the public infected some light-house keepers. Several attendants at California's Pigeon Point Light assuaged their loneliness and boredom by telling tall tales to unknowing visitors. (U.S. Coast Guard)

with the curious callers and began amusing themselves by embroidering their conversations with untruths. The first keeper at California's Pigeon Point Lighthouse, Capt. J.W. Patterson, met the press for an on-site interview just prior to lighting up for the first time in 1872. When a woman questioned him about the empty oil reservoirs in his lamps, he announced that the lamps required whale oil and could not be filled until someone caught and "tried out" a whale. The tendency to mislead the public must have been infectious at this station, for a subsequent keeper told visitors that if he drew aside the white drapes around the huge prism lens, its intense heat would burn their bodies to a crisp and melt the glass of the lantern windows. Everyone was duly impressed and commended the keeper for his courage in working under such hazardous conditions.

Dangerous optics did exist, but not at Pigeon Point. Its lens was kept covered more to protect it from visitors than to protect them from it. The keepers at New Jersey's Navesink Twin Lights, where many of the larger and more powerful optics were tested, wore special green-tinted glasses to protect their eyes while tending these beacons, but none of the old Fresnel lenses was capable of charring human skin. However, when Oak Island Lighthouse went into service in 1958 in North Carolina, it banished the darkness with a high-tech, dual-intensity flash of light. On the highest setting, for fog and extremely low visibility, the beacon was powerful enough to scorch the skin of anyone standing in the lantern room, and special goggles had to be worn to shield the eyes.

Keepers were forbidden to take pay or tips for giving tours of their stations. The 1902 *Instructions to Light-Keepers & Masters of Light-House Vessels* clearly stated:

Keepers must not make any charge nor receive any fee for admitting visitors to light-houses, or light-vessels, or for performing any service to humanity, or accomodation at their station, or on board the vessel on which they may be serving.

Keepers must be courteous and polite to all visitors and show them everything of interest about the station at such times as will not interfere with light-house duties. Keepers must not allow visitors to handle the apparatus or deface light-house property.

The instruction further stated that visitors could not tour a station after sunset or before sunrise and that they would not be allowed entry to a station if intoxicated. Keepers were warned to beware of visitors who might scratch their initials on glass windows, the lens prisms, and painted surfaces. They were also discouraged from accepting bonafide gifts from visitors, though no regulation to that effect was ever published. The practice of accepting gifts was difficult for the government to restrict and was considered by many personnel to be a benefit to morale on lonely outposts. Gifts came, welcomed by the government or not, especially on holidays and particularly for those who were marooned on offshore lights.

The Harbor of Refuge keepers got ribbon candy at Christmas, usually shattered in a thousand pieces from its bumpy trip out to the forsaken sentinel on the end of the breakwater at Lewes, Delaware. A number of lighthouse keepers in southern New England were given radios by Mrs. Edward Harkness of Waterford, Connecticut, who it's said had a soft spot in her heart for the sentinels along the shore. New London Ledge Light's crew also received gifts — books and magazines from women's clubs, and an occasional six-pack of beer dropped off by boaters, though alcohol

The keepers of "stag stations," where only men were allowed, spent their idle hours with hobbies such as woodcarving, painting, and reading. Ships' crews sometimes stopped at these isolated stations with gifts. The keepers of Scotch Cap Light posed in the 1920s with a Christmas tree given to them by a passing steamer. There were no trees on their barren Aleutian station, evergreen or otherwise. (U.S. Coast Guard)

was strictly forbidden. Local fishermen were generous, too, stopping by to present lobsters and fish as tokens of their appreciation for the men who kept the water-bound light.

Sympathetic folks ashore often adopted a lighthouse and sent the keepers letters and boxes of goodies, which might have included gum, candy, cigarettes, shaving supplies, writing paper, and homemade gifts of jams, pickles, cookies, or a knitted cap and mittens. Schoolchildren were especially fond of this activity. For many years, the families at Cape Neddick Light received mail and packages from youngsters in nearby York, Maine. One of the station's last Coast Guard keepers also visited the children at their school. Once a year, he made a special trip ashore to talk to the students about his life as a lightkeeper and to thank them for their kind letters and gifts. At times he confessed he felt like a visitor from another planet, so strangely did the children regard him.

Pastimes and Personal Pursuits

The lighthouse, by design, was a place of unending work, but when idle moments came keepers amused themselves in myriad ways. Some painted; Frank Jo Raymond learned to paint in his free time on Latimer Reef Light in the 1920s and was still making his living as a painter at his death in 1993. Logbook poetry reveals that many keepers enjoyed lyric pursuits; some were also zealous letter-writers and diarists. Collections were popular — shells, stamps, butterflies, and the like, some quite large and noteworthy. Laura Hecox collected native specimens and put together a small natural history museum in the old Santa Cruz Lighthouse in California. Her personal tours for visitors and friends were a delightful mix of natural history and pharology, the science of lighthouse keeping. Another California keeper raised horses for the stagecoach line, while Maria Israel of Old Point Loma Lighthouse made beautiful shell pictures and mirror frames.

Of course, reading was the mainstay of leisure time, and most lighthouses did not lack for books. Some stations had permanent libraries, but if there was no such resource the government, beginning in 1876, supplied books in big, portable oak bookcases that circulated among the lighthouses. James Gibbs, who as a young man served at Tillamook Light off the Oregon coast, discovered a

gold mine of books in a tomb-like room under the lantern and
secreted himself there to read whenever he could spare a few minutes. The passion paid off, as Gibbs later became a writer and
editor and is today recognized as a skillful author of West Coast
maritime history and lore.

The same appetite for books and literature infected Stephen
Jones at Harbor of Refuge Lighthouse in Delaware some 30 years
ago. His earliest encounter with the keeper he was to relieve involved a sparring match about what constitutes good writing. The
outgoing keeper was a collector of poems and stories, which on
the day of his departure were packed off the lighthouse in a box.
Roughly handled, the box broke open on a perilous ride down a
rope to a lurching boat. A shower of paper was caught by the
wind and settled on the sea around the lighthouse like so many
floating seagulls. The departing keeper desperately tried to retrieve his treasured collection, while the boat dispassionately pulled
away, its pilot unable to comprehend the importance of a box full
of yellowed papers.

*I had a classmate who fitted for college by the lamps of a lighthouse,
which was more light, we think, than the University afforded.*
                                                        Henry David Thoreau

*Author's Note: The hardships experienced by many lighthouse keepers
and their families, coupled with ridiculously low pay for difficult and
dangerous work, prompted a politicking prayer by an unknown author,
probably a lighthouse keeper from the Great Lakes region. The prayer is
in the collection of the Shore Village Museum, Rockland, Maine, and
was provided by Ken Black.*

A Prayer for the Lighthouse Keepers and Their Families

Heavenly Father, grant thy blessing in a very special manner
to the men and women and children in the great lighthouse family scattered up and down the coasts and islands in the Great Lakes
and rivers and various seas and oceans in the Great Water World.
They are Thy children, oh our Father, many of them a long way
from home and living in great solitude where life is a continual
tragedy, bitter because it is lonely, especially bitter when they be-

come discouraged and lose hope, and the pitiful little force within them fails to furnish them with light or joy. Oh God, our Father, our hearts are moved with deepest sympathy and our tears of sorrow bedim our eyes as we remember their hardships and deprivations and dangers that are ever with them. Raise up for them numerous friends, especially among Congressmen and Senators, that they may enact measures for the improvement of the condition of these, our brothers, and their patient wives and children who so bravely keep their lights burning brightly that our comrades, the masters of ships and sailors, "Who go down to the sea in ships, who do business in great waters," may know the right course to take in the storm and fog and darkness of the night.

Grant unto this people such blessings as they have never received before in an increase of pay that has long been withheld from them by the rich government they have so faithfully served, and bring them into new paths of happiness in this practical financial way that the personal joy and light that has become dimmed because of their condition may shine abroad into the world helping to proclaim the love of Christ, as they throw out the lifeline to perishing souls from the harbor of refuge and stand by with a helping hand as they cross the bar. Oh, our Father, keep us a brotherhood of light keepers united in thought and word and deed and mutual love that though we cannot unite our voices together unto Thee in prayer because of the thousands of miles of land and water that separate us, yet we unite our hearts in prayer to Thee, and share our sorrows and our joys together, and as we come down the long path of the afternoon to the darkening shadows, grant, oh Thou Blessed Savior, that Thou would join us as we cross the last bar and struggle for the farther shore, the lee shore of the land where the sun never goes down, and wilt Thou graciously and lovingly lead us into the land where sorrow is unknown and where there is no darkness for He who is the light of the world will be the light thereof, where never again shall come heartache or fear and where the hand of God our Father will forever wipe away all tears from our eyes. In Jesus' name we ask it. Amen.

CHAPTER 3

CHASING AWAY THE FOG

From a lighthouse beyond the harbor's mouth, a foghorn is heard at regular intervals, moaning like a mournful whale in labor.

—Eugene O'Neill

Destruction Island is a 30-acre hunk of rock and soil jutting up from the sea within sight of the Washington mainland some 20 miles south of LaPush. It rises to a plateau about 75 feet above water and is covered by a lush carpet of grass. Its flat top, along with an oblong shape, gives it the look of a huge dinner table with a green cloth draped over it; a white candle burns at one end of the table — the Destruction Island Lighthouse.

When the lighthouse was first commissioned in 1891, there was no fog signal at the station, an obvious oversight considering the unpredictable personality of the ocean off Puget Sound. It was only two years until complaints by shipping interests and fishermen induced the government to install a steam-powered siren. It shrieked its admonition to steer clear of the rocks for many seasons before growing so hoarse and petulant it had to be replaced. Perhaps because of the need to distinguish it from other nearby signals, it was changed from a siren to a diaphragm horn, the kind that bellows in a deep voice so like that of an angry bull.

At the time this change was made, there were a number of cows pastured on the island; they had been ferried out and lifted up the precipice in a sling. Grazing was good, and there was no need for a fence, since the island dropped off abruptly on all sides and there was no escape except into the sea. To keep his bovine stock replenished, the lighthouse keeper also owned a bull. Alone amid a harem of submissive cows, this fine specimen was quite content, even docile, until one morning when a low, threatening

A lighthouse keeper checks the foghorns at his station. Their deafening concussion could knock seagulls from the air and seriously impair human hearing. Fog signaling was a large part of the work at some lighthouses. Their honks, howls, screeches, groans, and whistles could be heard as much as 30% of the year. (Nautical Research Center)

bawl pierced the air over the green pasture and sent the cows rushing in every direction.

The alarmed bull snorted, pawed the ground, and scanned the island for evidence of an intruder. He saw nothing that even remotely resembled a rival bull, but a moment later another horrendous bellow sounded. The noise appeared to be coming from a small white building at one end of the island near the lighthouse — a new barn, the old bull thought to himself, housing a younger and more virulent male who had arrived to challenge his supremacy. In a blur of horns and hooves, the bull went racing toward his opponent, determined to protect himself and his territory.

As he crashed through the small picket fence surrounding the fog signal building, the roar echoed across the island again, and workmen scrambled to safety behind the oil tanks. The bull charged the building and smashed in the door; next, he rammed the ladders and tool boxes, followed by a few crates and empty barrels. When he set his aim on the oil tanks, the men ran for the lighthouse.

It was several hours before the bull's rampage ended, probably more from fatigue than surrender. The fog signal was stopped long enough to fashion a makeshift enclosure and lure the beleaguered beast inside it. Even then, the pen required strengthening when the horn's low-throated tones resumed. Only after many weeks and several persistent fogs did the Destruction Island bull come to terms with his invisible nemesis.

Voices in the Fog
Keeping a lighthouse often meant also keeping a fog signal. A light is useful only in good visibility. In a fog, the beam's range is reduced, sometimes drastically, and some other means of warning must be issued. Before there were horns, sirens, whistles, or bells, people banged pans, beat drums, or shouted into the murk to aid the mariner caught in the mists. It wasn't until 1719 that the first official fog signal was put into operation in America, and not surprisingly, it was a lighthouse keeper who came up with the novel idea of firing "a Great Gun to answer Shipps in a Fogg."

The site was Boston Bay, one of the busiest ports in the colo-

The fog cannon at Boston Light was America's first official fog signal. It was fired every half-hour during periods of poor visibility to help ships steer clear of Little Brewster Island and its surrounding shoals. The cannon was retired to the U.S. Coast Guard Academy at New London, Connecticut, some years ago but was later returned to Boston Light as a memento of that sentinel's unique distinction as the first official light station in America. (U.S. Coast Guard Archives)

nies and riddled with islands, rocks, and sandbars. John Hayes, the second keeper of the Boston Lighthouse, quickly recognized the need for a fog signal when he heard ships firing their guns in the murk to tell each other their positions. Boston Light, feeble even in clear weather, could not be seen in the fog. Hayes suggested to the Massachusetts Bay Colony that a cannon be set up near the lighthouse and fired with regularity to serve as warning. It was agreed the cannon would be fired every half hour when fog shrouded the bay. John Hayes got more than he bargained for — little sleep, headaches from the concussion of the gun, and only a small increase in salary for his effort. Long after the gun gave up its duties to other fog warning devices, it was moved to the grounds of the U.S. Coast Guard Academy in New London, Connecticut, where it remained until May 1993, when Coast Guard officials decided it should be returned to the Boston Light for exhibit.

Guns were placed at other lighthouses, too, some as late as the mid-1800s. Point Bonita Lighthouse on the northern hinge of the Golden Gate was given a fog cannon by the Benicia Arsenal in

1855. A retired army sergeant, who thought he deserved the peace
and solitude of lighthouse life, was hired to operate the beacon
and the gun. He quickly discovered that the strength of character
that had sustained him in battle was no match for San Francisco
fogs. He resigned only two months after his appointment, saying:
"I cannot find any person here to relieve me, not [for] five minutes; I have been up three days and nights and had only two hours
rest. I was nearly used up." The sergeant was replaced, and a few
months later the cannon was also gone, upstaged by a mechanical
fogbell that struck automatically. At $2000 a year for gunpowder,
the demanding cannon had proven too expensive for both its keepers and Congress.

It was the clarity and simplicity of a bell that most appealed to
the government when the time came to get serious about fog signals. Unfortunately, many foggy days had passed and thousands
of bewildered vessels had run aground in fogs before any orga-
nized effort was made to solve the problem. In this case, and with
definite pun intended, it was a concerted effort: The variety of
bell tones created and the melodies written for them could have
inspired a symphony. At the very least, they left local residents
humming their lilting songs and waxing sentimental about a particular tone that reminded them of home.

West Quoddy Lighthouse was given the nation's first fogbell
in 1820. It weighed 500 pounds and had to be struck by hand
when the fog rolled in at Lubec, Maine. For this tedious work, the
keeper received a paltry $60 a year, in addition to his regular
lightkeeper's pay. Of course, on foggy days he was expected to
tend the light and the fogbell equally. Having a wife and children
to help was imperative, though many spouses received no compensation for their work. When the fog was thick for days on end,
devotion and solicitude often clashed with job satisfaction, and
sometimes even sanity. No doubt the West Quoddy lightkeeper
made many colorful remarks in his logbook after hammering the
bell through a few Down East pea-soupers.

But not all fogbells were considered a bane to the job. One
keeper at a Maine lighthouse rigged up a long rope from the fogbell
clapper to his bedroom and before retiring each night would spend
an idle hour or two ringing the bell to amuse himself. Keeper

The first fogbell in use in America rang out from West Quoddy Lighthouse at the border between Maine and New Brunswick. Today this red and white candy-striped sentinel is a favorite with tourists and photographers. (Elinor De Wire)

Lancelot Rowe and his wife, at Massachusetts' Thachers Island Twin Lights, welcomed a new daughter into their family in 1853 at the same time a new fogbell was installed. The couple decided the bell was tolling a birth announcement and were so enamored of its pure, clear tone they named their new baby Belle Thacher Rowe.

By 1860, titanic fogbells were being cast for use at lighthouses. Mechanical strikers had been developed to free the keeper from manually sounding the bell. Among the biggest of the bells was the one installed in 1885 at Ediz Hook Lighthouse in Puget Sound. It weighed a hefty 3150 pounds and was rung every 15 seconds by an automatic striker. A pyramidal structure called the bellhouse enclosed a clockworks and weights suspended below the bell to power its striker. The clock needed to be wound every few hours but was otherwise self-sufficient. When the huge bell at Ediz Hook struck, it set all the metal parts of the station vibrating and humming sympathetically and sometimes loosened rocks and soil around the station.

The bell at Trinidad Head Lighthouse in northern California was even larger — two tons. The government decided to anchor it

Mechanical strikers were developed for fogbells shortly after the Civil War. This one at Connecticut's Bridgeport Lighthouse was operated by a rod connected to a clockworks system inside the tower. The clock had to be wound every few hours. Certain metallic tones carried well across the waves. (U.S. Coast Guard Archives)

into the cliff beneath the lighthouse to direct its sound seaward. The fact that its loud bongs were pointed away from the keeper and his family was an unplanned bonus. The weights for this bell were suspended on cables down the cliff face and were exposed to the sea. In 1900, as the keeper was tending the fogbell, the cables snapped and the weights plunged into the sea, never to be recovered.

Some lightkeepers had dogs who entertained themselves and hordes of visitors by ringing the fogbells; but fog was neither a source of amusement for those who traveled in it nor for those who worked to penetrate its vapors with beacons and bells. A multitude of inventions passed in review in the 19th century to make fog signaling easier and more effective. For example, the keepers at Maine's Whitehead Lighthouse operated a curious tidal fog signal. It consisted of a bell with its striker attached to a wooden timber suspended on the sea; as the timber bounced about in the waves, the bell tolled irregularly. It appeared not to have been a particularly popular idea, since it was utilized at this lighthouse

A parade of fog signals served at Whitehead Lighthouse, on an island off Rockland, Maine. This photo shows a bell tower and fogbell with automatic striking mechanism (enclosed in the box to the right of the bell). At other times Whitehead Light had a steam signal and a tidal signal, a curious bell rung by the motion of waves coming ashore on the island. (U.S. Coast Guard Archives)

alone and was replaced by a steam fog signal near the beginning of the Civil War.

Equally novel was a fog whistle actuated by air coming through a blowhole at Southeast Farallon Lighthouse. A chimney was built over the blowhole and fitted at the top with a locomotive steam whistle. A visitor to the station in 1870 noted that the whistle was blown "somewhat as an idle boy would blow his penny trumpet," entirely at the discretion of the sea. The invention was more problematic than practical and must have been a great torment in the lighthouse keepers' lives. It didn't work at all at low tide, and on foggy days when it was sorely needed, the signal was mute, since the wind is normally calm during periods of fog, and sea action inside the cave below the blowhole was not sufficient to force air through the whistle. On the other hand, when the weather was clear and windy, with seawater rushing into the cave, the whistle screamed continuously, as if it were a runaway train. Unfortunately, nature exerted considerably more control over this contraption than did its keepers. During a violent storm, the chimney was blown off the blowhole by a powerful sea, and the government gave up on the idea.

Fogbells were used, especially at smaller light stations, well into the latter part of the 19th century, and some still exist today, though mostly for nostalgia purposes. In the 1850s, bells were overshadowed by a new kind of fog signal, one that improved warnings for the mariner but created enormous work for the lighthouse keeper. The foghorn required that its caretaker possess mechanical ability, in order to keep its cantankerous boiler working properly, and the knowledge of a steam engine operator to ensure that the boiler fire was properly stoked and the pressure just right. It meant that fewer women entered the lightkeeping profession or retained their jobs as keepers. Whether by personal choice or because of the government's lack of confidence in their abilities, women increasingly gave up their positions to men as work at lighthouses became more mechanized.

Horns, with their low and throaty groans, were installed at fog-plagued stations on nearly every coast. Among the earlier ones were the Daboll Trumpets, huge wooden megaphones facing the sea and large enough for the keepers to stand inside. An experi-

A Coast Guard keeper's wife stands over the windy old chimney hole built atop a natural blowhole on Southeast Farallon Island. The rush of air through the blowhole powered a fog whistle at the light station on Southeast Farallon in the 1870s. This photo was taken about 1955. (San Francisco Archives)

Connecticut inventor Celadon Daboll contrived fog trumpets to amplify sound and tested them at several lighthouses in the mid-19th century. This enormous trumpet at Boston Light had a 17-foot-high opening. (National Archives)

Beavertail Lighthouse, at the entrance to Narragansett Bay, was a testing site for Daboll's fog trumpets and other strange fog signaling devices. An unusual Equine Trumpet was set up here in 1852, powered by the keeper's devoted horse, who plodded around a windlass. (National Archives)

mental model over 18 feet long was installed at Boston Light, but the most curious ones were tested at Rhode Island's Beavertail Lighthouse at the entrance to foggy Narragansett Bay. The 1852 Equine Trumpet was a true novelty, powered by the keeper's devoted horse plodding around a windlass hour upon hour to build up the compressed air needed for the trumpet's bellows.

As years passed, the variety and intensity of sounds produced by fog signals diversified, as did the descriptions given to them by local residents and newspaper reporters. The one at Sequin Lighthouse in Maine produced an ear-splitting honk powerful enough to knock seagulls out of the air. San Francisco Bay began to sound like a jungle cloaked in mist — whooping, growling, moaning, shrieking, and roaring. New York Harbor had its own unique concert, too. In 1905, when Great Captain Island Lighthouse received a spanking new fog siren, a local newspaper reporter indulged in some vivid purple prose to describe it. His exaggerated comparisons included: ". . . an army of panthers . . . the roar of a thousand mad bulls . . . wail of a lost soul . . . moan of a bottomless pit . . . and groan of a disabled elevator." If the neighbors lodged such complaints, think how the lighthouse keeper must have felt!

One of the noisiest places was Point Reyes Lighthouse on the precipitous California coast north of the Golden Gate. The San Andreas Fault runs out to sea here, but in the late 1800s the lighthouse keepers needed no reminders that the earth sometimes trembled beneath them. The incessant vibrations from the fog signal took care of that, blaring once a minute and gobbling up 140 pounds of coal an hour. During the worst spell of fog on Point Reyes, the horn ran for 176 hours straight, ravenously devouring 25,000 pounds of coal and disgorging deafening belches that could be heard 10 miles out to sea.

On the whole, lighthouse keepers carried out their fog signaling duties admirably. Wives boasted that fog softened their complexions and nourished their flowerbeds and gardens. Babies learned to sleep with the incessant din, and one mother even claimed that the first word uttered by her infant was not the usual "mama" or "dada," but "beeeee-ooooohhhhhhh!" Children helped out with the laborious task of ringing a bell or hauling coal and water for the boilers. The youngsters at Point Reyes had the ben-

The misery of serving at foggy Point Reyes Light, north of San Francisco, was expressed in one keeper's logbook: "Solitude, where are the charms that sages have seen in thy face? Better to dwell in the midst of alarms than reign in this horrible place." (U.S. Coast Guard)

efit of the long serpentine coal chute to use as a sliding board, though it took considerable courage to ride down it, and injury was often the end result. In November 1875, the head keeper wrote: "In letting Coal down today the belaying pin bent. The truck or hand car went with violent speed down the track, broke through the end of the shed and sleeping room and also doing serious damage to the car."

The noise at foggy stations, and the exhausting work that had to be done to keep them operating properly, didn't appeal to many. In 1926, the Superintendent of Lighthouses in San Francisco noted that he considered Point Reyes the most undesirable lighthouse in his district. He experienced difficulty in finding keepers to serve there. Those who did often seemed to go about their duties in a zombie-like state, stunned by the whir of wind and the oppressive clamor of the fog signal. In 1887, a San Francisco newspaper reported: "The sirens had been in operation for 176 consecutive hours and the jaded attendants looked as if they had been on a protracted spree."

Two lightkeepers at Block Island Southeast Light work in the fog signal house in the 1940s. Cantankerous engines for steam signals, like this one, required hours of work and gobbled tons of coal each year. (U.S. Coast Guard Archives)

The fog signal house at Block Island Southeast Light was typical of many in New
England at the turn of the century. The station horse, in the background at far
left, no doubt grew accustomed to the groan of the horns. (U.S. Coast Guard
Archives)

Attention to the fog signal transcended all other activities at a
lighthouse when the air was thick, and this exacted a price, both
in time spent tending it and the impact it had on its attendants.
Coast Guard keeper Marvin Gerbers became so accustomed to
the foghorn at West Point Lighthouse in Puget Sound that he
automatically paused every 27 seconds in his conversations with
visitors, knowing the foghorn would drown out his words. Apparently the habit followed him even after retirement, when his new
friends noted a curious but regular stop-start pattern in his speech,
as if his brain were still planning for loud interruptions.

If patience was lacking in the keeper of a lighthouse fog signal, a sense of humor was the next best thing. It amused lighthouse keepers to tell visiting children that a horn's burst of noise
was an attempt to scare away the fog — Boooo! Boooo! — or to
attract whales much as a hunter's duck call attracts ducks. The din
was sometimes blamed on old Neptune's conch horn, or Poseidon
blowing his nose. J.W. Patterson of Pigeon Point Lighthouse, who
could as easily have been a standup comic as a lightkeeper, was
quoted by a San Francisco reporter as stating that the station fog
signal's voice was that of two irritable bulls lifted up by their tails,

first the smaller one and then the bigger one. Given the variety of experimental fog devices the Lighthouse Service tested, two miserable bovines don't seem all that outlandish.

> *Gongs in white surplices,*
> *beshrouded wails,*
> *Far strum of fog horns. . .*
> *signals dispersed in veils.*
> *—Hart Crane*

CHAPTER 4

NEXT TO NATURE

The sea-bird wheeling round it, with the din
Of wings and winds and solitary cries,
Blinded and maddened by the light within,
Dashes himself against the glare, and dies.
–Henry Wadsworth Longfellow
The Lighthouse

When Captain Charles A. Sterling was assigned as keeper of Virginia's Hog Island Lighthouse in 1903, he was so inspired by the beauty of the place that he wrote a small book about it and had it privately printed. His work was a psalm of sorts, extolling the great turrets of pine, oak, and red cedar; wildflowers so abundant an apron-full could be gathered in minutes; and birds — wild geese, brants, mallards, and black ducks — rising from the water at dawn in silhouetted phalanxes of wings. Sterling's pastoral pen gave a touch of literary quality to the station logbook, but he knew, as all lightkeepers knew, that the edge of the sea was not always a friendly, placid place.

Three years before Sterling's tenure as keeper of Hog Island Light, nature had seemed to go berserk for a few days. The ordeal began the evening of February 22, 1900, with the air cold and still and the sea a stretch of smooth, black satin. Nothing seemed out of order as the keepers lit up that night. The tower's first-order lens shimmered brightly from its pedestal 150 feet above the sea. It guided vessels through Great Matchipungo Inlet, the main artery into Hog Island Bay on a narrow finger of Virginia soil separating the Chesapeake from the Atlantic. Thirty miles to the north, Assateague Lighthouse spilled its light seaward, and only 20 miles south lay Hog Island's companion sentinel at Cape Charles. The keeper who took the first watch could see both of these beacons from the top of Hog Island Lighthouse, reassurance that all was well and no bad weather lay ahead.

Lured by the light within, birds collide with the lantern panes and tower walls at almost every lighthouse in the nation. Some towers, particularly those along the great migration routes, attract more birds than others. (U.S. Coast Guard Archives)

But shortly after twilight, the tranquil evening turned to chaos. About 7 p.m. the keeper on watch was distracted from his reading by what sounded like a sudden rush of wind outside the lighthouse. He dropped his book and quickly went to the foot of the ladder leading up to the lantern. Above him the lens turned silently in its mercury float, casting amber beads of light down into the watchroom. Nothing seemed out of order. The keeper returned to his chair and was about to resume reading when the sound came again, a whisper of air sweeping by the lantern, faint at first, then much louder. The keeper rushed up the steep ladder and cautiously poked his head into the round room. A flurry of wingbeats greeted his ears, and something streaked by the windows, its sleek body reflected in the beams of the lighthouse. Another feathered raider flew in close, then another. Suddenly, hundreds of birds appeared and began pelting the lantern panes and the tower. The keeper instinctively covered his face each time a bird thumped against the glass, and he wondered how the panes stood such abuse. Feeling helpless, he waited, thinking the confused creatures would soon abandon their senseless self-battery.

A large brant rammed the window and fell to the deck twitching, its neck broken. Several ducks followed to their deaths. Then came the geese, their huge dark bodies slamming the column of iron legs and braces in slow, ponderous waves. A particularly large one circled the tower several times honking loudly, as if lining up on its target; then with missile speed it bombed the lighthouse and shot through the glass, colliding with a lens panel and shattering it. Almost immediately a second bird came through the opening, hit the damaged lens, and lodged in the twisted prisms.

By now, hundreds of frenzied birds were hitting the lighthouse. Their panicked squeals and whirling feathers filled the lantern and forced the keeper down the watchroom ladder, where he met his comrade headed up the stairs with two shotguns. The plan was to fire several shots into the air in hopes of frightening away the confused flock. The men had tried this on other occasions when birds flew at the lighthouse, and it usually worked, but not on this night. The flock was too large, and the noise of a thousand wings drowned out the shotgun blast. Like a huge hypnotic eye, the lighthouse beacon had drawn the birds to their deaths, either by collision with the metal tower or laceration in its glass windows and lens.

What normally lasted only a few minutes became a nightmare for the men. The birds would not relent but continued pelting the lighthouse and crashing through the lantern for the better part of the night. In desperation, the keepers turned their guns on the birds and fired until the gun barrels were hot. When they had used up all the ammunition, they grabbed whatever was at hand to repel their attackers — buckets, oil cans, mops, a chair, the brass dustpan. By morning, 68 geese, brants, and ducks lay dead around the base of the tower. Mangled bodies were strewn about the lantern and deck, and blood was spattered over the lens and what remained of the lantern windows. But somehow the light had not been extinguished. The men were able to clean up the mess and keep the light going the next evening. For added protection, they rigged a mesh screen around the broken lantern windows.

Serenity returned to marshy Hog Island for a night or two; then, as if from some bizarre science fiction tale, the birds came back again to assault the tower. The men were paranoid at the sight of the returning marauders and fought them this time with clubs and broom handles, knocking more than 150 birds to the ground in an hour's time. But the effort proved useless against so large an army. Dazed and exhausted, the keepers retreated to the lower section of the tower. Shortly before sunrise the squall of feathers and shattered glass ceased. The men climbed to the top of the tower and found the light extinguished. With no blinding beam to attack, the birds had given up the fight.

In its annual report for 1900, the Lighthouse Board noted that Hog Island had suffered one of the worst bird attacks on record at a U.S. lighthouse. No explanation was offered as to the cause of the incident, save the suggestion that the beacon had so disoriented a large flock of birds as to cause severe panic, which fed upon itself for hours. Why the second attack occurred remains a mystery. The station was cleaned up, and the costly damage to the lens was repaired. Hog Island Lighthouse served mariners for another 48 years before being decommissioned. During this time there were occasional collisions by birds, but never again an invasion so incomprehensible and terrifying as in the winter of 1900.

Blinded by the Light
Birds, for reasons still not completely understood, often slam into structures on the ground. Lighthouses are among the most vulnerable obstacles due to their sheer height and piercing beams. Almost all lighthouse logbooks mention these tragic occurrences from time to time, some with emotion, others as if such events were as natural as the combers kissing the beach. A British writer with *Cornhill Magazine* in the 19th century likened birds hitting lighthouses to giant moths lured by the flame of a huge candle. John J. Floherty, in *Sentinels of the Sea*, was less poetic in his observation of a lone duck that broke away from its flock while passing over Long Island to dive-bomb tall Fire Island Lighthouse. It flew at the tower repeatedly, quacking and banking sharply until at last it made a wide circle and, like a kamikaze, hit the tower and fell crumpled to the earth. Floherty, like so many keepers of the lights, wondered why a single bird had chosen to leave its flock and challenge the lighthouse in a duel it could not win.

Seldom are such collisions considered attacks. Most are accidental, with no serious harm to anything or anyone except, of course, the unfortunate fowl. Lighthouses that stand in the path of the great migrations have been fitted with bird screens to protect the lantern glass and lenses. These also prevent birds from perching on the gallery railing and soiling the deck and windows.

At Aransas Pass Lighthouse, leading into Texas' Corpus Christi Bay, a bird screen was installed in 1867 after hundreds of birds sought sanctuary in the tower during an unusual cold snap. The lighthouse was undergoing repairs of damage inflicted during the Civil War, and its lantern cap appears to have been temporarily off. Seeking warmth, birds flew inside the tower by the hundreds, transforming the Aransas Pass Light into an enormous birdcage. Most died of the intense cold, and along with the thousands of frozen fish that were thrown ashore in the storm, created a stench that surpassed anyone's description. The cleanup effort was massive, and when repairs to the station were completed, the government ordered the bird screen installed around the lantern to prevent further problems.

Bird collisions with lighthouses haven't always meant trouble. The more resourceful lightkeepers made the best of these unfortunate incidents. At desolate Boon Island Lighthouse, nine miles off York Beach, Maine, Keeper William W. Williams (records don't indicate whether his middle name was also William) was often marooned on the station for weeks without contact with the mainland or a delivery of supplies. He served 27 years at this lonely outpost in the late 1800s, never complaining or requesting a transfer to some bucolic mainland station. He felt lucky to have had a respected government job, and with typical Down East resolve, stuck to his duties and lived frugally. When life became miserable, he and his assistant opened the Bible for words of encouragement, prayed, and made the best of it.

One Thanksgiving there was no turkey for the platter, nor any other kind of meat since the sea had been too rough to fish. Keeper Williams had not been able to get ashore for groceries for some weeks, nor were his wife and children, living on the mainland, able to pay him a visit with turkey in hand. Williams and his assistant resigned themselves to the possibility that Thanksgiving dinner would be boiled potatoes and bread. On the eve of the holi-

A birdscreen encircles the lantern at Aransas Pass Lighthouse on the lower Texas coast. This tower has frequently been plagued by birds and was actually damaged by them shortly after the Civil War. (U.S. Coast Guard)

day, however, a flock of ducks flew over, and several of them hit the tower. The next day they appeared on the Thanksgiving table stuffed with bread and escorted by roasted potatoes, all slathered with rich, gamy gravy. The men were convinced their prayers had been answered, albeit in a round-about way.

Of course, not all encounters with birds were fatal, else bird authority Roger Tory Peterson might certainly not have expressed

The upper section of Oahu's Barbers Point Lighthouse was protected by a birdscreen during World War II, as well as a camouflage daymark on the tower. An awards ceremony for Jack Dempsey was being held here when the photo was taken. (U.S. Coast Guard Archives)

a yearning to spend a night on a lighthouse when the birds were flying. The keepers of Boston's Graves Lighthouse were cheered by feeding and watching the rock plovers around the tower. Atlantic puffins that lived in burrows on Matinicus Rock in its early years of service were quite comical but also fascinating, dressed in their tidy little tuxedos and wearing buffoon faces. Southeast Farallon Island Light was situated amidst a seabird rookery of considerable size, which made cleaning the lantern windows a never-ending task, but kept the lighthouse kitchen in eggs during the nesting season.

In 1860, the Smithsonian Institution recognized the unique status of lighthouse keepers when it formally requested that several Texas lightkeepers collect wild bird eggs for study. In addition, ornithologists began to recognize the usefulness of lighthouses as research bases. Keepers were often in the company of scientists studying some aspect of the natural world, and they were occasionally called upon to gather data. Even today, the National Audobon Society utilizes lighthouse sites for its bird counts and field studies, and a number of coastal bird sanctuaries and wildlife refuges surround lighthouses.

On picturesque Block Island, in the track of the great Atlantic Flyway, birds of many species pause in their migrations to rest and feed on this small lambchop-shaped island. Sadly, many have collided with the lighthouses on the north and southeast points of the island. Barbara Beebe Gaspar, daughter of a Block Island lightkeeper, recalls that in the 1930s and 1940s, the injured birds were gathered up and taken to a local ornithologist named Mrs. Dickens who examined them and, if able, nursed the injured back to health. Some died, of course, and these were added to Mrs. Dickens' collection of stuffed birds. A number of these specimens are still on display in the island's history museum. No doubt it was the Beebe children's experiences with these birds and Mrs. Dickens' assortment of feathered stiffs that inspired Gaspar's brother, Howard Beebe, to learn taxidermy.

Gaspar and her siblings also had plenty of live birds to entertain them as they grew up on Block Island's rustic North Light. Gaspar confessed that she tried, rather unsuccessfully, to tame seagulls, but was sometimes able to catch a sandpiper with an offering of food — no easy task, considering this bird's speed and good sense of hearing. "I would be very gentle and would only keep them for a little while," Gaspar recalled. "I guess I just wanted to cuddle them a bit."

The families at Kilauea Lighthouse had a much bigger gathering of avians around their windy home on Kauai, Hawaii. Today, the lighthouse is the centerpiece of Kilauea National Wildlife Refuge, but back in 1913, when the station was established as a landfall beacon for trans-Pacific voyages, life there could only be described as an extended vacation: The trade winds blew soothingly over the point, tousling the green banners of sugar cane in nearby fields. Fruit trees strained to hold up their bounty of guavas, mangos, papayas, and coconuts. There were seals wallowing on the rocks below the lighthouse, and the sea moaned and sighed as it moved in and out of the caves along Kilauea's steep cliffs. There were birds, too, thousands of them, reeling overhead, waddling or hopping along the ground, and skimming the sapphire brine

Kilauea Lighthouse on the northern tip of Kauai was a lightkeeper's tropical paradise. Wildlife abounds here, especially birds. Today the tower is part of the Kilauea National Wildlife Refuge. (U.S. Coast Guard)

in search of the plentiful fish that splashed unabashed and begged to be caught.

Duty at the lighthouse had its demands, though, which included caring for the powerful sentinel with its 4-ton clamshell lens. But Kilauea's keepers also had time to watch the island's acrobatic aviators: red-footed boobies, wedge-tailed shearwaters, great frigate birds, and Laysan albatrosses, better known as gooney birds because of their clumsy locomotion on the ground. Many of the men who tended this lighthouse were capable guides whose walking tours of the area were a naturalist's dream. A few keepers served with flair. In the 1920s, there was Fred Robbins, a native Hawaiian who dumbfounded visitors by diving into the sea and swimming to an offshore islet called Mokuaeae Rock. To make his intrepid swim all the more daring, Robbins sometimes waited until sharks were prowling the shallows between Kilauea Point and the tiny offshore isle, and he swam most of the distance underwater, adding suspense to the performance. The finale saw him scaling the slippery, wet rockface of Mokuaeae as a legion of seabirds took to the air and onlookers cheered incredulously. Robbins' ancestral beliefs, which included reverence for a shark god, plus his superior swimming skill and knowledge of the waters off Kauai, left him with little fear of the sea.

Fine-Feathered Omen

Like their compatriots, the sailors, lighthouse keepers were often superstitious about the natural world around them. Many keepers had jumped to dry land after retiring from sea or suffering an injury that left them unfit to serve aboard a ship, and they brought ashore a sea chest full of musty amulets and salty superstitions. Among these was the sincere belief that the behavior of animals offered clues about such things as fishing success, the weather, or a person's fate. As with the mariner, the lightkeeper sometimes carried these ideas to extreme. In one case, a bird was thought to have delivered a warning of an approaching storm and a message of impending disaster to the keepers of the Harbor of Refuge Lighthouse off Lewes, Delaware.

The light was situated at the end of a two-mile long rock breakwater and was, in its prime, the beckoning beam for ships headed

Situated at the end of a long breakwater, the Harbor of Refuge Lighthouse at Lewes, Delaware, looks like a seaside wedding cake. The foghorns project from the side of the tower and a TV antenna juts up from the lantern in this 1962 photo. This tower replaced an earlier one destroyed in a 1920 storm. (Courtesy of Stephen Jones)

into Philadelphia. Inside the breakwater was the beneficent Harbor of Refuge, where vessels could take shelter from the fury of storm winds and waves. Though the lighthouse was called by the same name, it may as well have stood watch at the gates of hell, for it was entirely exposed to the full force of storms moving up the Atlantic Seaboard toward New England. The destruction of the first light tower at Harbor of Refuge in the 1930s was caused by just such a storm. It was an almost tragic affair that, not surprisingly, has tendered its share of strange stories, the most popular one involving a delicate white bird and an anxious, obsessed keeper.

The man in this tale had undoubtedly brought his seaman's superstitions ashore, if indeed the Harbor of Refuge Light could be considered ashore, exposed and solitary as it was on the end of the stone breakwater. He believed everything that happened on the lighthouse held a message of sorts; thus he spent much of his time interpreting events, especially during the long, bleak hours of night when the tower creaked, and the wind sang high-pitched chants through the cracks in the walls, and the beam of light swept slowly over King Neptune's watery court, first white and then red where the jagged points of the sea god's trident protruded up-ward.

One night, as the man worked alone in the lantern, a delicate white bird, unlike any other he had ever seen, came tapping at the lighthouse windows with its beak, as if bearing some urgent news from the sea. Aboard ship, the appearance of such a bird would have been considered a harbinger of doom, since many old salts believed certain types of birds held the souls of drowned sailors. Alone in the lantern, with the soulful eyes of this night visitor fixed upon him, the keeper felt certain its stopover on the lonely sentinel was no accident.

Throughout the long hours of darkness, the keeper pondered the bird and its rhythmic tapping in sets of three: Tap, tap . . . tap. Perhaps he fell asleep, or was so caught up in his reverie he did not notice when the bird flew off. The eastern sky began to glow orange, with a tattered strata of high ruddy clouds to the south. A freighter appeared on the horizon and steamed close enough to the lighthouse to hail its keepers. The message from the signal-man was foreboding: A storm was wheeling up the coast from Cape Hatteras, with a rough time ahead for the lightkeepers out on Harbor of Refuge.

Anxiety over the approaching cyclone did its work on the keeper's idle mind. He began to console himself by analyzing the bird's visit and postulating what it might have meant. Three taps, two together and one alone. Daft from the portents of storm — the swells, the high-pitched squeals of the first winds squeezing through the crevices around windows and doors, the absence of birds in the sky — the keeper decided his night visitor had brought a warning: If two men remained on the light, one would surely die.

Unable to persuade his partner to seek safety ashore, the keeper resigned himself to the fact that he would have to take the station boat and row for Lewes if both men were to be saved. This he did, barely making it to the docks inside the harbor before the storm-pushed seas were running. Out on the lighthouse, the other keeper was baffled by his comrade's behavior, but he determined to batten down the lighthouse and ride out the blow. He knew of nothing more craven or punishable in the eyes of the Lighthouse Service than a lightkeeper deserting his station when those at sea needed him most.

A wall of dark clouds marching up from the south in the late afternoon necessitated lighting the lantern early. The surf began to batter the lower section of the tower before nightfall, and little by little the waves crept upward until the metal walls shuddered and the lens rocked in its brass cradle. As the intensity of wind and seas increased, it became clear that the tower would not hold together, so the keeper lashed himself to a supporting beam, one firmly anchored into the concrete caisson, and waited for the final moment. His hope was that the tower's foundation would remain firm and that by securing himself to it he would not be swept into the maelstrom and drowned.

The hurricane raged for several hours after dark, then retreated off to the northeast. When daylight came, the apprehensive keeper on the docks at Lewes looked out to the end of the breakwater in hopes that the lighthouse would magically appear in a swirl of spray. When it became obvious that the tower was gone, he commandeered a fishing boat to take him to the site, certain his friend had somehow survived. In his heart he firmly believed the bird's warning. His confidence was satisfied when the boat pulled alongside the mangled remains of the Harbor of Refuge Lighthouse, and the limp but breathing personage of the other keeper was found tethered to one of the broken metal supports.

A Naturalist's Paradise
When Stephen Jones enlisted in the Coast Guard in the 1960s, he

Stephen Jones spent a year on Harbor of Refuge Lighthouse in 1962 and later recounted his raw experiences in a book. Now a noted author and college professor, Jones assumes the role of Captain Cat in this promotional photo for a 1994 production of "Under Milkwood." His feline companion is "Cricket." (Courtesy of Richard Gipstein and Noank Historical Society)

was sent to Harbor of Refuge Light, to the tower that replaced the original one lost in the 1930s storm. Jones was somewhat content on the station, largely because he enjoyed the solitude which allowed him to read and write. Twenty years after serving on the light, he wrote about it in *Harbor of Refuge*, a tome that candidly tells of a year spent as an offshore lighthouse keeper in Delaware Bay. Much of Jones' current view of the world still passes through the prism of a lighthouse lens, polished by a degree in English from Columbia and years of experience as an author and college professor.

During Jones' time on the station, there were birds and bugs, hordes of them. He kept track of the many different kinds, and also kept a list of the various types of fish seen around the lighthouse. At night he put a spotlight on the water and watched what swam into his ken. The unexpected and the unexplainable were almost always there, a fair weather bird that should have flown elsewhere for the winter, or a swarm of bees far from the nectar of the mainland. Jones learned to look as never before. His perception of color evolved into a kind of super-vision, driven by the ambience of sea, rocks, and sky. Gray was not just gray, but a dozen shades — foggy, misty, smoky, dusky, ashen, silver, somber, slate, dun. The same was true of blue and green.

The entymologist might have enjoyed a brief tour of duty at Harbor of Refuge, for there was no end to the variety and quantity of insects at this lighthouse. Stephen Jones comically recounted days on the station when living with arthropods was a given: "We had a squadron of houseflies . . . so many that even the twice-blest flywhipper had proved ineffectual, and we had not been able to open our mouths to eat without risking an unappetizing thickening of each morsel." Jones told of insects arriving on the light in waves, with a particular species featured each time. One week it was bees; the next week it was moths, then flies, then beetles.

At Grand Island Lighthouse in Lake Superior, the station log for July 22, 1872, told of a busy night shooing big blue moths off the lantern windows. The exasperated keeper used a large feather

The sea was unpredictable at times, as it was at California's Trinidad Lighthouse in 1914. A freak wave hit the 196-foot cliff below this sentinel, scaled it, and washed over the tiny tower, momentarily stopping the lens from turning. Obviously, the keeper and his family feared no such wave when this peaceful picture was taken a few years before. (Nautical Research Center)

duster to chase away the aggravating insects. In large enough numbers, they could so obscure the light as to reduce its range several
miles. Their wings left a fine blue dust on the lens, and many of
them perished in the lamps, crisply fried in the oil or incinerated
in the wicks. Cleaning up after such a night was a painstaking
chore.

A year later, this same lighthouse logbook witnessed the keeper
philosophically musing about a visitation by an owl: "At 2:30 a.m.
an eared owl (the large kind) sat perched upon the railing of the
tower, as sedate and important as a judge advocate upon a court-
martial. But when the bull's eye of the lens would flash upon him,
he would throw up his wings and cast down his head as much to
say, I submit!"

The natural world around lighthouses contained assorted denizens, some remarkably inspiring and some unwelcomed, even
feared. Bears raided the trash cans at Alaskan lighthouses; bull
seals belligerently stood their ground at Oregon's Heceta Head
Light; wolves howled in the night around Split Rock Light in Minnesota. Even imaginary creatures disrupted keepers' routines:

The natural world of lighthouses contained assorted denizens, including bears.
Alaskan lightkeeper Ted Pedersen shows off two of the trophies he shot in the
1930s while at Cape Sarichef Light in the Aleutians. (U.S. Coast Guard)

"I, Amos Story of Gloucester, in the County of Essex, mariner, depose and say, that on the tenth day of August A.D. 1817, I saw a strange marine animal, that I believe to be a serpent, at the southward and eastward of Ten Pound Island, in the harbour of Gloucester. . . .

His head appeared shaped much like the head of a sea turtle and he carried his head from ten to twelve inches above the surface of the water. His head at that distance appeared much larger than the head of any dog I ever saw. . . ."

No one knows what Amos Story really saw at Ten Pound Island Lighthouse, but a number of witnesses corroborated the report, which has been recounted time and again as the legend of the "Gloucester Sea Monster."

There were serpents, however — real ones that caused consternation at several light stations. San Luis Obispo Light in California had abundant rattlesnakes before the surrounding area was developed. Hilda Settlemier recalled that her husband, who tended the lighthouse in the early part of this century, was not afraid of the snakes, though he certainly gave them due respect, and he was somewhat grateful for their presence, for their voracious appetite for rodents and bugs was a boon. And, the district lighthouse inspector was terrified of them.

Settlemier cleverly used the menace of snakebite to discourage the inspector from prolonged, scrutinizing visits. There were certain buildings the inspector intentionally passed by, being reminded by Keeper Settlemier that rattlers liked to doze on the cool stones of the foundation. By the time he got around to examining the lighthouse, the phobic inspector was so ruffled he gave it only a cursory inspection. All this worked in Settlemeir's favor, of course; his inspections were brief and without fanfare.

At Texas' Matagorda Lighthouse in 1929, Keeper Arthur Barr wrote in his logbook of his fear and hatred of the snakes around the lighthouse. There were many kinds, but rattlesnakes and water moccasins caused the greatest concern. During exceptionally high tides and storm surges, large numbers of them appeared at the station and sought sanctuary in the buildings. Barr's neighbor at Pass Cavallo Lighthouse went so far as to write to the government requesting that antivenom be kept at the Texas stations for use in case of snakebite. The request was granted.

Snakes were a serious problem at certain Gulf Coast lighthouses, including Matagorda Light in Texas. Keepers' concerns caused the government to issue anti-venom kits for snakebite. (U.S. Coast Guard)

A popular tall tale told around Cape Canaveral, Florida, contends that the lightkeeper who served there just before the turn of the century was beseiged by snakes that were attracted to the cool metal stairs and concrete platform of Cape Canaveral Light. According to this unsubstantiated story, he went a bit daft one day and rounded up a rabble of the reptiles in a burlap bag. He then tossed them into a vat of boiling water, cooked them well, and skimmed off the snake oil that rose to the surface. No finer oil could be found in the wilds of Florida in the late 1800s. The keeper supposedly used it to lubricate the intricate clockwork mechanism of the lens. (When he wasn't conducting a rattler roundup, we might suppose he wrestled alligators.)

Tested By the Elements
Living with the sea right outside the front door meant living with wind and water, in all their vibrant moods. Battery Point Lighthouse was built with its front door facing the sea, but keepers soon learned that getting in and out depended on the weather. Some days the wind blew so hard against the door it could not be

opened. If visitors came knocking, they were told to go around to the back door, and hopefully they made the trip without getting a saltwater washdown.

At Cape Cod's Highland Lighthouse, anything hung out to air or dry, from the station flag to the family laundry, was handily rent by the merciless wind. Salt spray and sandblast were the enemies of the lightkeepers, with each leaving its signature in a different way. The windows of the lighthouse required constant cleaning and occasional replacement when the blowing sand so frosted the panes that the light was obscured. White and crusty salt buildup was a never-ending problem, as were ice and bird droppings. Cleaning windows was no task for the fearful of heights. Less steady keepers were apt to tie a rope about their waists or design a long-handled mop to reach the upper windows. After about 1820, special handholds were built into the window frames on many lighthouses to the give the keepers something to grasp when it was windy or slippery. Some still rigged ropes and belts for use during gales when it was critical to keep the windows clear. Falls were rare, but logbooks frequently received comments about the tedious task of cleaning the lantern panes.

Wind and water caused another serious concern for the lighthouse keeper — erosion. The families at Cape Henlopen Light on the Delaware shore saw their home and the lighthouse slowly undermined by the relentless march of the dunes. Only months before the station toppled in 1926, the family was evacuated. Similarly, the sea invaded the premises of Charleston Lighthouse, which stood high and dry on Morris Island until this century. Today, the tower is completely surrounded by water. Even when the foundation of a tower began to give way, the government was slow to abandon it. Cape Romain and Rockland Lake lighthouses are two that continued to operate after erosion left them listing. Their keepers had the added challenge of walking about on slanted floors.

Ice sometimes made just getting in the door of a lighthouse a challenge. On the remote, offshore Great Lakes lights at Stannard Rock and Spectacle Reef, keepers were taken off the stations at the close of the shipping season around the first of December. The towers were locked and in later years a small, low-power beacon was left on for the winter. In March, the keepers returned to

Moving sand and erosive wind and water undermined the colonial sentinel at Cape Henlopen, Delaware, causing it to topple in April 1926. The keeper and his family had evacuated the station a few months before this photo was taken in 1925. (National Archives)

Hudson River currents undermined the foundation of Rockland Lake Lighthouse and caused the lighthouse to lean miserably, giving its keepers the added challenge of walking and sleeping on slanted floors. (National Archives)

their stations with fresh supplies and lit up again for the busy summer shipping season. Landing at these wave-swept towers was difficult, but keepers would sometimes encounter a more serious problem — a shroud of ice, several feet thick, over the entire station. Their first task in the brisk spring air was wielding picks and sledgehammers to free up the entry door. Several more hours would be spent clearing away the layers of winter ice from the lantern and the foghorns.

Ice was a very serious problem for keepers stationed on waterbound lighthouses in Chesapeake and Delaware bays, as well as on Lake Champlain and the Hudson River. Although riprap was piled around the legs and platforms of these sentinels to protect them from moving ice, often they could not withstand the mighty pressure of the ice breakup in spring. A number of lighthouses were sheared off their pilings or stove in, sometimes with their attendants helplessly standing by.

August Lorenz tended Colchester Reef Lighthouse on Lake Champlain from 1909 to 1931. Most winters the lake froze over entirely and the keeper was treated to visits by ice fishermen and shoreside residents who braved the frozen lake on foot or in horse-drawn sleighs. Having watched many unfortunate souls fall through

Ice threatened lighthouses on the Great Lakes and in northern bays and rivers. The keepers at Racine Reef Light, Wisconsin (above), were forced to pull their boat across the ice to reach open water when Lake Michigan froze around the tower. (National Archives) In the Chesapeake and Delaware bays, the spring thaw pushed lighthouses off their foundations (below) or destroyed them completely. (U.S. Coast Guard Archives)

the ice, and pulled them out both alive and drowned, August determined that such a fate would never befall him. Whenever he ventured out on the frozen lake he carried a long, spiked pole that he could use to snag the ice and pull himself out in the event he crashed through the lake. Fortunately, he never needed it for this purpose, but it did come in handy on another occasion.

It was spring, and the lake had begun to break up and clog in places with huge cakes of ice. On this particular day, a brisk southwest wind pushed the floe around the lighthouse. During the day, Lorenz kept watch over the ice floe to see that it moved along without too much interference, but throughout the dark evening hours he could only listen to the grinding and rending of ice along the sides of the lighthouse's stone caisson. He was worried that the ice would pile up against the stones on a windy night and push the lighthouse off its foundation.

That evening, it almost happened. Lorenz was in the lantern working when a terrible crash and screech of wood splintering sent him rushing down the stairs. As he entered the lighthouse kitchen, oil lamp in hand, the southwest corner of the room split open, and huge pieces of ice pushed through. Lorenz danced about the kitchen in fright, avoiding the small frozen chunks that scuttered across the floor. After a minute or two the wind reversed, and the monstrous intrusion of ice slid back out, leaving a gaping hole in the kitchen wall.

Residents ashore grew uneasy at the sounds coming from the lake that night, the ice gnawing at the lighthouse foundation; they worried for August Lorenz's safety. Imagine their relief the next morning when the familiar profile of the keeper was seen at the railing of the lighthouse deck. Later in the day he was gingerly leaping about on the ice surrounding the lighthouse. His dory, ripped from its davits and carried away during the night, was sitting upside-down on a floating cake of ice not far from the lighthouse. He was determined to rescue it, since he had saved his own money to buy the dory, and he wasn't about to let the lake have it. The wind was slowly moving the little ice cake toward him, and at the right moment he reached out with the long pole — the one he always carried while on the ice — and snagged the vagabond vessel.

Winter's blast turned some lighthouses, such as this one at St. Joseph North Pierhead on Lake Michigan, into ice castles. While pretty, such frosty ornamentation created enormous work for the lightkeepers of these stations and the tender crews who maintained them. (National Oceanic & Atmospheric Administration)

The keepers at Sharp's Island Lighthouse in the Chesapeake Bay had a much different experience with ice breakup. Their lighthouse was a screwpile structure, a round house perched atop iron spindle legs anchored in the muck under eight feet of water. The

Screwpile lighthouses, like this one at Thomas Point, Maryland, were especially vulnerable to destruction from ice flows. Huge, moving cakes of ice could shear a tower off its pilings and send it to the bottom, or in the case of Sharp's Island Light, on a derelict voyage with its terrified attendants aboard. (U.S. Coast Guard Archives)

few stones placed around the base of the legs to further stabilize the structure did little to hold off an ice floe late in the winter of 1881. As large sheets moved southward out of the Choptank River, they crunched against the riprap and rammed the iron legs of the little sentinel.

The keepers watched powerlessly, knowing it was only a matter of time until a large floe collided with the lighthouse and sent it to the bottom. Amazingly, when the fatal blow finally came, it cleanly severed the lighthouse from its iron legs. The structure leaned over on its side with a loud groan, sank into the muck for a moment, then surfaced and floated like a boat. For sixteen hours it drifted aimlessly on the bay, with its relieved but uneasy attendants along for the ride. The derelict lighthouse was spotted by numerous people ashore and by the few vessels brave enough to ply the ice-riddled bay. It finally went aground miles south of its home. The keepers were not only able to get safely ashore, but they also made several trips back to the lighthouse to retrieve many of the valuable tools and furnishings. These men of unusual mettle had kept to their post despite its vagrant travels, and for that they were highly commended by the Lighthouse Service.

I was not too young before I left Boston Light to have appreciated some natural beauty, and the one thing I shall always remember is the way big soft snowflakes fell through the twelve golden rays. The majority of people never see such scenes and therefore cannot love and appreciate them as I did.

–Jeannette Lee Haskins
Lightkeeper's Daughter

CHAPTER 5

TEMPEST AND TIDE

Throw out the life-line across the dark wave,
There is a brother whom someone
should save...
—Edward Smith Ufford

When the Boston Lighthouse was first built in 1716, the Massachusetts Bay Colony forbid the use of a lightning rod for fear that such an instrument would be viewed by the powers of heaven as intent to interfere with divine strokes. After the lighthouse was struck and damaged by lightning some 12 times in ten years, twice setting it on fire, a lightning rod was installed. The justification was that a lighthouse, reaching skyward higher than any other structure, was too much of a temptation for the powers above. Thereafter, the Boston Lighthouse suffered no serious injury due to lightning.

Lightning has been responsible for innumerable tragedies at lighthouses. When thunder rolled across the heavens and lightning flashed, the lightkeeper had reason to worry. A lighthouse was often the tallest structure in its particular landscape, and it contained plenty of metal parts to escort a bolt from the blue down to the ground. Even with lightning rods installed, some lighthouses were unsafe.

Bodie Island Lighthouse on the Outer Banks of North Carolina towered 150 feet over the dunes when it was placed in service after the Civil War. It was the third tower on this site, guiding vessels through the perilous Oregon Inlet, where many skeletons of ships lay rotting in the notorious "Graveyard of the Atlantic." The huge brick tower enclosed an iron stairway with ten spirals ascending to the watch room and a small iron ladder leading from that space into the lantern. Toward the end of the 19th century, the rod somehow became detached from the ground wire. The keeper was unaware of the problem until a violent thunderstorm passed through the area one summer afternoon and a powerful bolt of lightning hit the cupola on the lofty tower. Unfortunately, the keeper happened to be on the stairs at the time. The bolt coursed its proper path along the grounding wire until it reached the floor of the watchroom, where it jumped onto the stairs. The keeper was almost at the bottom of the stairs when a severe jolt entered his arm and ripped through his body. He survived, but was paralyzed on one side of his body for many months.

A similar strike occurred at Lake Champlain's Danskammer Light in 1914. James Weist, the keeper, was at his desk in the watch room when lightning hit the tower and traveled down the outside wall and in the window next to his seat. It knocked him to the floor, causing him to lose all feeling and movement on his left side. Still, he remained on watch for the rest of the night, put out the light at dawn and covered it with the lens drape, then slid down the tower stairs on his good side. Wondering why he had not come for breakfast, his wife went to look for him and found him trying to crawl to the house using one arm and one foot.

After Boston Light was struck by lightning several times in its first few decades, the Puritans decided to install a lightning rod. Their beliefs forbade the use of lightning rods, as these were thought to interfere with divine strokes from heaven, but the tall Boston Light was deemed too great a temptation for the powers above. (National Archives)

Though unable to walk for some time, he continued to work with his wife's assistance. Eventually, he recovered full use of his right arm and leg.

Throw Out the Lifeline

The schooner *Australia* left Boothbay, Maine, about 5:00 in the evening on January 27, 1885, in fair weather, headed for Boston with its captain, J. W. Lewis, and two crewmen, Irving Pierce and William Kellar. Not long after the vessel put to sea, the weather deteriorated, and by midnight a storm was pounding southern Maine. The temperature had dropped to well below freezing. Blinding snow pelted the little schooner, and ice encased its masts, rigging, and deck so heavily the men were forced to jettison the cargo. The captain considered running for the safety of Portland Harbor, but when the battered mainsail gave way under the immense pressure of its icy jacket, there was no choice other than to stand off until the storm let up.

That same night, just a few miles south of Portland, Marcus Hanna was standing watch in the fog signal building at the Cape Elizabeth Twin Lights. Both beacons were brightly lit, and the fog whistle was screaming a warning through the blizzard; but neither the lights nor the sound could penetrate the air. In the roar of the storm, Hanna did not hear the hull of the *Australia* grinding against the ledge and the shouts of its stranded men.

He was quite sick with a cold that evening and anticipating daylight, when he would be relieved by his assistant, Hiram Staples, and could head for the warmth of his house and bed. Staples arrived promptly just before dawn and admonished Hanna to button up and wrap a scarf about his face before starting for the house. The temperature was about 22 degrees, but with the wind howling relentlessly at 35-40 mph, the air felt like -20 degrees. The trek from the fog signal building to the warm kitchen sapped Hanna's strength. So deep were the drifts of snow and so powerful was the icy wind, he was forced to crawl on hands and knees, using the dispersed glow of the two beacons to navigate. His wife had been keeping watch for him and was ready with hot coffee, but first she had to pry the scarf from his face, since his warm breath had condensed inside it and frozen the wool to his beard.

As soon as he was warmly settled in bed, Mrs. Hanna bundled up and went to each of the towers to extinguish the lamps. While wiping down the windows in the lantern of the east tower she spied a dark silhouette on the rocky shore below, a gray shape that could only mean a ship ashore. Quickly, she returned to the house and awakened her husband. Without a selfish thought for his health, Hanna pulled on his foul weather gear and headed for the fog signal building to alert his assistant. The vessel had been pushed onshore bow first only a few hundred yards from the station, so the men decided to use a heavy rope, weighted on the end, to throw a lifeline to the schooner. They needed to work quickly, though; the tide was rising, and each wave threatened to break up the vessel and added to its already thick cloak of ice. The two crewmen were hanging in the rigging, too cold to cry out any longer and stiff from the ice that covered them. Captain Lewis had been swept away in the darkness hours before, unable to hold on until help arrived.

While Staples trudged to the nearby lifesaving station to alert the surfmen, Hanna worked his way along the slippery rocks northeast of the light towers, getting as close as possible to the schooner and hoarsely shouting encouragement to its crewmen. Stepping into the surf up to his thighs, he braced himself against some rocks and began hurling the weighted rope at the ship. Time and again he threw the makeshift monkey's fist at the vessel and saw it miss its mark or slide away before the men could grab it. Weakened by his illness and exertion, Hanna's brain began to reel. He stumbled out of the surf and lay down on the rocks to regain his strength. Staples would return soon, he thought, and the lifesavers would have a gun to hurl the lifeline.

His eyes fluttered with the urge for sleep. Hanna fought to rouse himself, knowing the torpor signaled trouble. He was freezing to death; he had to get up and move, otherwise he would join the doomed men of the *Australia*. He forced himself to his feet and began to dance wildly, flailing his arms and legs and beating himself. He became alert again, enough to see that during his brief stupor the schooner had begun to break apart under the stress of the incoming tide. Hanna waded out into the surf and renewed his efforts, casting the rope over the ship on his first try.

It landed beside Irving Pierce and snagged on a spar. Pierce was barely alive, and though he saw the lifeline he was unable to move his frozen hands to save himself.

Hanna shouted encouragement to Pierce from shore, as did William Kellar, who hung in the rigging only a few feet away and could plainly see Pierce's distress. Minutes passed, then Pierce suddenly broke out of his icy shell, grasped the rope, and wrapped it about his waist. Hanna mustered what little strength he could and signaled to Pierce to drop into the sea. With the rope tied securely around him, Hanna began hauling in the man, uttering a song-like prayer to keep himself awake and pulling. Pierce bobbed up and down on his shoreward journey like a buoy loose from its moorings. Hanna feared the crewman would die on the way, yet he continued to pull and hum and pray until the shape of a man emerged from the surf at his knees. With his last ounce of strength, Hanna pulled Pierce up on the rocks and collapsed beside him. A moment later he recoiled in horror as Pierce's gruesome visage came into focus: The man's eyes were iced shut and his jaw was frozen in a silent scream, with his lips blue and swollen.

Crying out to heaven for mercy, Hanna pulled himself up, untied the rope from around Pierce's body, and positioned himself in the boiling surf a second time. Kellar was still able to move and answered Hanna's reassuring call. The rope was thrown a dozen times before it landed within reach of Kellar, and when he had prepared himself for the horrid trip through the surf, he signaled Hanna and leaped into the turbulent water. Hallucinations racked Hanna's mind as he hauled the rope — hazy pictures of men walking on the sea and ships righting themselves and floating away under sunlit skies. The din of wind and surf seemed to grow farther away with each pull of the rope, and Hanna felt himself floating, drifting, sleeping. . . .

Staples loosened the bloody fingers locked dutifully on the rope and lifted his comrade tenderly, carrying him over the rocks as one might carry a sleeping child. The rope was taken by other hands, those of the U.S. Lifesaving Service, and Kellar was brought ashore safely, though as ghastly in appearance as his crewmate, Pierce. All three men — Pierce, Kellar, and Hanna — were taken temporarily to the warm fog signal building, since the storm was

The U.S. Lifesaving Service, established in 1878, often worked in company with the U.S. Lighthouse Service. This was certainly true in 1885 when lightkeeper Marcus Hanna was assisted at the wreck of the *Australia* by the surfmen of the Cape Elizabeth Lifesaving Station. (U.S. Coast Guard Archives)

still too wild to risk a trek to the house. Their frozen clothing was cut off, and treatment was begun for hypothermia. Hanna roused first and was carried by his wife and Staples to the house, where he was put to bed, his wife fearing pneumonia. A mere two days later he was up again, however, tending to the lights and assisting Staples with getting the rescued crewmen to Portland by sled. For his bravery and unselfish effort, Hanna received a gold lifesaving medal.

Marcus Hanna's devotion to duty and the preservation of life and property was not unusual in the Lighthouse Service. Lightkeepers considered rescuing a part of their profession, even after the establishment of the U.S. Lifesaving Service in 1871. They often worked side by side with the well-trained surfmen to deal with shipwrecks. When the Coast Guard assumed control of the lifesaving effort in 1915, the Lighthouse Service continued to assist, often handling emergencies that would have resulted in death

Records of destructive storms riddle the pages of lighthouse logbooks. Some turned into legends; others passed with little mention, as if the fateful tempest was an expected part of life. A terse January 27, 1839, entry in the logbook for Maine's Matinicus Twin Lights exemplifies such resignation: "Lighthouse tore down by the sea." The two towers pictured here replaced it. (National Archives)

and destruction had the victims not received assistance immediately.

Lighthouse keeper Fred Kreth, of Point Reyes Light, California, was commended for just such a rescue in the 1920s. The Coast Guard team at Bolinas Bay, California, had received a distress call concerning a fishing boat that had hit the rocks beneath Point Reyes Lighthouse. The three fishermen on board abandoned their boat, made it to shore, and were awaiting help on a narrow beach beneath the steep rockface Point Reyes Light overlooks. Above them, lightkeeper Fred Kreth studied the situation with concern. The tide was coming in, and he knew a Coast Guard boat would be unable to reach the men, due to the rough seas. Without much thought of the danger involved, Kreth fetched a long, stout rope and began rappelling down the cliff face.

Buffeting wind pushed him to and fro like a pendulum as he descended, and sharp rocks cut his hands. The fishermen, who had already been forced to take refuge on the slippery rocks because of the encroaching tide, must have suspected something was happening above them when a tiny avalanche of pebbles began falling. A 36-foot Coast Guard rescue boat approached cautiously, studied the situation, then signaled that a rescue would be accomplished from above. As the boat departed, the fishermen nodded optimistically, unaware that the Coast Guard had not seen Kreth, inching down the rockface.

A few hours later, Coast Guard rescuers arrived at a point 75 feet above the spot where the fishermen were stranded. A line was dropped with a message attached, indicating that the men should climb to safety. When no response came, a Coast Guardsman climbed down the rope to assist, assuming the men were too exhausted or frightened to climb up alone. He found the rocks deserted and feared the fishermen had either been swept away by the tide or had foolhardily tried to swim to safety. The Coast Guard team went directly to the lighthouse to place an emergency search and rescue call to the lifeboat station at Bolinas Bay. Fred Kreth met them at the door, with a cup of coffee in one hand and a plate of cinnamon buns balanced on top of the cup. Behind him in the warm kitchen, the rescued fishermen were comfortably seated at a table — warm, dry, and enjoying a hot mug-up.

A Killing Wind
September 21, 1938, is a date that will never be forgotten in Southern New England. Still fresh in the minds of many people who endured it, the horror of that day is said to have exceeded the sum of both the San Francisco earthquake and the great Chicago fire. Thousands were left homeless, hundreds died, among them lighthouse keepers, their spouses, and their children. The Hurricane of 1938 is indelibly written on the scrolls of human history as one of the greatest natural catastrophes of all time.

It arrived unannounced, at high tide, packing winds in excess of 100 mph. It left behind scars, both physical and emotional, that are still visible. Today, looking southwest from Beavertail, Rhode Island, toward the entrance to the Western Passage of the Narragansett Bay is a stump of brick and concrete caisson rising out of the water. There is nothing on it, save a small skeleton beacon to prevent ships from ramming it. Whale Rock Lighthouse stood here on the morning of September 21, 1938. Its keeper,

An April 1851 storm destroyed the first lighthouse at Minots Ledge, killing its two assistant keepers. The head keeper was ashore at the time, but he heard the gloomy death knell of the tower fogbell at midnight just before Minots Light disappeared beneath the waves. (National Archives)

Walter Eberley, was alone. His wife and six children lived on the mainland, close enough so that the children could signal to their father from shore, waving a large bedsheet or swinging a lantern at night. On the day of the hurricane, they watched from shore as the lighthouse was torn to pieces and disappeared beneath the churning bay with Eberley in it.

Even worse was the loss of five people, including the lightkeeper's wife and son, at Prudence Island Lighthouse farther inside the bay. Almost every lighthouse in the area suffered costly losses in life and property. District Superintendent George Eaton gave a sober preliminary damage assessment by telegram to the Bureau of Lighthouses the day after the storm:

PALMER ISLAND LIGHT DWELLING DESTROYED . . . KEEPERS WIFE DROWNED . . . PRUDENCE ISLAND DWELLING AND FOGBELL TOWER DESTROYED . . . KEEPERS WIFE AND BOY REPORTED DEAD . . . CASTLEHILL LIGHT GLASS TOWER DESTROYED . . . FOGBELL GONE . . . WOODHOLE GREAT HARBOR RANGE LIGHT DESTROYED . . . TARPAULIN COVE FOGBELL TOWER DESTROYED . . . WHALE ROCK LIGHTHOUSE DEMOLISHED TO BASE . . . WARWICK FOG SIGNAL HOUSE DESTROYED

Carl Chellis was the lightkeeper at Beavertail Lighthouse that year. Winds had reached hurricane force by mid-afternoon, when his children, Marion and Clayton, aged 7 and 12, were coming home from school from Jamestown on a bus with five other children. The bus had to cross over a narrow spit at Mackerel Cove. As it approached the cove, driver Norman Caswell saw two cars on the causeway and assumed it was safe to cross. As the bus started down onto the causeway, a huge sea rushed in and rolled it sideways. The bus flooded, but Caswell was able to open the door and let the children out. They climbed on the roof of the bus and began shouting for help. But before anyone could reach them, a second sea rushed in and swept them all away.

Only Caswell and Clayton Chellis survived. Young Chellis later told how he had held his sister's hand and had heard her frightened voice telling him to not let the water get in his eyes. He also remembered feeling her small hand yanked away forever. When his father arrived at the scene and was told little Marion had been drowned, he ran to the bus and began kicking out the windows and shouting in anger.

Arthur and Mabel Small were on Palmers Island Lighthouse at New Bedford, Massachusetts, when the hurricane hit. Through years of living on or near the sea, they had gained a sensitivity to the weather, and each suspected a bad blow was coming when the wind picked up a little before noon that day and the air thickened. It turned out to be worse than anything they had ever imagined. By late afternoon the island was awash, and Arthur Small sent his wife to high ground in the oil house, where he placed some boards across the rafters and lifted her up onto them. He promised to return as soon as he lit up the tower for the night. Both knew it was not only a duty but also a must that the light be kept operative until it refused to function.

Mabel Small watched as her husband attempted to get to the lighthouse. Time and again he fell, submerged, then resurfaced gasping for breath. By this time, much debris was floating in the water. As Mrs. Small watched helplessly, a piece of wood hit her husband and he disappeared underwater. She wasted no time getting down from the rafters and waded to the boathouse. As she fumbled with the moorings of the boat, she saw her husband reappear and signal to her to go back to the oilhouse. He could see something she could not — a huge sea rising up behind the boathouse. A moment later, it swallowed the little building and inundated the entire island. Arthur Small cried out to his wife, then was knocked unconscious by floating debris.

He awoke in a pile of wreckage a few hours later, and crawled inside the light tower which, suprisingly, was still intact. He was exhausted and dazed and soon collapsed. The following day, two friends of Small's rowed out to the disheveled station with a relief keeper. They found Small tending the light but obviously unfit for duty, as he was badly bruised and talking incoherently. Much of his conversation centered on his wife, who was nowhere to be found.

In a letter he later dictated to his son from a hospital bed, Small admitted he remembered nothing between the time his wife was swept away and waking up in the hospital two days later. Despite his ordeal and lapse of memory, he had managed to maintain the beacon and salvage some tools and parts of buildings. The Commissioner of Lighthouses gave him a high commendation for his performance during the hurricane, plus a two-year leave of absence with full pay to help him recover from the tragedy.

Mabel Small's obituary, which appeared in the *Fairhaven Star* on September 29, 1938, was a heartwarming tribute: "Living by and on the sea and knowing full well the might of God's awful elements as well as sunshine on a sandy, rock-strewn isle, nor by wind or tide dismayed, she tried to bring succor to her mate, who struggled in the raging tide. We, her friends who weep, may pause and say, 'There is no greater love than this'. . ."

Refuge from the Storm
Life at Bolivar Lighthouse at the entrance to Galveston, Texas, was anything but idyllic at the turn of the century. Nothing would grow in the sand around the tower, so the keepers spent much of their time rowing to a nearby settlement for food, which had to be nonperishable because of the Texas heat. Mosquitoes were thick, and soiled the lens and the brasswork. Birds crashed into the tower frequently and sometimes took refuge in the lantern if a cold snap

set in. And the heat and humidity could be oppressive on summer days when the Gulf breeze died down and the beach grass stood dry and unswaying. It exacerbated many a disagreement into a full-fledged fight that had to be settled through either a reprimand or a transfer of personnel, and sometimes even a dismissal.

But the real curse of Bolivar Light was its vulnerability to storms. Twice in its career it was tested by record-breaking cyclones that roared out of the equatorial latitudes, skirted Florida and the Yucatan, and slammed the Texas coast with full fury. Though it always stood firm when tropical corkscrews of wind and rain assaulted the coast, its keepers were terrified by the creaking and groaning of its metal joints and the way it slowly rocked

Black as the oil of its native state, Bolivar Light, at the entrance to Galveston, Texas, endured fierce hurricanes in 1900 and 1915. Both storms sent area residents into the tall tower for refuge after their homes were washed away. (U.S. Coast Guard)

Gulf hurricanes have been especially destructive to lighthouses. An 1893 storm nearly toppled Louisiana's Chandeleur Lighthouse (National Archives).

Horn Island Light off Mississippi, shown here around the turn of the century, was destroyed by the September 1906 hurricane, which also drowned the keeper, his wife, and little daughter. (U.S. Coast Guard Archives)

under the stress of hurricane winds. It was Bolivar's style of construction that helped it escape annihilation in such storms. The huge metal plates, held together by bolts the size of doorknobs, gave the tower slight flexibility when powerful winds buffeted it.

Harry C. Claiborne served at Bolivar Light through two of the most destructive storms in Texas. The 1900 hurricane struck on September 7 and 8, inundating Galveston and its surrounding shores with a monster storm surge and estimated 120-mph winds. Claiborne had just purchased a month's supply of provisions a few days before the storm. He probably had no idea how important the food would be in the days that followed, but no doubt he surmised there was trouble on the horizon when high, stratified clouds appeared on the eve of storm. Claiborne had experienced his share of Gulf hurricanes and could sense when one was bearing down on Texas. But he had never lost his fear of them, for he knew they brought death. The terrible cyclone of 1875 had killed four Texas lightkeepers at the Decros Point Lighthouse in Pass Cavallo.

Bolivar Lighthouse proved to be one of the most stable structures in the area in September 1900, in spite of its height. Those left homeless by the hurricane took refuge inside the big lighthouse, welcomed by Harry Claiborne and his wife, who dutifully fed her frightened guests meals of boiled beans and bread. Before the storm ended, 124 people had clambered onto its spiral stairs, two on a step, while in the bottom of the tower the water had risen to the chest of the lowest person. Keeper Claiborne stood watch in the lantern throughout the storm and at times was forced to cling to handholds to keep from falling as the 117-foot tower reeled in the gale.

Fifteen years later, another powerful hurricane hit the Texas coast in August. Keeper Claiborne stated in his logbook that the 1900 storm paled in comparison; this 1915 cyclone tore the keeper's house from its foundation and tossed it into a pit that the sea had gouged farther down the point. The assistant keeper's house, along with all other outbuildings and objects at the station, disappeared in the surge. Only the lighthouse remained, again a sanctuary from the tempest for dozens of local residents who had lost their homes. The beacon was still lit when the winds died down and the waters receded — a tribute to its two courageous keepers. But the oil tanks for the station had been washed away in the storm, so when the oil in the lamps was used up, the light went out.

An interesting sidenote concerning the storm was the bravery of Assistant Keeper J.P. Brooks, who stood watch in the lantern as the hurricane made landfall on the night of August 16. Brooks reported that the revolving mechanism of the light failed at about 9:15 that evening, and he was forced to turn it by hand. He remained in the lantern until the storm threatened to shatter the windows, then he trimmed the wicks and left the light shining on its own.

As he descended the stairs, stepping over one after another whimpering soul who had taken refuge, he felt wind howling up the shaft of the lighthouse. The iron door at the base of the tower had come open and water had risen some 6 feet high. Fearing the erosive force of the water would undermine the foundation and topple the lighthouse, Brooks tethered himself with a rope, jumped into the seething maelstrom in the bottom of the lighthouse, and attempted to close the door. After much effort he managed to secure the door and returned, bruised and spent, to join the shivering refugees on the tower stairs. When the waters receded, and the lighthouse door was opened, people fell to their knees at the sight of the devastated landscape before them. Nothing stood anywhere, as far as the eye could see, except the lighthouse.

The Ultimate Sacrifice
In 1827, Major John Flaherty was appointed keeper of the handsome stone lighthouse at Sand Key, which served as a seamark along the treacherous Florida Straits 9 miles south of Key West. His wife and five children went with him to live on the key in the quaint little government house next to the light. By all reports, it wasn't a bad life, though many advantages to be had at mainland lighthouses were missing here. The key was a sun-drenched strand in the shape of a bone, about 400 feet long, with no trees or shrubs, and not a bit of grass. Fresh water had to be brought out from the mainland, along with much of the food the family needed; but Rebecca Flaherty probably kept a potted garden of sorts grown in

soil she brought out from the mainland and quenched with dirty water from the laundry and dishes.

Despite its hardships, Sand Key had a charm about it that was difficult to describe to someone not acquainted with living on a semitropical isle. The children ran half-clothed, their bodies bronzed by the sun; they swam, sailed, and fished, often bringing a green turtle or shrimp or tender conchs to the kitchen for dinner. Sequestered away on a tiny stretch of sand meant no school, no colds and flu caught from other children, and not being tempted by the material possessions of those living in the midst of civilization.

The family was very content on the little isolated isle, until 1830. In that year, John Flaherty died, leaving his wife alone to raise the children. The government was obviously satisfied with the Flaherty family and sympathetic to their situation, for Mrs. Flaherty was immediately given the job of lightkeeper of Sand Key Lighthouse. Over the next 16 years, she disappointed no one. Flaherty and her children were liked by everyone in Key West, including the wreckers, whom it has been said were a cutthroat lot who profited by the misery of others and considered lighthouse keepers a bane to their business.

Flaherty's many friends in Key West included Barbara Mabrity, herself a widowed mother of eight who had been appointed keeper of Key West Light after the death of her husband Michael. The two women had much in common, and both made it a practice each night to look across the water for the other's light. Five strong hurricanes swept over Key West during Flaherty's tenure as keeper at Sand Key. One demolished her house and tore up the seawall protecting the key from rapid sand erosion. Another washed away half the sand on the key and exposed the jagged coral bed that served as its foundation. With every storm, the shape and size of the key changed, presaging the destruction that ultimately ended the career of the brick lighthouse and its valiant keeper.

October 10, 1846, arrived with a few high clouds rolling in from the east, as pleasant a day as could be wished for in South Florida in autumn. By evening, however, the sky looked ominous and the wind had increased. Flaherty probably suspected she was in for a stormy night and made preparations. The rain began shortly after dark and quickly turned into a cataclysm. Waves leaped over

Old Key West Lighthouse collapsed in an 1846 hurricane, killing seven of Keeper Barbara Mabrity's children, plus seven other people who had taken refuge in the tower. Mabrity and one of her children survived. Some of the bricks from the toppled tower may have been used to construct this replacement sentinel, which now serves as a museum. (National Archives)

the new seawall, rebuilt after the hurricane of 1844 had torn it apart, and stole sand from around the base of the new house and the tower. About the same time, the wind ripped away the roof of the house and torrents of rain poured in on the family. Gathering her children about her, Flaherty decided to seek refuge in the base of the tower, since it seemed to her a much more sturdy structure than the house. Huddled at the bottom of the lighthouse stairs, the family listened to the tempest outside and clung to one another each time the lighthouse shuddered under the stress of the wind and waves.

Back in Key West, Barbara Mabrity was struggling to protect her own family and to accommodate the dozen or so frightened townspeople who had come knocking at her door after their homes had blown away. Key West Lighthouse trembled miserably as the storm reached its zenith. Still, Mabrity climbed to the lantern to tend the lamps and to peer across the spume toward Sand Key. So much water was flying in the air she couldn't discern Flaherty's light, and she prayed for her friend who struggled alone with five children on a fickle patch of tropical sand.

No sooner had Mabrity started down the lighthouse stairs than the walls gave forth with an incredible groan, and cracks appeared, branching out like veins bleeding rain. She ran, holding the oil lamp in front of her, stumbling on the hem of her dress and screaming to the people below to escape. Bricks and bits of mortar came showering down, creating a cloud of dust in which Mabrity could feel arms and hands and faces, some she recognized as her own children's. The lamp was wrenched from her and exploded into flames. Pulling a small arm after her, she groped for the door, dashed through it, and deposited the frightened child outside. She wheeled immediately, thinking she might return to the lighthouse to save others. Before she could move a step, the entire lighthouse collapsed, burying seven of her children and seven other people who had taken refuge there.

The next morning, Mabrity's grief was not assuaged when she looked across the water toward Sand Key. There was nothing left to see. Not only had the lighthouse toppled, killing Rebecca Flaherty and her children, but all trace of the beacon, its human inhabitants, and the strip of sand had disappeared. The only consolation for the grieving Mabrity was that the deaths of her children, as well as those of her compatriot and her children, had been quick, and that a new light was shining somewhere for them all.

The Sea Comes Ashore

Barren Unimak Island sits far out in the Aleutians at the entrance to the Bering Sea. Two lighthouses stand watch there, one at Cape Sarichef on the west side of the island facing the Bering Sea, and the other at Scotch Cap facing the Pacific Ocean on the southwest side. They were nicknamed the "Tombstone Twins" when they were built in 1903 because of the many shipwrecks in the area. Only men served here, due to the isolation of the stations, and they were allowed a full year of leave after serving three years at either station. Mail came infrequently, as did supplies delivered by a tender out of Ketchikan, 1350 miles away.

Surprisingly, the weather at Unimak Island is moderate compared with the rest of Alaska. The Japan Current brings warmer waters northward to the tip of the Aleutians, and tremendous upwelling of the nutrient-rich seawater here attracts a variety of birds and marine animals. About 70 miles south of the islands is the Aleutian Trench, a steep submarine chasm 25,000 feet deep in some places that defines the northern crustal boundary in the chain of restless volcanoes that rim the Pacific. In fact, Unimak itself is the tip of a volcanic mountain that formed ages ago and pushed itself to the surface.

The Pacific, in spite of its serene name, is a restless expanse, besieged by hurricanes and typhoons and sometimes by the uneasiness of the sea floor itself. Earthquakes under or along the sea where crustal seams stretch and rub have spawned some of the mightiest waves on record. It was this kind of wave that hit Scotch Cap Lighthouse on April 1, 1946. Estimates vary considerably, but seismologists believe the wave could have been more than 100 feet high. It came on a calm, beautiful, and moonless night with the stars shining brightly above, the Milky Way arching overhead like a bride's veil, and the aurora shimmering in the north — a night when fear and death were unimaginable.

The Scotch Cap Lighthouse had been rebuilt in 1940 and was situated on a concrete pad about halfway up a cliff 92 feet above the sea. Its walls were reinforced concrete designed to withstand the heavy northern storms that occasionally hit the area, as well as the tremors. Five keepers lived there, operating the 80,000-candle-power beacon and a diaphone foghorn. Above the lighthouse on the cliff summit was a Radio Direction Finding Station with about a half dozen station personnel in residence.

The midwatch commenced as usual on the night of April 1, 1946. The weather was clear, men not on the watch were snoring softly in their beds, and the surf was rumbling rhythmically on the beach below, auguring no clue of what was about to happen. At 1:30 in the morning, the monotonous watch was interrupted by a jolt, a movement of the Earth's crust deep in the Aleutian Trench. The entire headland shuddered. Electricity failed for a moment, the walls and floors trembled, and things fell out of cabinets and lockers. The earthquake lasted about 30 seconds, then everything returned to normal. A second shorter but more severe jolt came 27 minutes later. No one thought much about it; tremors were a fact of life on Unimak Island.

This was not a typical tremor, however. Its epicenter was miles away, deep in the Aleutian Trench, where a huge wall of rock had been jarred loose and had tumbled to the sea floor. The shock of this undersea landslide had created a titanic column of energy that extended from the sea floor up to the surface and radiated out in all directions as a series of waves. Called seismic waves, or tsunami, these killers are nearly imperceptible in the open sea, but as they speed toward land a shoaling effect occurs causing them to telescope in size.

After the second tremor at Scotch Cap, the watchman at the Direction Finding Station contacted the lighthouse watch by telephone. The men compared the times and severity of the tremors, as dutifully recorded in their logbooks, then agreed to stay in touch throughout the night. Around 2:15, the watchman in the lighthouse heard a strange sound, like a hundred aircraft approaching. He rose, went to the door, and stepped outside to scan the horizon. There was nothing in the sky except a thousand stars; still the sound grew louder and louder until almost deafening, and the watchman sensed an eerie suspiration of the sea, as if it were being drawn outward. Then came a flash of water high in the air and the outline of a monster wave looming over the lighthouse.

The wave arched its back and struck the island with indescribable violence. The lighthouse was inundated as seawater rushed up the cliff and swirled through the Direction Finding Station. The crew at the summit escaped to higher ground, unable to see anything below them in the darkness. They could hear the sea moving about, and several more times during the night they heard smaller waves come ashore, but they heard no voices below and feared the lighthouse and its personnel were lost.

Dawn confirmed their worst suspicions: The lighthouse had been destroyed. Only its concrete pad remained, with a few mangled lengths of metal jutting up. The officer-in-charge at the Direction Finding Station numbly recorded in his log: "0700 —

On this page and the next, sobering before and after pictures of Scotch Cap Lighthouse on barren Unimak Island in the Aleutians attest to the power and unpredictability of the sea. In the pre-dawn hours of April 1, 1946, a tsunami estimated to have been 100 feet high swept over it. The only traces found of its five keepers were parts of two bodies. Today, a new lighthouse shines from a higher, safer elevation on the hill behind the destroyed sentinel, and a plaque commemorates the bravery of the five keepers who died in the 1946 seismic sea wave. (U.S. Coast Guard Photos)

Went to light station; debris strewn all over the place. Piece of human intestine found on hill."

No one will ever know what thoughts passed through the minds of the five lightkeepers as they were wrenched from their beds and battered to death in a wall of water. Parts of two bodies were recovered, but nothing else was found; no logbooks, no furniture, no clothing, no pieces of the lighthouse. Somewhere under the sea south of Scotch Cap, those things were scattered and are now resting full fathom five. The Coast Guard rebuilt Scotch Cap Lighthouse out of reach of the sea, 500 feet up, and placed a memorial plaque where the old sentinel had stood, inscribed with the names of the men who died. Small solace to the families of these men was knowing their loss spurred the establishment of the Pacific Tsunami Warning System, centered in Hawaii with a substation in Palmer, Alaska. Had such a system been in effect in 1946, a warning of the approaching tidal wave could have been issued in less than ten minutes after the earthquake occurred — plenty of time to get to higher ground.

"Wherefore is light given to him that is in misery..."

–Job III: 20

Let the Lower Lights Be Burning

Brightly beams our Father's mercy
From his lighthouse evermore;
But to us He gives the keeping
Of the lights along the shore.

> *Let the lower lights be burning!*
> *Send a gleam across the wave!*
> *Some poor fainting, struggling seaman*
> *You may rescue, you may save.*

Dark the night of sin has settled,
Loud the angry billows roar;
Eager eyes are watching, longing,
For the lights along the shore.

> *Let the lower lights be burning!*
> *Send a gleam across the wave!*
> *Some poor fainting, struggling seaman*
> *You may rescue, you may save.*

Trim your feeble lamp, my brother!
Some poor seaman tempest-tossed,
Trying now to make the harbor,
In the darkness may be lost.

> *Let the lower lights be burning!*
> *Send a gleam across the wave!*
> *Some poor fainting, struggling seaman*
> *You may rescue, you may save.*

(From *Christian Service Songs*)

CHAPTER 6

CONFLAGRATION

Every precaution must be taken against fire.
Fire buckets, when provided, must be kept
filled with water and ready for use in a fixed
place.
—Regulation 13
Instructions to Lightkeepers &
Masters of Lighthouse Vessels
1902

Southampton Shoal Lighthouse stood in San Francisco Bay in the early part of this century, a fine house with gabled windows and ornate iron deck railings, all poised on top of a dozen stout iron and concrete posts. "With its many windows, verandahs, and tower," wrote W.H. McCormick, "it looks far more like a seaside hotel than a lighthouse." The handsome, symmetrical appearance was not to last, for in 1906 the destructive San Francisco Earthquake shook the structure so severely its support posts ended up with an 11-degree list. They were realigned as much as possible, but passing boats could not fail to notice the odd tilt that remained in a few of the pilings. When viewed from a distance, the lighthouse resembled some strange arachnid creature wading through the bay on wobbly legs.

Throughout its career, Southampton Shoal Lighthouse was regarded as somewhat of an unpleasant assignment. Though only two miles from the shores of Berkeley, it was a cold and clammy place, and rarely did the keepers row ashore and back without being soaked to the skin by either rain or fog. The huge station fogbell, attached to one side of the lighthouse, gonged more often than it was quiet, causing everything in the station to rattle and vibrate with sympathy. The roof was frequently beseiged by seagulls, who found it a comfortable stopover on their way elsewhere. Unfortunately, they left behind a mess the keepers had to

On Christmas Day 1936, lightkeeper Albert Joost died in a San Francisco hospital of burns he received while working at Southampton Shoal Lighthouse. Joost's wife called for help, then remained at the station to tend the light while her husband was taken ashore. This sentinel on stilts was located two miles off Berkeley, California. (U.S. Coast Guard)

scrub away or else risk having it wash into the drinking water supply.

Still, some families adjusted well to Southampton Shoal Lighthouse, even growing to love the place. This was certainly true of the Joosts, who came to live at the station in the 1930s. Albert Joost was an experienced and well-respected lightkeeper when he arrived at Southampton Shoal, and his wife, though somewhat disabled by a deformity of one leg and foot, was his efficient and enthusiastic helpmate. But, in spite of their dedication and hard work, their life of lightkeeping bliss ended abruptly on Christmas Day 1936.

They were alone on the lighthouse over the holidays that year, with the assistant keeper, Simonson, ashore on a few days leave. Albert Joost decided to work on the station radio antenna and lit off a blowtorch so that he could do some soldering. The torch went out, and when Joost tried to relight it, there was a loud explosion caused by the igniting of vaporized gasoline that had escaped during the brief period when the torch was unlit. When Mrs. Joost reached her husband, his clothes were on fire, and he was struggling to use a Paragon fire extinguisher. She was able to smother the flames, but not before the keeper was seriously burned. Realizing the severity of his injuries, she helped him into the station boat and watched as he feebly rowed for Angel Island, where a doctor would be on call at the Fort McDowell clinic. His parting words to her were to light the beacon at sunset and look after the station.

The medical staff on Angel Island could do little for Joost, but rushed him by boat to a hospital in San Francisco. Meanwhile, Mrs. Joost remained at Southampton Shoal to tend the lighthouse. Alone on the bay sentinel, and anguished by the thought of her husband's travail ashore without her, she lit the lamps and dutifully took care of the night chores. A few hours later, the tender *Lupine* pulled alongside with a relief keeper named Spellman who found "Keeper Joost's wife had already lit up but [was] much excited on account of [the] accident to her husband. . . . Mrs. Joost left at 7 p.m. for the city. Reports from [the] hospital are that the keeper is in a serious position."

Spellman stood watch at the lighthouse that night and was relieved the following morning by the first assistant, who had been recalled from his shore leave. Simonson reported in the logbook for December 24: "I found the station in a very disorderly condition. Southwest corner of station on outside of keeper's quarters had been on fire and paint was burned off. Also deck showed where fire had started. Pieces of his [Joost's] burned clothing led to water tank on upper deck. Evidently he tried to get water to put out the fire on himself, then went inside and got a Paragon fire extinguisher as there was no pail on the upper deck. By the time he reached the extinguisher in the stairway he must have been a burning torch as the walls in the hall, door casings, and the floor were all stuck with pieces of burned clothing. The keeper apparently fell in the hall as the wall showed a half circle of charred clothing. How he ever managed to put out the fire on the outside after being burned like he must have been, and then lower the boat and go to the hospital at Fort McDowell all alone is something to think about."

Mrs. Joost was taken back to San Francisco where she spent Christmas Eve at her husband's bedside. He was bandaged beyond recognition and in horrible pain, but he must have felt her presence beside him, and he may have heard her reassurances that the light out on Southampton Shoal was lit and operating smoothly in the care of Simonson. He was never again to see the quaint lighthouse with curious listing legs; he died a few hours later on Christmas Day.

Dangerous Illuminants
Fire was a serious hazard at lighthouses, especially in the years prior to electric lights, when oil lamps and pressurized gas tanks were used. Boston Light, the first in the nation, caught fire in January 1720, only four years after it was established, as a result of ". . . the Lamps dropping on ye wooden Benches & snuff falling off & setting fire." The keeper, Captain John Hayes, was thoroughly interrogated concerning the blaze and fervently testified: "Ye said fire was not occasioned by ye least neglect of ye Memorialist." Hayes was exonerated of all blame, since he had an unblemished record of service at the lighthouse and had instituted a number of improvements.

The first Plymouth Twin Lights, within sight of the landing

The rebuilt wooden Plymouth Twin Lights replaced similar wood towers that burned in 1801 when an oil lamp overturned and set fire to the oil-soaked floor of the lantern. Wood was a poor choice of building material for lighthouses when flammable agents were used in the lamps. (U.S. Coast Guard Museum)

place of the Pilgrims, burned down in July 1801 because an oil lamp overturned and caught fire, consuming one wooden tower, then burning across the covered way joining the two towers and destroying the second one. The keeper, John Thomas, was not injured and even managed to save many of the materials inside the lights, including the precious drums of oil for the lamps. Local merchants were so concerned at not having a beacon for Plymouth Harbor, they contributed money and labor to help Thomas erect a temporary light. Two years later a new station was built, with John Thomas still in charge. Unfortunately, the government again opted for wooden towers rather than stone. These deteriorated so rapidly they needed to be replaced by a third set of twin towers in 1843.

Wood was, without a doubt, a poor material for use at lighthouses. Not only did the constant assault of sea air and dampness shorten the lifespan of wooden structures, but they were also vulnerable to fire due to the many combustible materials used in the lighthouse lantern. Myriad things, natural and unnatural, could set a lighthouse on fire, from mishandling the lamps to a well-directed bolt of lightning. Surprisingly, even the optic itself was a danger, since its powerful lens panels could focus sunlight into an intense beam capable of igniting dry grass or dead trees. Keepers kept their lenses draped with special cloths during the daylight hours to prevent sunlight from cracking the delicate prisms, but also to obstruct any incendiary rays that could start a fire at the station. Even so, circumstances sometimes arose that were entirely beyond anyone's control. . .

Fire at Thimble Shoal
In late December of 1909, an unseasonable blast of arctic air swept down from the north, bringing snow and bitter cold winds to the Chesapeake Bay. It had been a difficult year for Chesapeake shipping, with several vessels lost in mid-Atlantic storms. And now 1909 seemed determined to end as calamitously as it had begun. Two days after Christmas, the four-masted schooner *Malcolm Baxter Jr.* passed through the Virginia capes in a light gale, headed for Norfolk. It was joined by the steam tug *John Twohy Jr.* which hooked lines on the schooner and began the prodigous tow to port through the choppy bay waters. The gleam of Thimble Shoal Lighthouse shone to the northwest — a navigator's star to steer by on this cold and turbulent trip into Hampton Roads.

Inside the lighthouse two keepers, J.B. Thomas and T.L. Faulcher, were huddled around a little coal stove in the kitchen, with blankets wreathing their legs and wearing caps and mittens to stave off the bitter cold that seeped through every crack in the wooden lighthouse. Thimble Shoal was a screwpile light, a quaint little clapboard house built on iron legs that were screwed firmly into the bay floor. Riprap was piled around the structure to stabilize it against the ice pack that came racing down the bay every spring and crunched against the tower. But it wasn't ice the keepers had to fear this December night.

As the tug neared the lighthouse, the heavy towline jerked repeatedly under the strain of the big, bucking schooner; but the helmsman was able to keep things under control. Little by little, the vessels moved toward port in the churning bay, keeping the lighthouse to starboard. Then the unexpected happened: The steering mechanism of the *Baxter* locked up, and the tug could not handle the unruly schooner. The towline parted, and the *Baxter* surged out of control, on a collision course with the lighthouse.

It was too cold a night to do more than the obligatory duties of lightkeeping; hence neither keeper at Thimble Shoal strayed far from the stove unless absolutely necessary. Around midnight, Faulcher got up, threw more coal in the stove, and gave the bay a cursory glance. He saw nothing out of the ordinary — just some snow flurries over the rough waters and the blink of Old Point Comfort Lighthouse to the west. Without lingering by the window, he returned to his chair next to the stove. Thomas was slumbering peacefully beneath his blanket, a wool cap pulled down over his ears and slow, steady puffs of visible breath appearing with his every exhale.

Faulcher had just about dozed off himself when a thunderous crash and rending of wood and iron broke the silence of the evening. The entire structure shuddered, knocking the men out of their chairs and opening up a crack in the southeast wall that

A schooner rammed Thimble Shoal Lighthouse in Chesapeake Bay in the winter of 1909, starting a fire that destroyed the entire structure. The keepers barely escaped in the station boat. (U.S. Coast Guard Museum)

widened to admit the bowsprit of a ship. The *Baxter* had hit Thimble Shoal Light. As the keepers scrambled to avoid the unwelcome intruder, the stove overturned and hot coals spilled onto the wooden floorboards, setting fire to the lighthouse. Oil everywhere — in cans, on rags, and soaked into the floor — fed the flames. The keepers barely escaped to the station boat, lowering it into the bay just moments before the davits caught fire.

The crew of the *Baxter* worked furiously to disentangle the vessel from the burning lighthouse. Fortunately, the same seas and winds that had helped propel the schooner into the sentinel also helped push it out, and within minutes the maverick vessel was freed and surging on its way. The *Twohy* had been attempting to make fast a new towline when the schooner hit the lighthouse. Seeing the vessel clear of all danger from the fire, the tug crew concentrated on saving the two lightkeepers, who were fighting to keep their small boat from capsizing in the frigid bay water.

Luckily, it was only a few minutes before the wet, chilled men were pulled aboard the tug and treated for hypothermia. People had already begun gathering on shore to watch the lighthouse burn. It was a horrible scene: flames shooting skyward, tanks exploding, glass shattering from the tremendous heat, and an orange reflection dancing wildly on the water. In less than an hour the station was totally destroyed, with only its skeleton legs left standing in the water. But like the mythical phoenix, a new lighthouse arose from the ashes of the old one within a few years. This time, engineers sunk a concrete caisson beneath the tower to repel any wayward ship that might again try to challenge it.

Deadly Sparks, Lethal Vapors
Many of this country's lighthouses have beautiful names, like Charity Island, Fairport Harbor, Love Point, Rock of Ages, and Sombrero Key. Others sound ominous — Cape Fear, Poverty Point, Destruction Island, Cape Disappointment, Alligator Reef, Alcatraz. The most sinister title goes to Execution Rocks, a bleak heap of stone in the treacherous waters of Long Island Sound between New Rochelle and Sands Point, New York. The lighthouse there was built shortly after the Civil War, but the site has a much older history with a gruesome tale concerning its name.

In Colonial days, the British executed insurrectionists in a pit sunk into these same rocks. The condemned were chained to the walls of the pit at low tide and left to drown when the tide rose and flooded the hole. A popular legend relates that the executed patriots got their revenge during the Revolution, when a British ship pursuing George Washington and his troops hit the rocks and sank. The ghosts of all concerned have been reported, at one time or another, to haunt the rocks.

Another often-repeated story is that after the Revolution, the fledgling U.S. government made Execution Rocks a symbol of freedom by proclaiming that no one would ever again be chained to it. When the lighthouse was built a century later, that decree was honored when duty at the Execution Rocks Lighthouse was made voluntary. No one could be sent there against his or her wishes; all who served the light would arrive at their own request. Nothing in the current Coast Guard Archives file on Execution

A 1918 blaze ruined part of Execution Rocks Lighthouse in New York. Its keepers didn't wait for firefighters to arrive. They put out the fire before it swept through the buildings. Fire on a waterbound lighthouse like this one is as dangerous as fire on a ship at sea. (U.S. Coast Guard)

Rocks Light Station supports this legend, but a strange event does exist, suggesting that the interplay of good and evil is still at work here.

The January 1919 Lighthouse Service Bulletin carried the following report concerning a fire at Execution Rocks Light Station:

On December 8, 1918, a fire, the cause of which could not be determined, broke out at Execution Rocks Light Station, N.Y., damaging the station to the extent that the engine house was totally destroyed, the engine and machinery rendered useless, the brickwork of the oilhouse damaged and the roof thereof burned off, the stonework on the north and east sides of the tower badly chipped, windows on the east side of the tower burned out, woodwork in the lower hallway of the dwelling scorched, and the gutter on the east side of the dwelling and the eaves on the north end thereof burned away. The oil house, which was alongside the engine house, was full of oil, there being about 2000 gallons on hand; about one-half of this oil was burned, the remainder being removed from the oil house after the fire was extinguished. . . .

Credit is due the keeper and the second assistant keeper of the station, and also two Navy men. . .for their prompt action in attempting to prevent the fire from spreading. . . .

Even in recent years, fires have destroyed lighthouses and injured or killed their attendants. In 1960, a spark set off an explosion in the compressor room at Maryland's Bloody Point Bar Light. The two keepers suffered smoke inhalation and minor burns, but escaped in a powerboat just moments before gas tanks exploded and turned the lighthouse into a flaming inferno. The station, like Thimble Shoals Light, was constructed mostly of wood over a steel skeleton and was a total loss.

A more serious explosion at Makapu'u Point Light in Hawaii in April 1925 killed one keeper and left the other critically injured. The mammoth hyper-radiant lens at Makapu'u at the time was illuminated by an incandescent oil vapor lamp with three 55-mm mantles. About 3:00 A.M. on April 9, as the two keepers were about to change watch, a flash fire occurred. The Lighthouse Service Bulletin of June 1, 1925, described the fire:

A cylindrical tank containing alcohol for starting the oil vapor lamp stood upright on a small wooden stand about six feet inside of the main entrance door on the left and about two feet above the floor. The first assistant suggested to the second that he fill the alcohol lighter, and after drawing all the alcohol which would run from the faucet, it was discovered that some of it had dripped to the floor. The first assistant lighted a match, which ignited the alcohol on the floor, and the explosion followed.

Later examination revealed blistered varnish and paint on all vertical wood surfaces. A calendar in a window recess was charred at the edges, and a letter tacked on a cupboard was completely burned. Investigators surmised the entire room had momentarily been filled with intense heat. No damage was done to the tower or lighting apparatus, but the needless death of the first assistant spurred officials to release this warning:

This deplorable accident shows the necessity for the greatest caution in dealing with the many highly inflammable substances used in the work of the Lighthouse Service.

A similar accident at Stannard Rock Light in Lake Superior killed one keeper and left the other three stranded on the concrete pier at the base of the tower. Three days elapsed before a passing ship discovered them. Stannard Rock Light had not been converted to electricity until after World War II, though most major U.S. lighthouses had been electrified in the 1930s. The keepers had been glad to be rid of the hazardous kerosene lamps and stoves. The offshore station had operated over 60 years using flammable illuminants, both in the lantern and in the living quarters. Yet only a few years after electrification, the station's first and only fire gutted the tower.

It was caused by the explosion of gasoline and propane tanks that fueled the station power plant. The buildings on the station pier were destroyed and the interior of the tower was severely damaged. One of the four keepers, William Maxwell Houghton, was standing near the power plant at the time of the explosion and was killed instantly; another keeper was seriously injured. With radio communications out, the three survivors — Oscar Daniels, Walter Scobie, and Richard Horn — had no means of calling for help. Huddled together on the edge of the concrete pier, wearing only their thin summer uniforms, they waited two days before a passing vessel sighted them and notified the Coast Guard. The tender *Woodrush* hurried out to the station and rescued the men.

As a result of the incident, it was decided that Stannard Rock

Coast Guard firemen battle a recent blaze at Boon Island Lighthouse, 9 miles off the shores of southern Maine. Fire is an ever-present danger at lighthouses and was even more so when flammable illuminants were used. (U.S. Coast Guard)

Light would be made automatic. It was too remote and dangerous a place for people to live. The fire damage was repaired, automatic machinery was installed, and the beacon was downgraded to 6000-candlepower. For 80 years it had been a stag station, considered too harsh and isolated from society for women and children. The fire convinced the Coast Guard it was too cruel a place for men as well.

The Burning of Cape Florida Light

July 23, 1836, dawned as expected for a midsummer day on Key Biscayne, Florida. The night breeze off the sea subsided as the rising sun sent temperatures into the nineties. Smudge pots smoldered to repel the mosquitoes, while palmetto switches served as fans in the oppressive heat. By noon, all work at Cape Florida Lighthouse was halted, and the keepers were resting inside the dwelling house to escape the torrid afternoon swelter. They lay inert on their beds listening to the hum of the insects and the gentle rush of the combers on the beach in front of the tower. Every so often, one of the men would get up and walk to the kitchen for a drink of water.

The head keeper, James Dubose, had gone to visit his wife and children, whom he housed in Key West, a safe distance from the troubles that beset the Miami area during the Second Seminole War of 1835. His predecessor, William Cooley, had lost his entire family in the massacre and had resigned as keeper of the lighthouse. Dubose willingly took the appointment of temporary

Scars from an old fire can still be seen in this 1890 photo of Cape Florida Lighthouse at Key Biscayne. Seminoles attacked and burned the station in 1836, killing the keeper's assistant and leaving the keeper marooned in the lantern with no way to get down. (National Archives)

keeper because of the pay but refused to take his family to Cape Florida. Instead, he hired an assistant keeper, John Thompson, and an elderly black man named Aaron "Henry" Carter to help him with his lighthouse duties and to care for the station during his frequent trips to Key West.

In Dubose's absence, Thompson and Carter did only those things absolutely necessary to maintain the light. Their lethargy on the afternoon of July 23 prevented them from seeing several Seminole canoes approaching from the south. The Indians pushed their canoes onto the beach and quietly made their way through a stand of palms toward the keepers' dwelling. Fortunately, Thompson chose this moment to go to the kitchen for water. He glanced through the open doorway on his way to the bucket and saw several Seminoles creeping toward the house with rifles in hand. Quickly, he wakened Carter, and the two men bolted through a back window and ran for the lighthouse with the Seminoles in pursuit.

The keepers were able to get inside the tower and bar the door, though Thompson had been grazed by a bullet. While the Seminoles pounded the door from the outside with the butts of their rifles, Thompson and Carter gathered muskets, ball and buckshot, and a keg of gunpowder — all stored in the base of the lighthouse — and carried these up the tower's wooden stairs. In their haste, the men had upset a tin can of lamp oil on the floor of the lighthouse. It had soaked their shoes and pants as well, but at least they were armed. Thompson fired from the lighthouse windows as he ran up the stairs, with Carter echoing his assault from behind. When they reached the lantern, they engaged the Seminoles in a shoot-out for several minutes; then the Indians retreated into the trees.

The men dared to hope the marauders were gone, but as evening approached, the irate Seminoles returned and the shooting resumed. The renewed gunfire sent Thompson and Carter for cover inside the lantern. Little did they know that the volley of bullets was a ploy to provide two Indians with cover while they set fire to the locked pine door at the base of the lighthouse. It was only a matter of minutes until the flaming door tossed sparks onto the spilled oil, and the interior of the lighthouse was ablaze.

Thompson and Carter realized they were sitting at the top of a giant chimney with a furnace burning beneath it. Air was being sucked up the tower and fanned the flames, setting fire to the wooden stairway. The keepers attempted to chop the stairway loose from its upper anchorage, but were forced back by the intense heat of the fire below. They closed and barricaded the small entry door at the top of the stairs and took refuge in the lantern.

It wasn't a haven from the heat for long: The fire climbed up the stairs and burned through the entry door, fueled by the oil cans in the watch room and the flue-like effect of the hollow tower. The iron lantern grew hot as a skillet, and the glass windows and lamps shattered from the heat. The men were driven outside onto the iron gallery. As soon as the Indians saw them, they began shooting again. Thompson was hit in the leg and had two of his toes shot off. Carter, badly burned and suffering miserably, expressed his intention to commit suicide by jumping from the tower. Before Thompson could stop him, he stood up and was shot in the chest. He fell dead on the gallery.

Thompson's clothing caught fire. He rolled about on the gallery, tearing the clothes from his body, then felt the searing heat of the iron gallery floor against his bare skin. He realized he was being roasted alive and, like his companion, resolved to end the ordeal. The keg of gunpowder sat on the gallery near his feet. With what energy he had left, he grabbed the keg and hurled it into the fiery hole below, hoping to blow up the lighthouse and himself.

The concussion of the blast rocked the tower and threw Thompson against the gallery railing, but he was not killed. Smoke and ash filled the air. The lighthouse blazed like a torch for a few minutes, then quickly burned out. Thompson's plan had worked, but in an unexpected way: The gunpowder explosion had caused the flaming stairs to collapse to the bottom of the lighthouse and smother the conflagration. Thinking Thompson and Carter were dead, the Seminoles departed, but not before they looted the house and commandeered the keeper's sloop.

Now the worst ordeal began for Thompson. Badly burned and bleeding from gunshot wounds, he had no way to get down from the lantern, since the interior of the lighthouse had been gutted.

The iron gallery cooled slowly and the night breeze off the ocean
eased his suffering only slightly. He lapsed into a fitful sleep, over-
whelmed by thirst and plagued by hungry mosquitoes gnawing at
his bare, burned skin. When dawn came, he was awakened by the
buzzing of flies and the foul odor of rotting flesh — his own but
also that of his friend, Carter, whose bloated body lay in a con-
torted pose at the edge of the gallery. Summoning all his strength,
Thompson pushed Carter off the lantern and grimaced as the
dead weight hit the ground 65 feet below. He scanned the sea
with red, swollen eyes for any sign of help, but there was nothing
but trackless miles of turquoise water veiled by a canopy of clear
blue sky bearing a brutally hot sun. Thompson wriggled into a
small bit of shade beneath the overhang of the lantern roof to
escape the blistering rays, and slipped into unconsciousness.

Toward evening, Thompson awoke to voices on the ground
below. He pulled himself to the edge of the gallery and carefully
peered down, thinking that the Seminoles might have returned.
When he saw men in blue uniforms and a schooner anchored
offshore, he called out for help and feebly waved an arm. The
marines of the USS *Motto* stared up at the lantern in disbelief. The
poor tortured soul who greeted them had no clothing, no hair,
bloody stumps where several fingers and toes should have been,
and skin as blistered and raw as a hickory-smoked ham. But how
to get him down?

Several devices for getting a line to the top of the tower were
hastily tried, without success. As darkness fell, Thompson began
to lose hope. The mosquitoes returned, more vicious than the
night before, and the thirst and pain that wracked his body were
now unbearable. Though the men on the ground took turns
throughout the night yelling encouragement, Thompson rolled
onto his side and surrendered to the darkness devouring his brain.

The following morning, a kite carrying a line was launched at
the lantern, but it flew by and was carried out to sea, where it was
mutilated by the surf. The marines feared Thompson had died,
yet they worked tirelessly to reach him. Finally, someone thought
to attach a line to a ramrod and fire it from a musket. The line fell
over the lantern railing to the cheers of the marines. By some
miracle, Thompson roused and secured the line solidly enough to

allow a man to climb up and rescue him.

Thompson was taken aboard the USS *Motto* to Key West, where he was hospitalized. In a letter to the Lighthouse Service headquarters in Washington, D.C., the collector of customs in Key West wrote: "Thompson was brought to this place & is in a fair way to do well. Indeed his recovery is deemed certain, but it is feared he will be a cripple for life. He being a seaman by profession and only volunteering for a short time in this exposed situation, I have thought it but equitable to extend the agreed aid to sick and disabled seamen. This is the only aid I felt authorized to extend without the sanction of the department."

Thompson remained in Key West until he was able to travel, then was moved to Charleston, South Carolina, where, understandably, he took up work other than lighthouse keeping. Cape Florida Lighthouse was not repaired and relighted until 1846. Then in 1868 it was upstaged by the "Eyes of Miami" — the huge iron screwpile lighthouse out on Fowey Rocks. A century of darkness followed for the battered Cape Florida Light, but in 1966 it became part of the Bill Baggs State Recreational Area. It was ceremoniously relighted in 1978 and placed on the National Register of Historic Places. However, it still bears visible scars from the blaze of 1836, reminders of one man's death and another's painful trial by fire.

The Fiery Wrath of Pele

At the turn of the century, shipping bound for Hawaii needed a landfall beacon on the easternmost point of the Big Island of Hawaii. After the Panama Canal opened, the demand for a navigational aid here was restated, and with the coming of trans-Pacific air travel in the 1920s, it became obvious a light had to be built quickly. Cape Kumukahi Lighthouse answered that demand when it flashed on in 1929 on a lava-strewn point of land east of the active Kilauea volcano. But the tower was small and its light too weak to be seen far at sea. In 1934 a new steel skeleton tower replaced the flimsy wooden structure and a brilliant landfall light was installed, flashing 1,700,000 candlepower visible 19 miles at sea.

The land around the lighthouse was not arable, so the keep-

ers' homes had to be located about a half-mile away where a garden could be planted and livestock kept. One of the early keepers, Joe Pestrella, hauled loads of soil out to the lighthouse and
planted fruit trees and flowering shrubs, all at his own expense.
His assistant, Sidney Estrella, was also landscape-conscious and
worked alongside Pestrella to make the compound a more pleasant place.

In 1955 the men's nerves were tested when the Kilauea volcano erupted and threatened to bury the station. Cape Kumukahi
had received its name from a legendary chieftan who worshipped
the volcano goddess, Pele, but also displeased her with his scorn-
ful remarks about her bold behavior. In retaliation, Pele buried
the chieftain alive in lava and thus formed the cape where the
lighthouse stood watch. The keepers worried that Pele might bury
their lighthouse. Pestrella remained at the station during the eruption of 1955 and was highly commended for his bravery by being
selected Civil Servant of the Year in Hawaii.

A few years later, the lighthouse was again imperiled when
Pele awoke one January day and spewed her fiery anger over the
village of Kapoho, not far from the lighthouse. Pestrella, his wife
and baby, and a new assistant keeper named McDaniels packed
their belongings and prepared to leave their homes if the lava
flow threatened to burn the station. McDaniels and Pestrella's family departed a few days later when just such a threat occurred, but
Pestrella remained at the station until lava began its slow crawl
down the access road to the lighthouse. Then he set the beacon to
work automatically and joined his family on safer ground inland.

Attention was riveted on the lighthouse as the flow advanced
toward it, setting afire the lovely trees and shrubs Pestrella had
planted and devouring the outbuildings. When the wall of hot
coals and flame reached the lighthouse, something uncanny happened. The flow split and forked around the tower, forming two
orange rivers to the sea that added a considerable amount of new
real estate to the Big Island. Heat from the flow melted the electrical wiring in the emergency generator system and extinguished
the light, but the 115-foot tower stood firm. Native Hawaiians
claimed Pele spared the lighthouse because of its humane mission of saving lives. The Coast Guard was not convinced it was

Pele's clemency that saved the light, however. As soon as the eruption subsided, a maintenance crew was called in to install automatic machinery in the tower so that it might operate without a
keeper. Its cottages were not rebuilt, nor were the handsome
plantings Pestrella had cultivated replaced. There was no reason
to tempt volatile Pele again.

> . . .the lighthouse fire blazed
>   like a star in the midst of the
>   ocean.
>   –Thomas Moore

Lava flows approach Cape Kumukahi Lighthouse in 1960 during the eruption of
Kilauea Volcano. The lighthouse was abandoned when hot lava came too near,
but amazingly, the advancing flow forked around the tower. The intense heat
melted all the electrical wiring and put out the light. Local Hawaiians believe the
fire goddess, Pele, spared the skeleton tower because of its beneficent mission.
(U.S. Coast Guard)

CHAPTER 7

CHILDREN OF THE LIGHT

There was a poor boy with a tuberculosis hip,
the lightkeeper's son.
—Virginia Woolf
To the Lighthouse

Manitou Island Light Station, July 15, 1875:
"Principal Keeper started out at 8:00 P.M. in the station boat with wife for Copper Harbor in anticipation of an increase soon after arriving. When one and a half miles east of Horseshoe Harbor, Mrs. Corgan gave birth to a rollicking boy; all things lovely, had everything comfortable aboard. Sea a dead calm."
James Corgan, Principal Keeper

Childhood Memories
The late Norma Engel had warm memories of her childhood at Ballast Point Lighthouse in San Diego in the 1920s. Raised by loving parents whose dedication to the Lighthouse Service was as strong as their affections for each other, Engel learned to revere hard work and family values. Her father and mother gave 37 years of service at three California lighthouses, but her recollections of Ballast Point were the most vivid:

"I loved going up to the tower. From the outside walkway I could look down on the tops of the nearby dwellings and see all around. It was a wonderful lookout spot. . . . In the center of the tower stood a pedestal, and atop it a round object covered by a soft, dust-free linen cloth. It looked like a bird cage. Dad carefully pulled off the cloth and smiled down at me. Then he lifted me up to take a look at the beautiful lens. . . ."

Engel's father was transferred to Ballast Point Light in the 1920s after serving a difficult tour of duty at Point Bonita Light near San Francisco. There, the family had experienced isolation and hardship, including the 1906 earthquake which nearly de-

Charles E. McLeod, Jr. mimics his father's cross-legged pose in this snapshot of life at Point Retreat Lighthouse, Alaska, in 1928. With most of the old civilian lighthouse keepers gone, the memories of lighthouse children, like McLeod, have become vital ties to the past. (U.S. Coast Guard)

stroyed their house and left them living in its ramshackle shell for nearly two years before the government got around to rebuilding it. When Hermann Engel received the position at Ballast Point, he traveled ahead to the station with his two sons, then had his wife and daughter follow a few weeks later. Norma Engel and her mother took a steamer out of San Francisco to San Diego, and took a taxi to Fort Rosecrans. Since there was no telephone at the lighthouse, they were unable to call ahead to arrange for the buggy to meet them. In a downpour, they walked the long, muddy beach to the lighthouse wearing traveling dresses and with heavy bags in hand.

Engel's remembrances of Ballast Point are graphically recaptured in her book, *Three Beams of Light.* She was truly a child of the sea, swimming and rowing and fishing and beachcombing in the warm Southern California sun, with a schedule tempered by her parents' work, the shipping that passed Ballast Point, and the weather, which could be idyllic or dismal.

One of the most poignant stories from her childhood, though it happened some 70 years ago, rings familiar to us today, as we share concerns over the environment and the future of the sea. Norma Engel learned the appalling consequences of water pollution first-hand: "The stench of dirty oil lay heavy in the damp October air. A thick sheet of scum coated the surface of our cove. . . . I hated the careless ships that emptied their foul bilges along our shores."

Less than 10 years old at the time, Engel surveyed the shore that day, mindful of her mother's admonition to stay out of the filth on the beach. As she skipped stones and tossed oil-soaked kelp into the air with a stick, something that "resembled an oily brown mop" caught her attention. It turned out to be a baby fur seal, soaked with oil, hungry, and frightened. Engel rounded up her two older brothers, and together the children pulled the baby from the contaminated surf and carried it to the house in a piece of canvas. With kerosene, rags, and soap, they cleaned the seal, then fed it clams and fish. It was kept in a box and doused with seawater every few hours. After about a week, the family decided the sea had cleansed itself enough to welcome back its winsome little brine child. Ambivalent feelings accompanied the children on their way back to the cove when it came time to return "Fuzzy" to his natural home.

Despite her family's assurances that the seal would never return after it was released, it came back to Ballast Point a few weeks later. And not only did it return and allow the children to feed it and frolic with it again, the seal became so tame it followed everyone like a puppy, receiving handouts and allowing curious hands to fondle it. Fuzzy grew enormous, and feeding him from the

Norma Engle's childhood memories of Ballast Point Light Station at San Diego included an oil-soaked baby seal she tamed. This photo of the station, taken near the turn of the century, reveals its lovely gingerbread architecture. (U.S. Coast Guard Archives)

hand became risky business with those sharp teeth snapping near fingers. As time passed, he seemed to prefer to catch his own food on forays that took him farther and farther from shore. Engel's parents tried to prepare her for the inevitable: The seal, wild and free and responding to some inner urge to travel onward, left for good.

Saved By a Parrot

Donald Campbell lived at Portland Head Lighthouse shortly after the turn of the century. His father was an assistant to the legendary Zebadiah Prout, an old sailing master who had swallowed the anchor and taken the position of head keeper at Portland Head Light. Young Campbell was in awe of Prout and followed the white-haired keeper everywhere, listening to his yarns and begging to learn the duties of a lighthouse keeper. He was taught how to care for the beacon and the fog signal, how to identify vessels coming and going in the harbor, and he helped with the painting, machinery, and sundry domestic duties around the station. Prout also cautioned the boy about the dangers of life beside the sea, but Campbell learned this on his own one sunny September day. The experience left him with an even greater regard for Zebadiah Prout but an irrevocable fear of the sea that remained with him for the rest of his life.

It was the morning of his first day of school. He wore a new suit "of itchy green material" his mother had made a size too big so that he would not outgrow it too quickly. As he waited to be walked into town to board the trolley, he saw a toy sailboat tossing in the sea below the lighthouse. Determined to have the prize, he climbed down the ledge and waited until a wave brought the little boat near the rocks, which were still wet from the tide and covered with slick green slime. As Campbell reached for the toy, his leather shoes began to slide; he coasted down the rocks and into the sea where he began thrashing wildly, since he had not yet learned to swim.

It was Prout's droll green parrot that first spotted the boy foundering in the waves. The bird began a frenzied squawk, punctuated with all the phrases it had been taught by the keeper. Realizing the bird was alarmed by something, the keepers and their wives launched an immediate search for the cause, and in doing so discovered young Donald was missing. The station dog spotted the boy in the sea, still thrashing but losing strength. Zebadiah Prout, 61 years old, dove in and saved the child. The boy did not go to school that day, but was made to spend the rest of the morning and afternoon pondering the lesson he had learned. The following day he was sent to school wearing the dried-out green suit, which smelled like seaweed and salt, and carrying a note that explained to the teacher that he had been absent the previous day due to falling into the sea and nearly drowning.

Donald Campbell's childhood memories were charmingly captured in a little tome by Arthur H. Cameron titled *The Lighthouse at Portland Head.* The book records the boy's impressions of an incident that occurred a year after his near drowning. ". . . when I was seven, I saw Halley's Comet. Its astounding appearance has been seared into my memory forever. You would have to see it, as I did, in order to believe this mind boggling spectacle."

This most famous and unique celestial visitor was seen by many people in 1910, but those living along the shore had spectacular views of it due to the flat sea horizon. Comets are those huge chunks of ice that melt as they encounter the solar wind; they are most visible near sunrise and sunset, sweeping their diaphanous tails along nearly the same path traveled by the sun. Being at a lighthouse with a broad view of the ocean horizon, and nothing to obstruct it for 3000 miles, meant Campbell occupied a viewing platform that would have made any astronomer envious.

Young Campbell indicated that it was mid-morning when he first saw the comet to the southeast, that it took the entire crew of the lighthouse by surprise, and that he observed a swirling of its long tail and a glowing ball at its head. No doubt the swirling effect was caused by the boil of air low to the horizon; the glowing ball was the comet's nucleus, a 27-mile long iceball. Campbell observed the comet for several consecutive mornings before it faded from view, and its appearance caused much trepidation around Portland Head, frightening even the station dog, who growled at the sight of it blazing across the heavens. Apparently, the sequestered families at the lighthouse had not been reading the newspapers closely, else they would have known of the comet's arrival, for such events are very predictable, and the public had been informed of Comet Halley's visit weeks in advance.

Growing Up in Long Island Sound
"I think my life was different from other children's . . . in a lot of ways," remembered Ruth Carr Gross in a 1986 interview with Connecticut Public Television. She spent her childhood in the 1920s on Little Gull Lighthouse in Long Island Sound, and in the 1930s at Southeast Lighthouse on Block Island. At Little Gull there were three families, all living in a square duplex house next to a 90-foot granite tower. The island itself, 9 miles from civilization, was a modest parcel of rock and sand, with a concrete cap on top of it. Gross was 18 months old when her parents moved to the station and old enough to start school when she left Little Gull. She remembered that there was a small, pebbly beach and a won-

Marie Carr (right) poses with her daughter Ruth Carr Gross at the opening of an exhibit on lighthouses at Beavertail Light in 1990. They have graphic memories of life at Long Island Sound's Little Gull Light and Southeast Light. (Elinor De Wire)

derful swing her father put up in the boathouse. The main entertainment was roller skating on the concrete: "We learned to roller skate because there was a big platform around the lighthouse, and there wasn't much else to do."

The families at Little Gull were close, and the kids played together, mostly board games. Gross thought she had almost every board game on the market back then. She and her brother played in the kitchen in the evenings by lamplight, since there was no electricity at the station. There was no plumbing either. Water had to be pumped by hand, and toilet facilities consisted of one outdoor privy. Gross' mother, Mrs. Marie Carr, washed her family's clothes over a washboard and cooked the meals on a woodstove. With no refrigeration she had to be creative. The family ate a lot of fish and lobster in order to have fresh meat.

Gross sometimes went ashore with her mother to get milk. No cows could be kept on the station, yet Mrs. Carr was determined that her children would have milk every day. In spite of the difficulties involved, she gathered about her a network of devoted travelers who would either take her ashore to get the milk or bring it to her personally. Twice, Mrs. Carr nearly drowned in the pursuit of this wholesome liquid. Her husband, Earl Carr, went out to rescue her one evening as she returned from the city of New London in rough water. He took his two children along, though it was a dangerous trip, perhaps because he may have felt it was better the children not be left orphaned if both he and his wife drowned. Fortunately, no one drowned, and the milk made it to the lighthouse unspilled.

Gross, like many lighthouse children, never wished to be away from the sea. She eventually settled in the grand old sailing community at Newport, Rhode Island. Her memories of her upbringing remained pleasant ones, but she admitted there was one obvious disadvantage of growing up on a lighthouse: "It did make me very shy. It was difficult for me when I went to school on Block Island." Gross' father moved the family to Block Island Southeast Lighthouse when she was six. She had to repeat the first grade there due to her extreme shyness. Her brother, who was nine when the family arrived on Block Island, started first grade with her. He had not been able to attend school while his father kept Little Gull Light, and this had been the major reason Earl Carr had requested a transfer from the isolated station; he wanted his children to be able to attend school without being sent away from home. For children at Little Gull, school meant living ashore with another family and returning to the lighthouse only on weekends, holidays, and summer vacations.

Marjorie Congdon Pendleton's parents, Lawrence and Amy Congdon, took over the Little Gull lighthouse in 1921 when she was five, and the following year she went to Long Island to live with her grandmother and attend school. Going to the lighthouse in the summer was a treat, a time when her parents, especially her father, spoiled and pampered her because they saw so little of her the rest of the year.

When Pendleton was eight, the family moved to Watch Hill Lighthouse near Westerly, Rhode Island. She had happy and vivid memories of this home, with a cow grazing in the pasture, a little Scotty dog for a pet, and many friends from the surrounding com-

Marjorie Congdon Pendleton had happy memories of growing up at Rhode Island's Watch Hill Lighthouse, seen as a clump of buildings to the far right on this old picture postcard. Pendleton and her sister were enamored of the young men at the nearby Coast Guard Station. (Elinor De Wire Collection)

munity; they viewed her father as someone very important. "He was proud of his job, and everybody liked him," Pendleton recalled. "It was something to be a lighthouse keeper back then. People looked up to him." He was a figure larger than life in her memory, and she adored him, though he could be very strict.

For Pendleton and her sister, life was idyllic on the breezy point at Watch Hill Lighthouse. There were grand picnics with high school friends on the lighthouse grounds, and swimming parties. Their church youth group held its summer outing at the lighthouse. "It was a popular spot, and we were never at a loss for friends. The kids would come out fishing, berry-picking, or to the beach. I loved it; I still think of it often."

When Pendleton was 20 she married a local carpenter — Clifford Pendleton. Their wedding was held in the living room of the keeper's house at Watch Hill. She wore a beautiful long gown; it was 1937. The wedding party posed, somber-faced, for a photo in front of the oilhouse at the station. Afterwards, Pendleton and her husband lived on nearby Quonochontaug Beach, while her parents remained on duty at the lighthouse. A year later, the 1938 hurricane took the area by surprise and caused horrendous dam-

Lighthouse daughter Marjorie Congdon Pendleton (second from right) wears a solemn expression on her wedding day at Watch Hill Light in 1937. The groom (far right) was a local carpenter named Clifford Pendleton. Marjorie's sister, Edna, was her maid of honor, and Edna's husband, George McLaughlin, served as best man. The girls spent much of their childhood at this picturesque Rhode Island light station. (Courtesy of Marjorie Congdon Pendleton)

age. Pendleton spent most of that day trapped in a car holding her infant son over her shoulder to keep him above the surge waters that had swept inside the car and risen up to her chest. At Watch Hill Lighthouse, a few miles away, her parents worked tirelessly to keep the beacon going.

After the storm ended and a damage and loss assessment was made, it was discovered that the wedding gown was among the casualties: "We were lucky. We didn't lose anyone in our family. I saw my neighbors drown, and my husband was worried about all of us. He was stuck in an elevator in a bank in town because the power had failed. I know it's a small thing, but I was sad to have lost my wedding dress."

Childhood at Island Lights
Gustav Kobbe, an intrepid reporter for *Century Magazine* in the 1890s, loved adventure and out-of-the-ordinary places. Thus, it surprised no one when he traveled to remote spots such as Minots

Ledge Lighthouse, a mile off Cohasset, Massachusetts, and the
Matinicus Twin Lights, 23 miles off the Maine coast, and spent a
harrowing week aboard the Nantucket New South Shoals Lightship.
The articles that grew out of his experiences with the keepers of
the lights were brimming with stories of heroism and hardship,
happiness and devotion to duty. Kobbe made lighthouse keepers
seem superhuman, and he portrayed their children as little cher-
ubs of exceptional obedience, intelligence, and maturity.

While visiting Matinicus Twin Lights in 1892, Kobbe interviewed the grandchildren and nephews of the station's legendary
couple, Isaac Grant and Abbie Burgess Grant. No lighthouse marriage was ever more blessed with courage and a call to duty than
the Grants'. Abbie Grant's life is discussed in a later chapter; here
Kobbe extols her dutiful descendants and their peculiar upbringing on the rock ledges at Matinicus, which they felt was the happi-
est possible world. His description of the Grant children is more a
paean to childhood than an accurate recounting of activities and
events, though he seems not to have missed even the smallest
detail. From his report, there is ample evidence that children are
children no matter where they grow up — in a traditional quiet
little town or on a barren rock jutting out of the sea. However, the
children of Matinicus Rock were somewhat unique.

*Along the edge of their rocky home, and among the boulders, these
boys had roamed so often that what to a casual observer would seem
nothing more than reaches of fissured granite and a confused heap of
jagged rock had assumed for them that variety of form and feature which
we would look for in a highly diversified landscape. Every little indenta-
tion became a cove, every little pool among the rocks a pond, and for these
miniature topographical features they had names like Spear Point, Western Guzzle, Devil's Gulch, Fort George, Canoe Pond; while a mass of
boulders became the Rocky Mountains of this thirty-two acres of granite.*

*On Canoe Island they built a miniature fishing-village, with all its
accessories. Besides the dwelling they erected four little wharves, flakes
(the long tables on which fish are cleaned and split), and fish-houses —
all, of course, on a Lilliputian scale. On the pond they had various little
craft—the dories so characteristic of the New England coast, smacks, lobster sloops with club-sails, and even a steamer that had clockwork for an
engine and transported fish from the village to a port at the opposite end*

of Canoe Pond. On a point at the entrance to the village harbor they erected a miniature lighthouse. . . . The fame of this fishing village spread all over Penobscot Bay, fisherman often putting in at Matinicus Rock for a look at it.

To them, living on an island dependent on a small boat for the only communication with the rest of the world, going to school by letters and a correspondence course, exchanging most infrequent weekend visits and many letters with their little friends as their only companionship outside the family, providing their own amusement and sports, seems to them the most natural state of affairs in the world, and children who live otherwise are more to be pitied than blamed, perhaps, not to be envied.

Kobbe went on to tell of the boys' duck hunting on Matinicus Rock, a sport available year-round due to plentiful mussels on which the ducks fed, but made all the more challenging by the lack of cover on the isle. Kobbe also mentioned a small grave, a curious resting place in a rock crevice shut up with bricks and mortar. The grave was that of a little girl, a sister to the Grant boys, who was born on Matinicus Rock and lived out her entire life of two years on its secluded shores, never once setting foot on the mainland. "The thirty-two acres of granite, around which the sea was ever beating, formed her world, and there she now lies at rest," Kobbe poignantly penned. Seeing her grave touched him enormously. Beside his written remembrance of it is a sketch of the family — the keeper, his wife, and another child — sorrowfully bearing a tiny wooden box across the ledges.

The death of a child was as much a part of life on a lighthouse as elsewhere, but perhaps more magnified at certain lighthouses where isolation and the perils of the sea were the everyday experience. Lighthouse children sometimes died because medical help could not be summoned quickly enough; the weather might have been too rough or the doctor too far away. Childhood diseases and pneumonia took many at offshore stations. The lighthouse at isolated Southeast Farallon Island, 23 miles off San Francisco, was the scene of an overwhelming tragedy just before the turn of the century. The children of the two lightkeepers became seriously ill, and the parents were unable to get help in time to save all of them. The only communication the Farallon families had with the mainland before the advent of radio and telephone was the occa-

A 19th-century magazine article about Matinicus Rock Lighthouse contained a poignant sketch of a funeral procession for the keeper's infant daughter. Since there was little soil on the island, the baby's tiny casket was buried in a rock fissure which was then sealed with bricks and mortar. (*Harper's New Monthly Magazine*)

sional visit of the service tender, *Madrono*, bringing supplies, food, a few creature comforts, and perhaps an inspector. Rarely, the tender also brought a minister to see to the spiritual needs of the lightkeepers and a doctor to examine the crew and handle any medical complaints.

In the 1880s the elevated station, 317 feet above sea, was tended by Cyrus O'Caine and William Beaman. They lived with their wives and children in two sturdy houses below the tower. Between them, there were enough children to warrant a schoolteacher on the island, but no teacher was brave enough to accept the position, owing to its severe isolation and the dreary surroundings. Ralph Shanks, an authority on Redwood Coast lighthouses, believes the children's existence was far from miserable, despite the many hardships on Southeast Farallon: ". . . the children seemed to have loved their island life. There were countless, fascinating places to play and a multitude of animals and birds. Each Christmas season would see the *Madrono* arrive with presents and even a Christmas tree. Then the children had to stay away from the landing while presents were brought ashore. When the great day arrived, keeper Beaman played Santa Claus."

The tragedy occurred in the early 1890s when a ship headed into San Francisco passed Farallon Island, and bonfires were seen burning all around its shores, signaling distress. There was no place for the large vessel to dock, but realizing there was trouble, its skipper plowed full speed ahead to San Francisco and immediately notified the lighthouse service of the desperate signals he had observed out at Farallon Lighthouse. The following morning the *Madrono* steamed out to the island with a doctor on board. The 20-mile trip was rough, with the doctor becoming horribly seasick; but his ills were small compared to the situation at the lighthouse. Diphtheria had struck. The families had fed the bonfires for days before help arrived, but it came too late. Two of the O'Caine children died.

A few years later, the Beaman family experienced a similar crisis when their son became gravely ill. Determined not to let misfortune repeat itself, the Beamans wrapped the boy warmly in blankets and launched the station's small rowboat, taking along their infant daughter, who could not be separated from her mother. Keeper Beaman and one of his assistants took turns at the oars, fighting rough seas, rain, and even hail. It took them several hours to reach the San Francisco Lightship, where they rested but received no further assistance, since the lightship did not have a doctor on board, or a radio, and was not permitted to abandon its watch, even under such dire circumstances. It was, like all lightships, a kind of floating lighthouse, and the Beamans certainly understood why it had to remain anchored to its offshore berth.

With no help from the lightship crew, the family set out in the boat once more and were able to reach the treacherous bar off San Francisco. There they were sighted by a bay pilot who took them aboard and rushed to the city wharf. The boy was immediately taken to a hospital, but as with the O'Caine children, help came too late. He died shortly thereafter.

Illness at isolated stations brought suffering to many lighthouse families, but most agreed drowning was their greatest worry where the children were concerned. Very young children were often kept confined or tethered, and older children were drilled in the dangers of the water. The ocean was regarded as a friend and provider, but also an omnipotent force that could bring misfortune and tragedy. In the case of the O'Caines, two of their children were lost to illness — a situation they may have sadly accepted as being beyond human control — but a third O'Caine child drowned at Farallon Light, perhaps causing the parents considerably more grief because his senseless death could have been prevented.

In the years when families were permitted to live at dangerous outlying stations, parents were known to attach ropes to their small children so that they could safely play outside. The rope was short enough to keep a youngster away from the water's edge, and he or she quickly learned to move about without becoming entangled. Although this method seems somewhat crude to those of us who live ashore, it was a sensible practice at lighthouses. In larger families, children sometimes boasted about being old enough to be "off the rope." It meant that they fully understood the difference between the sea and the shore and had been inculcated with a trenchant measure of respect for the sea. Still, drowning was an ever-present danger, even for older children.

In fact, the first official lighthouse child in this country, teenaged Ann Worthylake of Boston Light, drowned in Boston Harbor in 1716 while her sisters watched helplessly from shore. With Ann were her father and mother and the station slave; all were lost when their skiff overturned and the bay water caught their heavily clothed bodies in its icy grip before a rescue could be launched. The names of countless more have been added to the list of children drowned in the Lighthouse Service.

Such losses seem unimaginable to us today, and indeed they must have been so in the past, even in a time when parents came to expect that some of their children might not live to adulthood.

But the sea was not always unkind. It could wash ashore gifts of immeasurable value, perhaps as a way of making amends for its glaring disregard for human life and property. The sea is an inanimate thing, of course, with no feelings and no need to assuage human loss and grief. But. . . .

A Gift from the Sea

Long ago, no one knows exactly when, at Hendricks Head Lighthouse in Maine, there lived an older lighthouse couple, much respected and loved by the people of the nearby village of Southport. Their home was a picturesque square tower overlooking the mouth of the Sheepscot River, so enchanting in appearance and character that it would later attract artists and wealthy summer residents. But the 19th century occupants of the lighthouse were a heartsick pair, for they had lost their only child in the mercurial sea that thrashed against the margins of Hendricks Head. Just as for the biblical Sarah and Abraham, their baby had been a gift in their later years. He drowned on a winter day when he was barely old enough to walk. It was a bitter ordeal, and it had made the couple wish they had not chosen to live by the water and keep a light; yet they knew more lives were saved than lost by the beacon, and that many of the ships passing Hendricks Head had children aboard — little ones whose well-being depended on safe navigation in and around the rock-riddled Sheepscot River.

In March after the drowning of their child, a ship came ashore on a shoal a short distance from the lighthouse. Blinding snow filled the air, and heavy waves swept over the deck of the wrecked vessel, sending its crew and passengers aloft, where a constant sea spray sheathed their bodies in ice. One by one they froze, some falling from their frigid roosts in the rigging while others clung to the yards and ropes, paralyzed in sundry poses of death. On shore, the keeper and his wife stood an exasperating watch, since the water was too rough to launch a rescue effort. They had already lost their child to the sea; there was no reason to risk losing each other. To keep a lighthouse meant showing a beacon in all manner of weather, and doing everything humanly possible to save those in distress. But sometimes nothing could be done, and the death vigil was kept with prayers and lamentations.

Titanic waves crashed over the rocks around Hendricks Head that afternoon, the blizzard roaring with such ferocity as to drown out all other sounds, even the desperate calls of the doomed crew. It was just as well, for when darkness descended on the morbid scene there began the awful ordeal of the ship's death. The wind had died down somewhat, enough to allow the keeper and his wife to start a bonfire on shore. What light it cast out to sea, along with that of the lighthouse beacon, illuminated the black hulk of the ship, grinding and creaking on the ledge in its final agony.

A large hole had been gouged in its belly, causing some of the cargo to disgorge with every great wave that passed through it. All manner of things were wrenched out into the bubbling surf: boxes and timbers — some with bodies frozen to them — a jacket, tattered bits of sail, barrels oozing molasses, an open book, and coconuts from the tropics, which looked quite odd bouncing about in frigid northern waters.

There was a bundle of sorts, too, something deliberately rolled up in a mattress from an officer's bunk and bound tightly with line. It bobbed with such energy that it caught the attention of the keeper's wife, who had been busily searching the debris for signs of life. She ordered her spouse to run for the boathook and retrieve the parcel, for it looked like nothing she had ever seen come ashore from a ship. The task proved more difficult than imagined, but the closer the bundle came to the boathook the more certain were the keeper and his wife that it contained something important; they could hear sounds coming from inside it. Wet, chilled, and strained, they finally managed to pull the saturated package from the surf and roll it near the fire. It was quickly unbound, and its contents disclosed — a wooden box containing a blanket and a screaming baby girl.

Visits from St. Nick
During his radio talks in the 1940s and 1950s, the late New England historian, Edward Rowe Snow, often reminisced about his visits to lighthouses and his impressions of the difficult and reclu-

A seagull keeps watch on a misty summer evening at Marshall Point Lighthouse at Port Clyde, Maine. The light's caretakers operate a small museum in the keeper's quarters. (Elinor De Wire)

Left: Coast Guard lightkeeper Scott Gamble tickle[s] Shadwell, the station dog at Boston Lighthouse in 199[?]. The German shepherd was named for a black sla[ve] who belonged to the light's first keeper. (Elinor [De] Wire)

Below: The 1871 Presque Isle Light on the northwe[st]ern shores of Lake Huron is the younger of two sen[ti]nels tended by the Garrity family. Their collective se[r]vice at this and other lighthouses in the Great Lak[es] was more than 175 years. (Michigan Travel Bureau[)]

Opposite Top: Diminutive Isle au Haut Lighthouse [is] framed in the dining room window of "The Keepe[r's] House," a Maine bed-and-breakfast inn that lets gue[sts] escape telephones, TV, traffic, even electricity. The i[nn] is lit by oil lamps and heated with fireplaces and stov[es.] (Courtesy of Jeff Burke)

Opposite Bottom Left: Georgia Norwood, now a gra[nd]mother living in Boothbay, Maine, holds the no[vel] *Storm Child,* based on her life as a lighthouse child [in] the 1930s at Boston Light. (Courtesy of Wil[bur] Emerson)

Opposite Bottom Right: A poignant tribute to Mai[ne] lighthouse keeper Abbie Burgess Grant was this sm[all] lighthouse placed on her grave in the 1940s by his[to]rian and writer Edward Rowe Snow. As a teenager [in] the 1850s, she assisted her father at Matinicus R[ock] Twin lights, then went on to marry a lightkeeper a[nd] work at Whitehead Light. (Elinor De Wire)

International Chimney advertises its specialty on a yellow banner at Southeast Lighthouse on Block Island. The company successfully relocated the tower and attached keeper's quarters in August 1993 to a new home away from an eroding cliff. The project cost over $2 million, a price tag Block Islanders willingly raised to save their sentinel. (Elinor De Wire)

INTERNATIONAL CHIMNEY ~ EXPERT HOUSE MOVERS

Every December, the Cape Neddick Light Station becomes a lighthouse Christmas card at York, Maine. The tiny island sentinel is the subject of numerous memorable tales, including a cat that swam the channel between the lighthouse and the mainland, and a little boy who rode across the water in an aerial box to meet his school bus. (Jonathan De Wire)

sive lives led by lighthouse keepers and their families. Few could spin a yarn as aptly as Snow, and certainly the foregoing effort to relate the tale of the Hendricks Head baby pales in comparison with Snow's version. His stories captivated audiences everywhere and sent many a wide-eyed youth, the author included, rushing to the library to find his books. With titles like *Incredible Mysteries and Legends of the Sea*, or *Ghosts, Gales and Gold*, he held his readers spellbound.

Snow's lighthouse stories, including the one just recounted, are mentioned in numerous places in this book; hence it's only fitting that his contribution to lighthouse history and lore be included. Even more fitting is his inclusion in this chapter on lighthouse children, for he was well-known to them, playing a role that touched the hearts of many and survives as one of the best examples of gratitude for the work of lighthouse keepers and their families. For nearly 50 years, Snow was the "Flying Santa Over the Lighthouses." The sound of his plane circling overhead was as much a part of Christmas for lighthouse families as a trimmed

The tradition of the Flying Santa Over the Lighthouses was begun by Bill Wincapaw and continued by Edward Rowe Snow. Snow is seen here in the 1940s preparing to drop a Christmas bundle to the families at Boston Light. (Courtesy of Anna-Myrle Snow and Barbara Beebe Gaspar)

and lighted tree, carols, and the manger scene. Some children even thought he lived in heaven.

"I can remember the presents landing on the ledges out back and getting them when the tide went out," recalled Maurice Babcock, Jr., whose father was the last civilian keeper at Boston Light. The packages he so patiently waited to retrieve contained candy, balloons, books, gum, marbles, yo-yos, crayons, and the like. Though everything was usually soggy and pulverized, it was appreciated beyond words — a gift sent down from the sky from a man whose adoration of the Lighthouse Service traced back to his childhood and stories of his seagoing ancestors.

Snow was not the first person to think of keeping Christmas for the lightkeepers and their children. In the 1920s the tradition of the lighthouse Santa was begun by Bill Wincapaw, an aviator who felt he owed his life to the beam of a lighthouse. Returning to an airfield one stormy December night, he became disoriented and was able to find his way only after recognizing Maine's Dice Head Lighthouse. In gratitude, he dropped a package to the family there the day before Christmas. As it plummeted to the ground and into the hands of the excited keeper and his family, the idea occurred to Wincapaw that all lighthouse families ought to be remembered during the holidays for their benevolent services, especially at Christmas when the symbolism of a light to guide the way was foremost in everyone's heart.

Soon Wincapaw was making merry over a number of light-houses with packages full of gifts, most donated. By the time Snow took over the mission in the 1930s, dozens of New England senti-nels were on Santa's list. Snow added more during his years as the Flying Santa, eventually flying as far as the Gulf of Mexico, the Great Lakes, and the West Coast. His experiences as self-appointed St. Nick of the sentinels were related in some of his books and in many of his radio shows. He had several harrowing flights in bad weather, but most of the trips were memorable for other reasons. On one trip over Gloucester, Massachusetts, in the late 1930s, he was surprised to find that the family at Ten Pound Island Light had a special gift waiting for him.

Mrs. Edward Hopkins, whose husband kept the Ten Pound Island Lighthouse, was listening to the radio one morning a few days before Christmas when she heard that the Flying Santa, alias Edward Rowe Snow, was taking off that day from Boston Airport on his annual flight over the New England lighthouses. He had dropped gifts to the Hopkins family for several years in a row, and everyone was quite fond of him, especially the Hopkins' young son. The boy had gone ashore in the rowboat to attend school that morning, not knowing Santa was on the way. As usual, before returning home in the afternoon, he picked up a newspaper for his parents. To his surprise, the front page featured a picture of the Ten Pound Island Lighthouse with a huge "Merry Christmas" spelled out on the ground.

When the boy reached the lighthouse and handed the paper to his parents, his mother smiled knowingly. For years she had wanted to do something special for Edward Rowe Snow when he flew over to drop his Christmas bundle; finally she had done it, with front page coverage, too. Modestly, she told her husband and son how she had heard about Snow's flyby on the radio and had rushed outside and nailed newspapers to the ground to spell out a giant "Merry Christmas." Snow had snapped a picture of the unique greeting as he flew over the lighthouse, and later that day gave the film to a Boston newspaper, just in time for the evening edition.

School Days

Philmore Wass, in his splendid book *Lighthouse in My Life,* included a chapter called "Island Learning." It told how the children on Maine's Libby Island Lighthouse received their schooling, not via bus to some cozy building with classrooms, a principal, and a playground; rather in the extra bedroom of the lighthouse with a teacher sent out to the station to live with the family. Imagine being a child and having a teacher around 24 hours a day! It didn't seem to harm Wass; he went on to earn a doctorate from Columbia University. His book recalls the uniqueness of a childhood at an offshore lighthouse, with the chapter on schooling a fascinating glimpse into the means by which families, and the government, handled the difficulties of educating their lighthouse progeny.

Schooling for lighthouse children was a problem for those

Lighthouse child Philmore Wass toddles beside Miss Vera Sargeant outside
Maine's Libby Island Lighthouse in the 1920s. Sargeant was the itinerant schoolteacher for Wass' older brothers and sisters. She spent her school year traveling
to offshore lighthouses to educate the keepers' children. (Courtesy of Philmore
Wass)

assigned to offshore stations. On islands near the mainland, children were rowed to shore each morning during the school year to catch a bus or walk to the nearest school. The families at more distant island and rock lighthouses solved the problem by boarding the children ashore during the school year, or by home schooling them, which in some states was an acceptable practice as long as the children could demonstrate grade level achievement in the event they were later able to attend public school.

If a station had enough children, the government arranged for a visiting teacher. Maine had a number of these visiting schoolmarms, always women, who made the rounds at offshore lighthouses, staying a few weeks at each station. Great Duck Island Lighthouse in the Mount Desert region of Maine had 16 children romping about in 1902, free from books, pencils, and slates. Keeper Nathan Reed, father of the horde, requested a resident teacher, since there were two other keepers with children, and several children of a fisherman who lived on the island. The government not only sent a teacher, it also had a tiny schoolhouse built on Duck Island. Rena Reed, daughter of the lightkeeper, attended the little school and was so inspired by her lighthouse teacher that she went on to study at Castine Normal School and, upon graduation as a teacher, returned to Duck Island to instruct.

The Lighthouse Service did what it could, with what little funds were available, to assist keepers on outlying stations with getting an education for their children; but the responsibility increasingly fell on local communities. Maine, with its many offshore island lighthouses, was forced to address the need for teachers who could travel among the islands so that children would not have to be separated from their families in order to attend school ashore. In the summer of 1915, the Department of Education of the State of Maine assigned a teacher to work at the offshore lighthouses. A report in the Lighthouse Service Bulletin read:

". . .the Bureau is informed that it is the intention to hereafter employ one teacher for about 10 months in the year who will travel from station to station, taking a vacation for two months (December and January) in the winter. The State furnishes transportation expenses of teachers, salaries, and books, and the keepers furnish board at their own expense, and when opportunity permits and it does not interfere with the

other work of the [Lighthouse] Service, the teacher is transported by ten-
ders or station power boats. This arrangement has thus far proven very
satisfactory, and it is believed that it will be further improved.

Philmore Wass recalled that his itinerant teacher in the 1920s, Miss Vera Sargeant, stayed with the families at Libby Island Light for a few weeks, then handed over lesson plans to the parents when she was ready to leave for the next station. "It was a hit-or-miss kind of schooling that depended greatly on the seriousness of the parents in wanting their children to have a good educa-tion," wrote Wass. The room in which his school was held had tables, boards painted black for chalk writing, which Wass said did not work very well, a stove for heat, a skylight, and a special stairway that allowed the children of the other keepers to enter without tramping through the immaculately kept house. When the traveling teacher was away, Wass' mother took over the les-sons, and they were usually taught in the kitchen so that she could work and tutor at the same time.

Wass recalled that the government supplied few books for light-house children's schooling. He memorized most of the stories from the reading book his siblings used and often recited them to his friend. His experience with the itinerant teacher was casual, however, since he was not old enough to be included in the pro-gram, and it ended in 1922 — just as he turned the right age to start school. Thereafter, his parents rented a cottage ashore where his mother and the school-aged children lived on weekdays dur-ing the school year, except for the winter term, when the cottage was too cold for habitation, even with the stove fully fired. On weekends, weather permitting, they joined their father, Hervey Wass, out on Libby Island Light. Like many schoolchildren of today, Philmore Wass regarded summer as parole from the prison of school.

Of course, no lighthouse was ever devoid of books or writing materials, and it is safe to conclude that reading and writing and educating oneself were a great part of daily life there, even if ob-taining a formal education sometimes proved difficult. When Nathaniel Hawthorne visited the home of lighthouse keeper Tho-mas Laighton in New Hampshire, he was struck by the quantity of books in the keeper's personal library. These, along with the graphic experiences of living on the sea, certainly contributed to Laighton's daughter's success as a poet. Not all keepers had such expansive personal libraries, but there was no dearth of books. The government began supplying portable libraries to lighthouses in 1876. The idea was to absorb idle time and to educate, but also to present desirable models for behavior and to distract keepers and their families from the loneliness and monotony. Library books were carefully selected to reflect the Lighthouse Service's attitudes toward work and family and to assist in the upbringing and education of lighthouse children. There was a strong Christian bent to the reading, as well as inclusion of classical tomes and books on practical matters: Homer's *Iliad* might have occupied a space next to the Holy Bible, which might have been sandwiched between a guidebook on social manners and a volume of poetry.

Each library came in its own oak case with doors and a key, so it could be set upright as a piece of furniture. Four times a year, the libraries were exchanged by the visiting supply tender. Each library was numbered and contained about 50 different titles to assure that there was always something new to read. The number of popular poets and authors mentioned in lighthouse diaries and logbooks attests to the use these libraries received. Reading was ubiquitous to the entire lightkeeping corps, children included. When there was time to spare, and the wind was howling outside the lighthouse door, it was comforting to curl up with a good book.

A Harrowing Trip to School

In 1967 the *Boston Globe* carried a story about young Rickie Winchester, son of lighthouse keeper David Winchester who tended the Cape Neddick Light Station off York, Maine. Reporter Douglas Crocket launched the news story with this catchy opener: "He's certainly the only 7-year-old on earth who literally flies over pounding seas just to get to the second grade."

When Rickie's family first arrived at the lighthouse by boat, they found a strange conveyance rigged up between the island and the shore. It was a steel cable hovering some 50 feet over the narrow channel, to which was attached a wooden box about the size of a laundry basket. The family soon learned that the box was a convenient receptacle for sending and receiving parcels. Mail was delivered in this way, and groceries could be conveyed across the cable. It was an ingenious contraption, but keeper Winchester, more clever and daring than his predecessors, used it in a unique way.

Getting Rickie across the channel every morning to the school bus was troublesome and perilous, especially if the tide was ripping through the channel. The box on the cable began to look very tempting. No doubt Winchester tested it with various objects, and perhaps even the family dog, before commending his son to its smelly interior. "Don't stand up on the way across," he probably admonished the boy, "and be careful not to get a splinter."

So began Rickie's daily rides across the little tidal isthmus to the waiting schoolbus. He must have been the envy of his mainland friends, literally getting a lift every morning and bragging that he had traveled over the sea to get to school. When asked by the *Boston Globe* reporter if he made the crossing with trepidation, Rickie replied: "No, it doesn't ever scare me. It didn't even scare me the first time."

His imaginative mode of transportation, more sensible in Winchester's opinion than braving the fickle tides each day, was not to last. It became such a media topic that the Coast Guard grew concerned, not only for the safety of the boy but also for the image of "Semper Paratus." Tourists had begun to line the shore each day to watch the spectacle of Rickie's ride to school. There was a distinct polarity of views on the whole affair. Some people were enormously amused, while others expressed worry over the little boy who was forced to depend on a wobbly wooden box to get to school. A hasty Coast Guard investigation was conducted, the box was found to be unsafe as a means of human transportation, and Rickie went back to riding across the channel in the station boat. Even so, he could still brag that he had crossed the briny blue to get to school. Few children could top that.

Block Island Childhood

Growing up on a lighthouse was special in many ways; almost everyone who lived it says so. Barbara Beebe Gaspar credited her many practical skills and her weather sense with living on a lonely strand of beach on Block Island, Rhode Island: "You get in touch with nature, and so much of your life hinges on knowing what's going to happen with the weather. You get to a point where you know when it's going to rain or the fog is coming." Her mother was so accurate at interpreting natural signs that she received calls from local people asking for weather forecasts.

Gaspar's early memories of lighthouse life included visits to the waterbound Ledge Lighthouse in Long Island Sound where her father served as keeper from 1927 until 1938. She was allowed to go out to the lighthouse on weekends and in the summer during school vacation. She loved to fish from the upper deck, always with a rope tied around her waist in case she fell.

Gaspar lived in nearby New London with her mother and siblings. Her parents, separated by a mile of water, communicated with each other every night by "flashlight code." Howard Beebe climbed to the upper level of the lighthouse, flashlight in hand, and at the appointed time began sending a message to his wife. Mrs. Beebe answered from the upstairs window of her house in New London. It was a way to assure one another that all was well and to convey the feelings and frustrations of being apart.

The family moved to Block Island North Lighthouse after the 1938 hurricane, which caused considerable damage to Ledge Light and necessitated lengthy repairs before it could be placed back in service. Howard Beebe gratefully accepted his new assignment, knowing it meant he could be with his family year-round. A fishing boat out of New London, the *Mandalay*, took the keeper, his children, and their belongings on the two-hour trip across Long Island Sound to Old Harbor, Block Island. From there they were taken by car to the northern tip of the island, where they crossed Sachem Pond in a rowboat, then walked the long sandy spit to the lighthouse. Mrs. Beebe, who had recently given birth to a little boy, joined the family later.

At Block Island's North Light, on a small finger of sand surrounded by water on three sides, Gaspar learned to garden and to cook alongside her mother in the lighthouse kitchen with its wood stove and hand-pump sink. The family often ate blancmange for dessert, made from the seaweed around their home. Gaspar also honed her fishing skills and had her choice of casting into the

Block Island North Light (top) was home to Howard Beebe and his family in the 1930s and 1940s. Barbara, oldest of the children, is third from right. She now lives in Providence, Rhode Island, and occasionally gives talks about her life as a lighthouse child. (Courtesy of Barbara Beebe Gaspar)

saltwater off the lighthouse or in the brackish Sachem Pond. With her bedroom on the second floor of the lighthouse, she could hear the hum and click of the lens mechanism at night in the lantern above her. She grew accustomed to its familiar nocturnal rhythms and was usually the first to notice if anything was amiss with the light.

Gaspar walked two miles along the long windy spit to meet the rattling old bus that took her to the small school in Old Harbor. The wind was so strong one afternoon that it shredded her raincoat as she returned home on foot across the sandspit. Another time a winter storm hit as Gaspar and her sister and brother were returning from school. Frozen rain pelted them, and when they reached the lighthouse it looked like an ice castle. Gaspar's father had to toss a rope out to the children and pull them, one at a time, over the ice-slick brickwork surrounding the lighthouse.

A Poet's Childhood Memories

A century before Barbara Gaspar's experiences as a lighthouse child, young Celia Thaxter also took part in the daily routine of keeping a light with her father, Thomas Laighton, who tended White Island Lighthouse in the Isles of Shoals off New Hampshire. The family arrived at the sentinel in 1839 by boat when Thaxter was four years old and her brother Oscar was an infant; years later, she described her vivid memories of seeing White Island for the first time:

"It was at sunset in autumn that we were set ashore on that loneliest, lovely rock, where the lighthouse looked down on us like some tall, black-capped giant, and filled me with awe and wonder. At its base a few goats were grouped on the rock, standing out dark against the red sky as I looked up at them. The stars were beginning to twinkle; the sound of many waters half bewildered me. Someone began to light the lamps in the tower. Rich red and golden, they swung around in mid-air; everything was strange and fascinating and new."

Amusements were simple for Thaxter and her brother: They gathered shells and wildflowers and wove necklaces from them; they climbed among the rocks of the island, and on winter days when the weather was bad they played indoors at the windows

Poet Celia Thaxter drew much of her inspiration from her childhood home at White Island Lighthouse in the Isles of Shoals, New Hampshire. She and her brother often played in the covered way connecting the house and the tower. (U.S. Coast Guard Archives)

with pennies, which they warmed in their hands and pressed on the frosty glass to make small peepholes. Thaxter said the pennies were of no other use, for there was no place on White Island to spend them.

The family saw their share of storms and destruction. Thaxter recalled one gale when her father had to bring the cow into the kitchen to prevent the animal from being blown off the island. It was the same storm that sank the *Pocahontas*, a brig from Cadiz that was headed for Newburyport, Massachusetts. Thaxter had tended the lights that night for her father, and as darkness lifted over the Isles of Shoals and rain battered the keeper's cozy house, Thaxter and her mother heard the brig firing its guns in distress. Nothing could be done to save the doomed ship; it struck a sandbar and everyone aboard was lost. Years later, Celia Thaxter recounted the terror of the storm in "The Wreck of the Pocahontas":

The thick storm seemed to break apart
To show us, staggering to her grave,
The fated brig. We had no heart
To look, for naught could save.

One glimpse of black hull heaving slow,
Then closed the mists o'er canvas torn
And tangled ropes swept to and fro
From masts that raked forlorn. "

Celia Thaxter's fame as a poet is well-known today. She plucked her images of sea, and sky, and shoal, and shipwreck from her experiences as the daughter of a lighthouse keeper. She remained in the Isles of Shoals her entire life, for like many lighthouse children, she could never separate herself from the sea and the great beacon watching over it. She had lived with their murmurings about her almost from the beginning and must have felt that her lungs were meant to draw salt breath for all of her years. Celia Thaxter died in 1894 on Appledore Island in the Isles of Shoals, within sight of the lighthouse her father and she had tended on White Island.

Storm Child

Everyone envied little Georgia Norwood in the 1930s, the first child born at America's oldest light station. Her parents, Ralph and Josephine Norwood, came to the Boston Light from secluded Great Point Lighthouse on Nantucket. A September 1938 article in the *Boston Post* described the big Norwood family:

"Mrs. Ralph Norwood is proud of the fact that she is the mother of nine children, all of whom are hale, hearty, and happy on the island playground, with historic Boston Light in their front yard. Mrs. Norwood, only thirty-three, is believed by her friends to be the youngest mother of nine children in this section of the state, if not New England."

When Georgia Norwood was five years old, her family life at the island lighthouse caught the attention of writer Ruth Carmen, who cast little Georgia as the main character in her novel *Storm Child*. The book's jacket claimed: "The deft pen of Ruth Carmen weaves an exciting saga of the little known and supposedly lonely frontier — the lighthouse. The lives of these sea heroes are vividly depicted in this tangy and gripping drama. To them, storms, shipwrecks, and rescues came often. Yet in this rough and salty atmosphere you'll find humor, romance, and a most unusual love story."

In a 1986 biography of Georgia Norwood, written by her son,

Young Georgia Norwood gained fame in 1937 when a novelist based a book on her life as a lighthouse child. Her island home was at Boston Light, where she grew up with eight brothers and sisters. This reverse image of Boston Light was taken in 1990. (Elinor De Wire)

Willie Emerson, almost 50 years after her childhood at *Boston Light*, she recalled her dislike for the hype surrounding Storm Child: ". . . that summer many tourists visited Boston Light; all summer, coming in all kinds of boats and beautiful yachts, big and small. Seems someone always wanted a picture and I soon grew weary of that. I would hide behind Daddy's chair so they couldn't find me. . . ."

There was much excitement in 1937 as the book gained popularity, and the author began making arrangements for a movie based on the story. Georgia traveled with her mother and Ruth Carmen to several cities to make appearances. She was interviewed on the radio show "We the People" in New York, went to the World's Fair in Chicago, and hosted a party for a girls' orphanage in Washington, D.C. Her Shirley Temple looks and winning smile made her the ideal candidate for the film's starring role.

When it was suggested that Georgia be taken to the West Coast for a screen test, her parents protested, for this meant a separation from their child. Georgia had cried miserably when the whole idea was explained to her: "I want to go back to Boston Light," she begged. She had no desire to travel by train to a place so far from her island home and her close-knit family. The Norwoods, whose quiet, family-centered lifestyle had been disrupted by the entire affair, realized the best thing they could do for little Georgia was to take her home and "get on with a normal life."

In December 1938, a local newspaper out of Hull, Massachusetts, carried a letter from Ralph Norwood explaining his family's involvement with *Storm Child* and his reasons for severing relations with Ruth Carmen and her Hollywood entourage. Norwood wrote: "I did consent in the late summer of 1937, upon the promise of Mr. Yorkson [Carmen's publisher] of certain large sums of money, to be paid in regular installments, to permit the use of my daughter's picture, and name, in promotion of the book *Storm Child*. While no written contract was made between us, we did make a verbal contract which was witnessed by five persons."

Norwood went on to explain that the deal had not been honored and that Yorkson had misrepresented the Norwood family to the press. He added that all affiliation with Yorkson and Carmen had been broken off and that no further use of Georgia's name or likeness would be permitted.

So ended the brief, meteoric child-star career of Georgia Norwood, alleged to have been the first and only child ever born at a lighthouse. Had Ruth Carmen done her homework before making such a claim, she would have discovered that hundreds of children came into the world at lighthouses, many under less agreeable conditions than Georgia's arrival. Her first cries were uttered on a calm spring day, and she at least had a doctor in attendance. Some arrived in the teeth of a gale, with their mothers alone and afraid.

> *For those that never know the light,*
> *The darkness is a sullen thing;*
> *And they, the children of the night.*
> *Seem lost in fortune's winnowing.*
> *—Edith Arlington Robinson*
> *"The Children of the Night"*

Author's Note: In the 1980s, Captain Stetson Turner, Master of a
Supertanker, gave this poem from memory to the docents at
Maine's Shore Village Museum. As a child, Turner lived on Great
Duck Island Lighthouse and Bear Island Lighthouse, both in
Maine.

Lighthouse Keepers

Lighthouse keepers have it easy,
All year long their homes are breezy;
Noises don't disturb their labors,
For they haven't any neighbors.

They don't need big wastebaskets
For old papers, orange peels, or gaskets;
Just one careless motion
And their trash drops in the ocean.

They don't need nine holes or twenty,
They get exercise aplenty;
One trip up the spiral stairway
Equals three around the fairway.

Window shades are never needed,
They can dress or strip unheeded;
Wakeful brats don't have conniptions,
Neighbors don't give long descriptions.

When I'm old and don't need pity,
I shall leave the sullied city,
Climb a lighthouse, bar the door,
And trim my wicks forevermore.

CHAPTER 8

KEEPERS IN SKIRTS

*The lighthouse women were made of wonder-
ful fiber.*

–Hans Christian Adamson

The Lighthouse Service has always been dominated by men. They decided where lighthouses were to be established, built and outfitted them, appointed the keepers, and conducted inspections. Men far outnumbered women as lightkeepers, and the few women who did manage to receive appointments to lighthouses almost always had connections of some sort, either through family ties or friendships with government officials. But in this presumed man's world, a few rare women dared. Their contributions, whether officially recognized or not, were enormous.

With the exception of "stag stations" where women and children were forbidden, lighthouse keeping was largely a family occupation. The government was more than pleased with the domestic talents a wife and daughters brought to a station. Like life on a farm, everyone pitched in at a lighthouse, and almost always everyone, including the ladies, knew how to run the place. Those who gained official appointments as keepers worked as hard and were inspected with the same scrutiny as the men, but they were usually paid less. In addition, there was no prescribed uniform for women lightkeepers until control of lighthouses was handed over to the U.S. Coast Guard in 1939.

Even so, it was nearly 50 years later that the U.S. Coast Guard appointed a woman lightkeeper. Jeni Burr was the first "woman in uniform" to keep a lighthouse. In 1980 the Coast Guard assigned her to New Dungeness Lighthouse in the Strait of San Juan de Fuca, across from Vancouver Island. Burr and her husband were very content living in the 75-year-old keeper's house with a menagerie of cats and dogs and the rush and surge of Puget Sound just outside their front door. The eight-mile-long sandy spit connecting the light station to shore was sometimes a treacherous strand to travel. Occasionally, the tide swept over it, temporarily leaving the couple like castaways in their own home. Storms tossed large pieces of driftwood onto the spit. While some of these made lovely conversation pieces on her lawn, the larger ones could block the access road and force Burr to use her boat to get ashore until the road was made passable.

Coast Guard keeper Karen McLean — the last woman to keep a lighthouse in the U.S. — thought her work was much different than the lady "wickies" who preceded her. She served as a lightkeeper on the Kennebec River, Maine, from 1983 to 1986, watching over the small beacons and fog signals at Doubling Point, Squirrel Point, and the Kennebec River Range Lights. McLean had her two small children with her during working hours, much like the women who tended lighthouses in earlier days, but modern conveniences made life considerably easier for her than it was for lighthouse women a century ago.

When McLean needed to work outdoors, a remote radio system hooked up to the baby's room allowed her to hear if the child cried. There was also an outside bell rigged so that she could hear the phone when it rang. The fog signal at Squirrel Point, three miles away, was operated by a remote switch in McLean's office, and a special alarm system alerted her if any of the four beacons in her care failed.

Still, there was plenty of hard work to do. She put new shingles on the roofs of the two range lighthouses, did light carpentry work and some minor electrical repairs, and kept everything painted and polished and the lawn well-groomed. Her home was frequently visited by vacationers longing to get a first-hand look at the bucolic life of a lighthouse keeper; hence she took great pride in its appearance. Anyone stopping by quickly grew envious of her: She earned a good salary while staying home with her children and lived in a picturesque house with a breathtaking view of the river. Karen McLean was among the few lighthouse keepers who exemplified the quiet life we've come to associate with the nostalgia and romance of lighthouse keeping.

The first official lady lightkeeper on record was Hannah Thomas of Plymouth, Massachusetts. That settlement's first beacon

The last Coast Guard woman to work as a lighthouse keeper was Karen McLean, who tended a set of range lights, two small beacons, and two fog signals on Maine's Kennebec River in the mid-1980s. Like women in the old Lighthouse Service, she was able to keep her children, Dylan and Allie-Rose, with her while she worked. (Elinor De Wire)

was built on the Thomas family's property in 1769, at the end of a long finger of land the Pilgrims had named the Gurnet, in honor of a fish that was plentiful in the waters of their European homeland. The colony's arrangement with John and Hannah Thomas was typical of the day: The land was not purchased, rather John Thomas allowed the lighthouse to be built on his property so long as his family was allowed to tend it. The rent paid to him for the use of his land was a paltry five shillings a year.

Plymouth's 20-foot towers were listed as twin lights, a unique style of lighthouse construction involving two separate towers, two lanterns, and twice the usual work for the keeper. Mrs. Thomas assisted her husband at first, then assumed full responsibility for the station after his death. Probably unaware of her uncommon status, she performed the same duties as her male counterparts in addition to keeping her home and raising a family. Apparently, her work was satisfactory, for in 1790 when the lighthouse was

Fanny Salter, the last civilian woman to keep a lighthouse, shines the lens at Maryland's Turkey Point Lighthouse for a publicity photo in the 1930s. She retired a short time later because arthritis in her feet made it difficult to climb the lighthouse stairs. (U.S. Coast Guard Museum)

Helpmate and assistant to her husband, Maria Israel served at Old Point Loma Lighthouse from 1873 to 1891. When she wasn't busy tending the light or keeping house, she made shell pictures to sell to tourists. (National Park Service)

ceded to the federal government, Mrs. Thomas was still the official keeper, receiving her annual five shillings in rent but also a
lightkeeper's salary that equalled about $200 a year. She was be-
coming feeble, though, and her son was doing most of the work.
At the recommendation of an old family friend, General Benjamin
Lincoln, who had served with John Thomas during the Revolu-
tionary War, Hannah Thomas stepped down, and the younger
John Thomas assumed the job.

Lighthouse Widows

Women most often received appointments to lighthouses because their spouses, who had formerly held the positions, died
while on duty. This was the case with Hannah Thomas and became an unofficial rule concerning the appointment of most of
the women in the Lighthouse Service. The government, it seemed,
had few reservations about hiring women with several years of
apprentice-type experience. By 1851, 30 widows had succeeded
their husbands at American lighthouses. A few daughters of lighthouse keepers obtained their jobs in this manner, too. Records
indicate that as a group, women had longer careers and moved
less frequently than the men, and reports of lighthouse inspectors
showed the majority of them to be exceptionally tidy and meticu-
lous.

Widowed Clara Emory Maddocks kept Maine's Owl's Head
Lighthouse for several decades, and in addition to household
chores, rearing children, church work, and tending the high, promontory lighthouse, she rang the station fogbell by hand in periods
of poor visibility. At Owl's Head, that could be as much as 2000
hours a year!

As a retired centenarian in the 1940s, Maddocks recalled many
unusual events during her tenure at Owl's Head. Storms often
tossed spray over her house, 80 feet above the water. Getting to
the tower was an accomplishment in itself when weather was bad,
since the house and tower were separated by a long, curving ramp
and stairway. Maddocks experienced one winter so cold the bay
froze over completely, and her lighthouse became a rinkside lamp
post for skaters and people riding over the ice in horse-drawn
sleighs.

Eleven shipwrecks occurred around Owl's Head during Maddocks' years as keeper, and she participated in many rescue efforts. One rescue in particular stands out, as it was her loyal old milk cow that had fallen over the cliff and had to be hauled up the precipice with ropes and pulleys. The bewildered bovine was returned to the pasture unharmed, and no fee was charged to Keeper Maddocks by those who helped, for her benevolent occupation was revered by all.

Betty Humphrey of Monhegan Island Light in Muscongus Bay, Maine, served a keepership of 18 years following the death of her husband, Joseph Humphrey, in December 1861. Mrs. Humphrey's two sons had enlisted in the Union Army a few months before their father's death. Alone, and with incredible courage, she kept to her post, even when Confederate raiders sank several vessels just off the island. Her youngest son died on Southern soil; the elder boy was wounded but returned to help with the lighthouse work. In 1880, when Humphrey retired from lightkeeping, she was earning $700 a year, $100 less than her husband had earned at his death.

California's "grande dame" of lighthouses was Emily Fish, the respected widow of a Monterey doctor and a woman of considerable beauty and social grace. Born in Michigan, she had lived in China, followed her husband from camp to camp during the Civil War, and was a well-known socialite in San Francisco, where her husband took up private practice and taught at the University of California.

Neither Fish's husband nor anyone in her family had been lighthouse keepers, yet she was able to secure a position at Point Pinos Light in 1893, two years after her husband's death. Fish was 40 at the time and knew nothing about the operation of a lighthouse, but she was charming and intelligent, and she knew people — lots of them. It's likely her son-in-law, Henry Nichols, got the job for her. He was the Twelfth District Lighthouse Inspector and no doubt had considerable voice in the selection of lightkeepers for his district.

Regardless of how she obtained the position, Fish met the challenge of keeping the little Cape Cod-style sentinel on the wind-blown Point of Pines with grace and fortitude. Not only did she perform all the duties expected of her, but she brought finesse to the job as well. Her thoroughbred horses roamed the 95-acre reservation, along with milk cows and French poodles. The bleak lawn was transformed into a colorful tapestry of grass and flowers fringed with cypress hedge and a picket fence. Her gardening talents were superb, as many of Monterey's notables discovered at the dinner parties she held in the lighthouse.

A Chinese servant named Que assisted Fish with the gardens and livestock, and she frequently hired additional help when a special project arose. But it's doubtful she allowed anyone to care for the kerosene lamps in the lighthouse or polish its prism lens. Despite the chores of housekeeping and lighthouse keeping, she managed to stay quite busy in the social circle of Monterey, holding offices in clubs and societies and striking a comely profile as she drove her carriage around town with her favorite poodle on the cushions beside her. This was a woman without financial worries, keeping a lighthouse and its grounds as if it were a hobby, yet seriously devoted to her work.

Fish's daughter, Juliet Nichols, undoubtedly used her married name to obtain a position at San Francisco's Angel Island Light-

POINT PINOS LIGHT HOUSE.

Pleasant little Point Pinos Lighthouse was home to Emily Fish in the 1890s, one of the Lighthouse Service's most elegant keepers. She was a widow and California socialite who undoubtedly obtained her position by virtue of her son-in-law's work as Twelfth Lighthouse District Inspector. (Elinor De Wire Collection)

house in 1902 after the death of her husband, District Inspector
Henry Nichols. This sentinel at Angel Island was often plagued by
fog, and Mrs. Nichols, like many women keeping lights and fog
signals after the age of machinery, was not always able to repair
the fog mechanism when it broke down. On several occasions she
resorted to manual (should we say "womanual"?) labor. She reported in her log that once she "struck the bell by hand for 20
hours 35 minutes, until the fog lifted." Two days later it returned,
and she "stood all night on the platform outside and struck the
bell with a nail hammer."

On the blustery shores of Lake Michigan, Harriet Colfax recorded a number of fierce storms during her 50-year career as
keeper of Michigan City Lighthouse in Indiana. Her 1861 appointment as lightkeeper was, no doubt, a result of her blood kinship
with a certain high government official, namely Vice President
Schuyler Colfax, who was Harriet's cousin. Even so, Miss Colfax
proved herself able and courageous. She worked beyond the age
of 80, heating oil for the lamps on her kitchen woodstove, then
carrying it out a long, blustery pier and up into the lighthouse.

In cold weather, the oil would often congeal in its metal can
before Colfax reached the lantern, and she would have to return
to her house and heat it again. During one storm, she had just left
the lighthouse and started back along the pier when a terrific gust
of wind pushed waves over the pier. She heard wood splintering
behind her and turned in time to see the entire lighthouse blow
over and disappear into the murk of Lake Michigan. Had she dal-
lied in the tower she, too, would have gone to her death.

Living conditions for lightkeepers varied, but one aspect common to most was economy. The houses were spartan, furnished
with the basic necessities and sometimes less. Everyone was expected to skimp and scrape; opulence was almost unheard of. At
times a keeper's home was utterly primitive: Maine keeper Kate
Nevins got by living in the beached hulk of a wrecked steamer
while tending Winter Island Light, since there was no house there
in her day. At California's Point Bonita Light, a tent served two
large families for over a year after the 1906 earthquake destroyed
the dwelling houses. There were few comforts and conveniences;
lighthouse women knew hardship, even in the 20th century.

Complaints were few, however, and for those who despaired, anguish often grew into contentment. Such was the case for petite Katie Walker. She was miserable at first sight of the squat, spark-plug lighthouse where her husband was assigned in the 1870s. It was on their first night of duty at Robbins Reef Light that she informed Jacob Walker: "I won't stay. The sight of water which-ever way I look makes me lonesome and blue."

The feisty, German-born woman had fallen in love with Jacob Walker while he was keeper of Sandy Hook Lighthouse in north-ern New Jersey and imagined her life as a lighthouse keeper's wife would be as idyllic and wonderful as at Sandy Hook, firmly an-chored to solid ground with a road leading to it and neighbors to visit and flowers growing by the door. Robbins Reef Lighthouse was altogether different. It stood on a concrete platform on the west side of the main channel of New York Bay. There were plenty of neighbors — yes, thousands of them peering across the water each day from Staten Island and Brooklyn.

Katie Walker refused to unpack her bags when she first ar-rived at Robbins Reef, but love eventually won out. Slowly, things were put away and she set about making the place a comfortable home. The Walker's two children also lived on Robbins Reef. When they were old enough to attend school, Mrs. Walker rowed them to Staten Island on weekday mornings and returned for them in the afternoon. These trips honed her boat-handling skills, which would later prove invaluable in the saving of lives.

When Jacob Walker died of pneumonia in 1886, his wife was devastated. Her children were grown, and she felt she knew no life other than lighthouse keeping. For weeks after his death, she stared out a window toward Staten Island Cemetery where he was buried, wondering what to do. The idea came to her that Jacob Walker wanted her to continue caring for the lighthouse. "Mind the light, Katie!" had been his parting words to her. And so she applied for the keeper's job.

It was a year until she was officially given the appointment. The Lighthouse Board was concerned that a woman under five feet tall and less than 100 pounds could not manage the equip-ment and handle the boat. Mrs. Walker's past performance, along with a well-tended light during the months following her husband's death, convinced everyone she could do the job. In her opinion, she was better suited to the task than most men. Living within sight of the Statue of Liberty was reassurance that a woman could keep a lamp lifted high and shining bright.

Her size and spunk were severely tested over the next 35 years. It was not so much the lighthouse that demanded stamina, but the people who traveled in and out of New York Harbor. In her career as keeper, Walker would be credited with more than 50 rescues. She found most people ungrateful for her help and unable to grasp how near to death they had come. The one castaway she thought had truly appreciated her efforts was not a person, but a little Scotty dog that had gone down with the crew of a three-masted schooner.

When Walker pulled the dog into her boat on the end of an oar, he was barely alive. She hurried back to the lighthouse with the Scotty and five crewmen from the schooner. The little dog appeared dead in the lamplight inside the lighthouse kitchen, but resolute Katie Walker poured warm coffee down his throat and massaged his body; amazingly, he was revived. The dog was too weak to be taken to the mainland when a boat arrived for the castaway crew a few hours later, so Walker was asked to look after him until he was well enough to travel.

A few weeks later, the schooner's skipper returned to the lighthouse to retrieve his pet. The little dog had recovered nicely and was bounding about the catwalk as chipper as ever, barking at every ship that passed. While Walker and the skipper visited over a cup of coffee, the Scotty padded about the little round lighthouse, tail wagging and eyes bright. He might have considered the possibility that his two favorite people were intending a long hiatus together on this iron and concrete ship with a go-nowhere mission. That would have satisfied him, for the lighthouse had become a pleasant home, and he had grown to love the small woman's gentle ways.

It was not to be so. Coffee and conversation ended, and the little dog felt himself pressed against the woman's breast one last time, then handed down the ladder into the skipper's waiting arms. Katie Walker thought the dog looked back at her with tears in his huge brown eyes, sadness at having to leave the dedicated little lady lightkeeper who had felt even a dog's life was important to save. There were certainly tears in Walker's eyes.

Daughters on Duty

Not every matron to trim the wicks was a paragon of womanhood. A few were sloppy in their daily tasks, some generated a never-ending string of complaints to the government, and occasionally one was just plain bored with the whole idea of tending a light and fog signal. Nancy Rose, who kept Stony Point Lighthouse on the Hudson River in the late 1800s and retired at age 79 after almost a half-century of service, admitted: "Nothing ever happens up here. One year is exactly like another, and except for the weather, nothing changes."

Her daughter was equally unenthused: "I can't remember anything that has ever happened, except once our cow died, and several times it's been bad years for the chickens. But even the one wreck wasn't really what you might call a wreck, for nobody was hurt, and it wasn't Mother's fault anyhow, for both the lights were burning as brightly as ever."

Nancy's son added that he would rather pick huckleberries over the mountain than keep a lighthouse. The whole family agreed the spectacular view up and down the Hudson had grown uninspiring, and with more and more tourists and picnickers invading the point every year, the Roses longed for a comfortable cottage in the village.

Wives and daughters certainly had reason to be unhappy at some lighthouses. Cloistered years spent on lonely islands and rock stations took a toll, especially on teenagers. For the women and girls, especially, there was a profound need for social life and for the trinkets and trappings of the comfortable mainlanders. When Philmore Wass approached his older sister about an interview for his book detailing the family's years in the Lighthouse Service, she declined; she had hated their lighthouse life and, understandably, didn't want to discuss it.

But not all daughters of lighthouse keepers considered their home a dismal dungeon from which there was little opportunity of escape. Some had a penchant for following in the footsteps of their fathers, either as keepers themselves or married to lighthouse keepers. Perhaps they became so enamored of the sea and guarding those who traveled on it that they wanted to live apart from neither. This was surely the case with young Abigail Burgess Grant of Matinicus Rock, Maine. Known as "Abbie," her courage and devotion grew into a legend that survives today, even though the lonely lights at Matinicus Rock long ago lost their keeper.

Abbie's father, Samuel Burgess, had received his appointment as keeper of the twin lights at Matinicus Rock in 1853, but due to his wife's poor health he was forced to work also as a lobsterman to afford a doctor and medicines. When her father was away tending the lobster traps or ashore for supplies, Abbie ran the lights. Though only 14 years old when she began assisting her father, she learned quickly and was, according to the fishermen of Penobscot Bay, as able-bodied as the official keeper.

In January 1856, when Abbie Burgess was 17, her father was detained ashore 22 miles away while a storm raged over Matinicus Rock. Alone at the light station with a sick mother and small frightened sisters, she worked tirelessly to keep the lamps burning in both towers and soothe everyone's fears. As the storm's intensity increased, the old keeper's house began to collapse. Abbie moved her mother and sisters into the north tower, away from the brunt of the storm's wind and waves, then hurried out to the chicken coop to rescue her pet hens. These proved wise decisions, since the old house and chicken coop were washed away at the height of the storm, and the eggs produced by the hens in the days that followed were the only food the women had until Keeper Burgess could safely return with provisions.

With the election of President Lincoln, Samuel Burgess lost his job. Lighthouse keepers' appointments were politically controlled at that time, and since Burgess was not affiliated with the elected party, he was replaced. Dutifully, he packed up his family and turned the station over to John Grant, a loyal Republican. Not wishing to leave Grant in the lurch, however, Samuel Burgess left his capable daughter behind to acquaint the new keeper with the workings of the station.

Abbie Burgess was then about 22 years old and well known to sailors and coastal residents of Maine. Her devotion to the twin lights and her skillful methods heartily impressed John Grant, but

A 19th-century artist sketched the legendary Abbie Burgess with her pet hens. The young girl gained fame for keeping the Matinicus Twin Lights burning through a fierce storm in 1856 while her father was detained ashore. (Shore Village Museum)

even more, they impressed Grant's assistant keeper, who also happened to be his son. Within a few weeks of his arrival, Isaac Grant was in love with the willowy, quiet girl and proposed marriage. No one will ever know whether she consented out of passion for Isaac or love of the lights, but the couple seemed happy as they took their vows at the station the following year.

Abbie Burgess Grant was appointed second assistant upon her marriage, though she had considerably more experience and ex-

The fabled "Army of Two" at Scituate Lighthouse in Massachusetts were Rebecca and Abigail Bates, teenage daughters of the lightkeeper. They supposedly repelled an attack on the town in September 1814 by hiding behind a hillock near the lighthouse and playing martial music to frighten away English soldiers anchored offshore on a man-of-war. (*St. Nicholas Magazine*)

pertise in lighthouse keeping than her husband or father-in-law. Still, it was not customary to promote or pay a woman more than the men with whom she served, so Abbie had to be content playing third string. She gave birth to four sturdy children at the rocky islet and had them nearly raised when her husband was transferred to Whitehead Lighthouse near Rockland. There the couple served until 1890, when Abbie's health forced their retirement.

Two years later she was gravely ill at only 52 years of age. She had lost all interest in living after leaving Whitehead Light, and shortly before her death in 1892 she confided to a friend that she hoped her gravestone would be in the form of a lighthouse. Somehow the request was forgotten, and a simple white marble stone was placed on her grave in the cemetery near Spruce Head. Fifty years later, New England author Edward Rowe Snow read about the heroic woman's wish and decided to honor it. He had a small lighthouse made and placed it at the foot of her grave as a memorial to her selfless devotion to keeping the lights. Knowing Abbie

Mississippi's Biloxi Light was home to Maria Younghans and her daughter, Miranda, whose combined service at the sentinel equaled 62 years. Younghans, a native of New Orleans, was appointed to keep the light in 1869 after the death of her husband, Perry Younghans. Miranda took over after her mother was no longer able to tend the light. (U.S. Coast Guard Archives)

Burgess Grant was also a lover of Tennyson, Snow read "Crossing the Bar" at her graveside.

Lightkeeper and Naturalist

California's most revered lighthouse daughter was Laura Hecox, the ninth of ten children born to preacher and lighthouse keeper Adna Hecox, who had traveled West with a wagon train in 1846 and was instrumental in having a lighthouse built at Santa Cruz. Laura Hecox's mother, Margaret, was a gifted writer who chronicled the family's wagon train trek westward in a book titled *California Caravan*.

Laura Hecox was no less ambitious than her parents. From childhood she was a curious and avid collector of natural history specimens. Her studies of the flora and fauna of the California coast won praise from scholars. She was regarded as one of the nation's foremost naturalists whose collection included fossils, Indian relics, shells, bird eggs, and marine specimens. She corresponded with a number of scientists, one of whom was so impressed by her professional documentation of California's natural history that he named a newly discovered specimen in her honor.

Hecox became keeper of Santa Cruz Lighthouse in 1883 following the death of her father. By then her collection took up an entire room in the lighthouse, and she delighted in showing her personal museum to visitors and giving tours of the station. She always insisted that visitors remove their shoes before going up into the lantern to view to tower's valuable fourth-order French lens. And woe betide the curious admirer who left a fingerprint on the shimmering prisms of the lens or its highly polished brasswork! Laura Hecox never married, and upon her retirement she gave her collection to the citizens of Santa Cruz and helped them establish a museum. She spent her remaining years giving tours of the new museum and reminiscing about her experiences as a lady lightkeeper.

Rescuer at Lime Rock

Perhaps the most famous lightkeeper's daughter in America was Ida Lewis, a tall, slight woman from Rhode Island who was as shy as she was well-known. She assisted her father, Captain Hosea Lewis, from 1857 until his death in 1872, and during that time she rescued a number of Newport Bay residents, including four careless youths, a drunken soldier, and a farmer's prize sheep. Her picture appeared in *Harper's Weekly* in 1869, along with an account noting that her rescue of a drowning man "was a most daring feat, and required courage and perserverence such as few of the male sex even are possessed of."

Suffrage leader Susan B. Anthony honored Ida Lewis with a passage in *Revolution* extolling her virtuous calling as a lightkeeper, but she was even more honored when President Ulysses S. Grant

The quiet and solicitous nature of Ida Lewis, beloved heroine of Rhode Island's Lime Rock Lighthouse, shows in this portrait taken about 1890. Her devotion to saving lives earned her many honors. The Ida Lewis Yacht Club now occupies the old sentinel she tended for nearly 50 years. The Coast Guard recently honored her by giving her name to the first of a new class of buoy tenders. (U.S. Coast Guard Museum)

came to visit her and informed the crowd of curious onlookers that to see the heroine he would have gladly rolled up his trousers and waded out to Lime Rock. Fortunately, he didn't have to get his feet wet; Ida Lewis took him to the lighthouse in her rowboat.

July 4, 1869, was declared "Ida Lewis Day" by the residents of Newport, Rhode Island. The shy Lewis was presented with numerous awards and a handsome new lifeboat. Several speeches were made, but when it came her turn to address the citizens who so adored her, bashful Ida Lewis asked a friend to deliver her words of thanks. She climbed into her new boat and rowed back to Lime Rock, happy to be away from the commotion and fanfare ashore.

Lewis received other awards, including three lifesaving medals, and was given honorary memberships in important organizations — some she had never heard of until their representatives came knocking at her door. Gifts and letters poured into her mailbox from all over the world. Some contained marriage proposals, and though she did wed a local fisherman in 1870, she separated from him a few months later and remained single the rest of her life. Once, when a reporter pried into her private life by pointing out that she was childless, Ida Lewis replied: "The light is my child."

Keeper George West and his wife, Alma (right), show off their garden outside their home at lonely Guard Island Lighthouse, Alaska. The woman in the center is unidentified, but perhaps she was a daughter or sister to the keeper. If so, social life would have been almost nonexistent for her. Such sequestered women often married sailors, fishermen, or other lightkeepers, for these were probably the only men they knew. (U.S. Coast Guard)

Despite her fame and capable work at Lime Rock, it took seven years for her to gain an official appointment as keeper of the lighthouse, even though she had assumed all of the duties immediately after her father's death. It was customary to give the position to the keeper's widow, but Mrs. Hosea Lewis was ill and could not meet the physical demands of keeping a busy harbor lighthouse. Only after Ida Lewis gained fame as a rescuer and proved herself highly fit for the job did Congress declare her appointment official. Her reputation also earned her an enviable salary of $750 a year.

Lewis continued to care for the lighthouse and kept the boaters out of trouble. Her last rescue was performed at age 64 when a friend who was rowing out to visit her fell overboard. Never content with a mediocre effort, she rescued both the woman and her boat. But her long, devoted career was nearly over. Tourists no longer flocked to Lime Rock to glimpse America's most famous rescuer, and the government had supposedly made plans to replace Lime Rock Light with a small sentinel on nearby Goat Island. Rumors ensued of Lewis' removal from the service due to her inability to keep up with technology and her stubbornness about following the rules imposed by the new Bureau of Lighthouses.

Ida Lewis was brokenhearted about the hearsay circulating in Newport, though she had not received any official word from the government concerning the future of Lime Rock Light or the quality of her performance. One morning, in the midst of the controversy, her brother found her unconscious on the floor of the lantern room. A blood vessel had burst in her head. She died later that day with her brother at her side. He felt certain the rumors of her possible dismissal had hastened her death. She was buried in a cemetery in Newport, and a few years afterward her beloved lighthouse became a yacht club named in her honor.

"A Sacred Duty"

The August 1929 issue of *Woman's World* contained a number of household hints and helpful articles, along with a stirring editorial on Thelma Austin, interim keeper of Point Fermin Lighthouse near Los Angeles. She was pegged as a woman braving danger and hardship to maintain the family tradition of lighthouse keeping. Her father had served at several California lighthouses, including Point Arena and Point Conception; hence Austin knew what isolation and hard work were all about. She also knew about marine disasters, having witnessed the freighter *Shasta* dashed to pieces on the rocks off Point Conception.

When her mother died suddenly at Point Fermin Light, Thelma Austin said her father "just seemed to waste away." He died in 1925, and Austin and her sister vowed to keep the light going in memory of their parents' dedication: "I felt that we had a sacred duty to perform: to promulgate the heroic work which our parents started." Her sister was a bit less inspired and ran off to marry a sailor not long afterwards.

Determined to remain at her father's post, Austin entreated the government to grant her the new appointment. She kept a good light and knew the job inside out. No bureaucrat in his right

mind could not have been moved by her situation. She had seen
to it that her five brothers were properly raised and sent into mili-
tary service — something she considered as noble as the lighthouse
service — and she was carrying on the duties of her father, who
had been a capable and well-liked government servant. On top of
that, she could pluck even the most irascible heartstrings:

"Why the sea and this lighthouse seem to me like a holy shrine,
and I'm afraid it would break my heart to give it up. But no matter
what happens, I will accept my fate with a brave heart, and just as
cheerfully as my parents would have done. When you have been
raised in the lighthouse atmosphere, as I have been, it is mighty
difficult to change your mode of living and accept any other line
of endeavor which does not offer romance and adventure."

Austin got the job and supplemented her low pay by working
as a dental assistant. In 1974, aging but still perky and talkative,
she attended the 100th Anniversary party for Point Fermin Light.

The Waving Girl
The monotony and loneliness of lighthouse life has been depicted
in many ways, but the story of Florence Martus of the Elba Island
Lights is perhaps the most sensitive portrayal of a woman's devotion to duty. Elba Island lies at the mouth of the Savannah River,
Georgia, and during the closing years of the 19th century its range
lights were tended by a disabled Civil War veteran named George
M. Martus. Decorated war veterans were often awarded jobs as
lighthouse keepers, perhaps as compensation for their physical
trauma in defense of their country; also they could receive appointments through family ties. This was certainly the case with
George Martus. He and his sister, Florence, had grown up shel-
tered and naive on Cockspur Island, where their widowed father
served as keeper of a small government beacon.

Florence Martus made up for the lack of excitement in her
childhood by taking an avid interest in local history. After her
father died, she went to live with her brother on Elba Island, where
he had been assigned as keeper of the two small range beacons
ships used to line up on approach to the river channel. It was the
first time teenage Florence had traveled any distance from
Cockspur Island and then only a few miles.

Life was pastoral and quiet on Elba Island, except that Fort Pulaski was nearby with its roughneck soldiers and martial activities. Lonely Florence Martus was fascinated with the fort and began giving tours of it to visitors. Everyone was astounded by her long, involved lectures and her extensive knowledge of local history. For young Florence, there was little else to keep her active mind alive and well — that is, until love came into her life.

It was in 1887, when she was 18 and still quite innocent, that a dashing Navy lieutenant visited Elba Island and began romancing her. He was from Cape Cod and had come down from his ship's berth in Savannah to join one of the tours Florence Martus gave of Fort Pulaski. Perhaps he intended to add her to a long list of conquests in various ports around the world; less likely he truly fell in love with her but was unable to keep his promise of marriage. Regardless, after a whirlwind romance, his ship lifted anchor and he departed with the assurance that he would return and marry Florence Martus as soon as possible. As a token of love, he gave her his white neckerchief, which she tearfully waved as his ship passed Elba Island on its way to ports unknown.

After several months and no word from her beau, Florence Martus began to wonder where he was and if he was thinking of her. She thought of him almost constantly and kept the neckerchief close to her heart, anticipating how wonderful it would feel to run down to the riverbank and wave it at his ship as he returned. Every vessel that passed received her most earnest scrutiny, even at night, but it was never his ship.

She began waving the neckerchief as if delirious with grief, but soon caught hold of her senses and decided she would wave it at every passing vessel in hopes someone who knew her lover would get word to him that she desperately awaited his return. Sailors of all places and nations entering the Savannah River were soon telling each other of the young girl who stood on the riverbank waving her white cloth in greeting. Florence Martus became known as "The Waving Girl of Elba Island." Her obsession then expanded to include swinging a lantern to ships by night, often accompanied by her timid collie.

Months turned into years, and still no word came from her fiancé. By then, the pain of rejection had been replaced by her passion for waving at ships. Newspaper reporters came and went, tourists stared curiously, and cameras flashed. By 1931, when George Martus retired from keeping the lights and gently led away his almost demented sister, she had been waving to ships for 44 years. She remained with him until his death, then was placed in a hospital where she died in 1943. Seamen and the people of Savannah have never forgotten Florence Martus, though. A statue on the Savannah waterfront recalls her unselfish devotion: Frozen in a pose of eternal greeting, the waving figure represents all women who have sacrificed to protect those who brave the sea.

Sighing, I climbed the lighthouse stair,
Half forgetting my grief and pain;
And while the day died, sweet and fair,
I lit the lamps again.
—Celia Thaxter
The Wreck of the Pocahontas

CHAPTER 9

COMPANIONS

Come show us the pathway;
The night is not friendly...
Iroquois

In *The Outermost House*, a naturalist's psalm to the mercurial backside beach at Cape Cod, Henry Beston wrote of things salvaged from wrecked ships:

"When the Coast Guard returned to the *Castagne* on the quiet morning after the wreck, they found a gray cat calmly waiting for them in the dead captain's cabin, and a chilled canary hunched up upon his perch. The bird died of the bitter cold while being taken ashore in a lifeboat, but the cat left a dynasty to carry on his name."

No doubt the lighthouse keeper at the Nauset Triple Lights assisted the able surfmen who responded to the wreck of the *Castagne* in the hours just before dawn in February 1914, if only to give temporary shelter to the tropical-clad survivors and help with the salvage of property, which in this case was a smelly cargo of guano. Old Cape Codders claim the gray cat brought ashore from the ship at daylight was given to the lifesavers in appreciation for their effort. They, in turn, presented the scrawny cat to the Nauset lightkeeper, who gratefully accepted her and put her to work eradicating rodents in the three little wooden lighthouses he tended.

Still another story from Cape Cod, or more likely a legend based partly on fact, relates that the Highland Lighthouse keeper at Truro had three cats, all rescued from wrecks and appropriately named Jetsam, Flotsam, and Lagan. The three were tailless, which agrees with the popular ditty: "Cape Cod cats, they have no tails; they lost them all in Nor'east gales." How much truth there is to these legends no one can say, but that cats were popular pets of lighthouse keepers is solid fact.

A mother cat and her kittens peer through an open lens panel at the Lighthouse Service Depot in Boston. Cats were excellent lighthouse pets, prized for their tidy habits and eagerness to rid light stations of rodents and insects. For the same reason, they were kept as pets in district warehouses. (Shore Village Museum)

Alan Villiers once remarked that every ship ought to have a cat. He spoke kindly of lighthouses throughout his life at sea, and though no one ever asked his opinion, likely Villiers also thought every lighthouse should have a cat. Very few didn't, as cats were good companions and useful in controlling pests. At times, cats were so effective at eliminating mice and rats on islands, they had to go elsewhere to quell their appetites. This was true of Sambo Tonkus, the resident cat at Maine's Cape Neddick Lighthouse in the 1930s.

Sambo was a burly tom weighing in at about 20 pounds and with a silky coat of bright orange stripes. He had been born on the Nubble, as Cape Neddick was called, and was passed down from keeper to keeper throughout his long life. In his prime he belonged to Keeper Eugene Coleman, who spoke of Sambo's great swimming ability and his charm with the tourists who stood on the mainland and peered across the channel at the Nubble and its picturesque little lighthouse.

Around mid-morning in warm weather, Sambo would amble down to the water's edge, jump in, and swim across to the mainland, stopping only to lick the salt from his fur before disappearing into the tall grass. By late afternoon he was back, looking as if he'd had a good time ashore and with a fat mouse clenched between his teeth. His determined dive into the channel started the cameras clicking. Tourists were willing to wait for hours just to capture the image of this unusual lighthouse cat returning home with a snack.

The feline tradition at the Nubble continued long after Sambo. Coast Guard keeper John Terry and his wife, Karyn, were among the last attendants of the lighthouse in the mid-1980s. They had two cats, not as well-known or as stouthearted as Sambo Tonkus, but equally loved and needed. Tiny and Tuffy chased seagulls, ate the bugs in the lantern, and raced up and down the lighthouse stairs, undaunted by heights. Karyn Terry often took walks around the small islet, and she warmly noted that she never went alone; the cats always tagged along.

Barbara Beebe Gaspar recalled having dozens of cats in her youth at Block Island North Light, 18 at once when she was a teenager. There were several wooden buildings on the station that attracted rodents; plus the lighthouse itself was plagued by mice and rats, especially in the fall when the first cold snap drove them to shelter. Eighteen cats ate well, with rodents to spare. Gaspar caught fish for the cats, too, and they sometimes ate the sea jellies that washed ashore. Feeding time at the lighthouse was met with a chorus of plaintive meows, and many lonesome hours were made

Coast Guard lightkeeper John Terry holds his two big cats, Tiny and Tuffy, in 1984 in the lantern room of Cape Neddick Light Station. This station, perched on a tiny islet a few hundred feet offshore at York, Maine, had a long tradition of lighthouse cats, some of them known for swimming ashore when they wanted to carouse with other cats or catch mainland mice. (Courtesy of Karyn Terry)

bearable by soft, whiskered faces rubbed against Gaspar's legs and hands, by purrs of contentment. She proudly remembered, "I loved them all and knew every one by name." Sadly, Gaspar lost some of her cats to poisoning. Living on a sequestered spit of sand was no guarantee of immunity from society's misdeeds, even for cats.

Connie Scovill Small was living on Dochet Island in the St. Croix River Lighthouse at the Maine-Canadian border when Scottie became a part of her life. It was shortly after World War II, and she and her husband, Elson, had gone to Calais to buy their first car, a new Pontiac. They decided to show off their prize to some family members who lived in Lubec. Elson Small was feeling in such a fine mood when their visit was over, he suggested they take home one of the kittens his sister-in-law had for adoption. Connie Small described her selection as "two yellow eyes peeking out of a ball of black." She named him Scottie because he reminded her of a Scottie dog.

Scottie turned out to have long angora fur and grew quite large on a diet of clams. He dug them out of the sand himself, and the Smalls opened them for him. Occasionally, he got into trouble, but always showed remorse and sometimes even offered atonement in the form of a gift. Connie Small recalled one day when Scottie made a mess of the upstairs bedspreads and was put outside as punishment. A short time later, he scratched to be let in and bounded across the kitchen floor with a wild duck in his mouth. The duck survived the harrowing experience and temporarily joined the chickens in the coop. It was later roasted for a fine dinner.

The Jennings family of Lovell's Island Range Lights in Boston Bay owned Frenchie, another long-haired New England lighthouse cat. He was the boyhood pet of Harold Jennings, who told of the fun he and Frenchie had exploring the island and playing by the water's edge in a little book called *A Lighthouse Family*. Like most Yankee cats, Frenchie thrived on a diet of fish and rodents and was quite independent. Not everyone was as fond of him as young Jennings, however, partly because of his grizzled appearance and independent lifestyle.

One autumn when Jennings was about ten years old, the Lighthouse Depot supply tender arrived to deliver coal for the stove and furnace in the keeper's house. Most of the crew were from the Cape Verde Islands and sang as they worked, which was a most delightful experience for the children in the Jennings family. Strong and tanned, each man could easily lift a 50-pound bag of coal onto his shoulder, carry it up from the launch, and pitch it some ten feet up to the coal bin door.

Jennings recalled that Frenchie came around the corner of the house that day as the men were unloading the coal and singing: "I don't know what they thought he was, but the bags dropped like dominoes, and they started running for the boat." After several minutes of pandemonium, with the foreman yelling and the men jabbering amongst themselves, Jennings appeared with Frenchie in his arms. Everyone settled down when it was realized that Frenchie, purring and docile, posed no threat.

The names of many cats pepper the pages of lighthouse logbooks. Despite what we've always thought about cats not taking to

Harold Jennings' boyhood at Lovells Island Range Lights in Boston Harbor was not without four-footed friends. In the top photo taken about 1933, Scotty waits with Harold (left) and his father, Captain Charles Jennings (right), as groceries are unloaded at the island. Below, Frenchie, the family's long-haired cat balances on the porch railing. One of the Lovells Island range lights can be seen in the background. (Courtesy of Harold Jennings)

water, they were ideal pets at lighthouses and adjusted well to living by the sea, or in some cases, on the sea. At Deer Island Light in Boston Bay, Keeper Tom Small had a swimming cat. The lighthouse was cast iron and looked like a wedding cake, with three tiers and a lovely ornamental lantern. It was built atop a cement caisson and had a ladder descending to the water. Tom Small's cat would climb down the ladder, hind feet first, leap into the bay, and dive for fish. When she caught one, she'd return to the ladder with the catch in her mouth. Writer Edward Rowe Snow was fascinated with this swimming cat. On one of his tours of the Boston Bay, he snapped a photograph of her aquatic antics and had it printed in one of his books.

Feline Legacy
The tradition of the lighthouse cat continued in the early 1990s at Boston Light, where a slinky black cat named Ida Lewis — in honor of the famous lady keeper of Lime Rock Light — ruled over the island. During a visit to Boston Light in May 1991 by members of the Island Preservation Association, Ida sauntered about like a queen. Coast Guard keeper Scott Gamble referred to her as "my kitty" and was seen holding her like an infant in arms. The officer-in-charge, Sandy Booth, boasted that Ida could handle a rat as big as herself and that the station dog was "at her beck and call." The third crewman at the station was on shore leave and could not be reached for comment, but it's likely Ida had bewitched him as well.

In some ways, her life was like that of cats that lived on lighthouses years ago. She was a foundling, adopted by the Coast Guard keepers from a city animal shelter. It seems many lighthouse cats started out as orphans or came upon bad times just prior to their adoption, and Ida was no exception: "She would have been destroyed, no doubt," said Scott Gamble. "Not many people adopt a full-grown cat, but we needed one ready to go to work. There are lots of rats here — big ones!"

Unlike her feline lighthouse forebears, Ida ate gourmet canned cat food. Each of the three keepers brought cat food back to the island when he returned from shore leave, along with his own groceries. Everyone shared the financial responsibility of feeding the pets, for they were cherished as friends and comrades. Ida

The tradition of lighthouse cats continues today at a number of lighthouse parks and museums. The author visited with Genie at Ponce de Leon Inlet Lighthouse Museum in Florida in 1982. Genie was among about a dozen cats in residence at the lighthouse at the time. (Jonathan De Wire)

shared in the occasional feasts of seafood and special treats dropped by passing boaters and grateful visitors. She even lapped up a little beer now and then. Fortunately for her, the Boston Light has been preserved as a monument to the Lighthouse Service by a special act of Congress. This legislation ensures that the station will always be cared for by human hands and will uphold the traditions of lightkeeping for future generations to enjoy. It also means that cats will always have a home there, for they are a part of that tradition and represent the thousands of cats that have lived at lighthouses along our American shores, giving companionship and comfort to the keepers.

Guardian of the Light
"Striker, don't eat the lady reporter! She justs wants to interview

Trick photography, or a detailed human-sized model? Either way, a Hawaiian
lightkeeper and his dog appear as giants beside Molokai Lighthouse. The dog's
inclusion in the photo gives evidence of its importance as a companion and
helper. (U.S. Coast Guard)

you." Striker's master was the keeper of Cape Cod's Highland Lighthouse at Truro in 1987. A stout chainlink fence separated Striker from his interviewer; he snarled in his most vicious guard dog voice. His owner described him as "some spaniel and mostly black lab, with a little rottweiler thrown in for fun." The small tufts of brown fur above his eyes, set into a big round face, convinced the interviewer that a little rottweiler was definitely included in this canine package. "He'll stop growling as soon as I let you inside the fence," assured the keeper. He did.

Striker turned out to be a congenial sort of pooch once he felt sure no one was invading his kingdom. He lived on the high bluff where Cape Cod legend says those three castaway cats once lived — Jetsam, Flotsam, and Lagan. Striker had arrived at Highland Light not by shipwreck, however, but by vehicle, a four-wheel vehicle made to travel the cape roads when sand blew over them. His job description contained the usual clauses about companionship and protection, but also a mention of tourists:

"If we didn't have Striker, they'd jump the fence and come right in the house," said the keeper. "They think we're here to give guided tours or something. It's terrible in the summer. Couldn't get a lick of work done without Striker; he keeps them on that side of the fence," he continued, gesturing to the parking area west of the lighthouse. "But he's as sweet as a kitten when we're ready for visitors — like you; see how he likes you now that you're inside the fence!"

Striker's unique assignment as a tourist repellant was a job more and more lighthouse dogs found themselves doing toward the end of the lightkeeping years. It wasn't so much the possible vandalism that concerned keepers as their privacy. Their occupation was special, and people wanted to have a glimpse of that life before it disappeared. Striker never rescued anyone from drowning, or rang the fogbell; he didn't fish or do tricks. He didn't haul supply packs up the cliffs at Highland as his predecessors might have done. He didn't meet any of the famous writers who have trudged by Highland Lighthouse in search of inspiration and verbiage for their journals. He simply kept the tourists at bay and was a friend to the keeper, and in 1987 that was enough.

Canine Keepers

Dogs as lighthouse pets have stories all their own — hundreds of them. Just like the cats, they had work to do, and they had distinct personalities and eccentricities from living by the water and being friends with the keepers. No particular species was preferred, though Newfoundlands and St. Bernards were prized by many lightkeepers for their strength and intelligence, which translated into ability as rescuers. Yet small dogs made fine lighthouse pets, too, as they adapted well to the limited space in some lighthouses and took up little room in a bunk or a boat.

No doubt there are a few old-timers who remember the fogbell dogs at Wood Island and Owls Head, Maine, in the 1930s. Sailor and Spot had something to do with tourism, too, but unlike Striker, their job was to entertain not repel. Sailor amused Saco Bay tourists by ringing the Wood Island Lighthouse fogbell whenever a boat passed. It was a salute worth cruising the bay for, since Sailor preceded his bell trick with all sorts of jumping antics and barking. The Orcutt family who kept the lighthouse had merely taught the dog to yank on the bell rope with his teeth. Sailor added the rest of the theatrics to his show and was an undisputed ham.

Spot was more serious about his fogbell ringing at Owls Head Lighthouse, at the entrance to Rockland Harbor. The dog could discern the distant horn of a vessel long before Keeper Augustus Hamor could hear it, and the spaniel also seemed to know the distress signal of a ship's horn. He performed many benevolent deeds during his life, not the least of which was saving the Matinicus mailboat from sure collision with the rocks during a heavy snowstorm.

On that day, Spot was asleep by the kitchen wood stove while Mrs. Hamor prepared supper. Her husband was on watch in the lighthouse, though its beam could do little to penetrate the blizzard outside. Above the high-pitched howl of wind, Spot heard the horn of a boat trying to pass around the promontory and make a safe entry into Rockland Harbor. He scratched to be let out and bounded into the snow, which had drifted so high only his head remained above it and he was able to move about only by making great leaps.

Using the natural compass all dogs seem to have in their heads, plus his good nose, Spot found the fogbell on the cliff below the lighthouse. Digging frantically, he exhumed the bell rope and began tugging, but frozen snow had so encased the bell it gave out only a muffled "clunk." The urgent moan of the boat's horn spurred on the dog. He made his way down to the water's edge and began to bark. By now Keeper Hamor also had realized the boat was in distress and heard the dog's insistent barking on the bank beneath the lighthouse. He watched as the boat suddenly steered away from the promontory, obviously having heard Spot's warning. Its lights soon disappeared in the snow, as did the sound of its horn.

Sailor, a handsome male Samoyed, keeps the Coast Guard keepers company in the 1950s at Anacapa Lighthouse in the Channel Islands off Southern California. This remote station is located about 20 miles off Port Hueneme, California. (U.S. Coast Guard Archives)

Keeper Hamor called Spot back to the house, and the near-frozen dog was brought inside and dried with a massage from loving hands and an old towel. Warm milk and the scatter rug by the wood stove were his reward. A few hours later, Mrs. Hamor received a phone call from the wife of the skipper of the Matinicus mailboat. She praised the dog for his valiant behavior, noting that the mailboat would surely have hit the bank had her husband not heard Spot's barking. The loyal spaniel lived to a ripe old age and, as all good dogs should, died peacefully in his sleep. The Hamor family buried him beneath the fogbell.

Newfoundlands have always been popular lighthouse dogs because of their great ability as swimmers. These gentle giants appear in many stories of bravery and rescue. The best-known of the lighthouse Newfoundlands was Milo, who also had a trace of St. Bernard blood, which made him a little more agile and quick. He lived at Egg Rock Lighthouse in the 1850s, about a mile off Nahant, Massachusetts, and belonged to Keeper George Taylor. It's said that when a construction crew came to the station to reno-vate the keeper's house, they grew so fond of Milo they built a special door for him so he could come and go as he pleased.

Milo rescued several children during his stay at Egg Rock. Often, he swam the mile-wide channel to the mainland to visit the people of Nahant and carouse with mainland dogs. On one occa-sion, Keeper Taylor saw Milo dive into the sea after a wild duck and swim out of sight to the east — away from land. When the dog didn't return by sundown, the family feared he had drowned. But the next afternoon a weary Milo was sighted swimming toward the island, this time from the west. Apparently, he had attempted to swim back to Egg Rock, missed the island, and gone on to the mainland. The ecstatic Taylor children launched a boat when they saw Milo swimming home and rowed out to meet him, pulling the giant dog into the boat and nearly capsizing in the process.

Marine painter Sir Edwin Henry Landseer used Milo as his model for the painting "Saved," which showed keeper Taylor's son, Fred, resting between the dog's huge paws. Sadly, Milo was absent a few years later when Fred Taylor's boat overturned in a narrow and dangerous waterway off Massachusetts called Shirley Gutt, and he drowned.

Coast Guard Dogs

Maine's Great Duck Island was a place of both delight and desolation in the years when families tended its lighthouse. Standing watch off the mainland, its insular attendants relied on each other for fellowship. At one time the keepers and their family members numbered more than 20, almost a commune. But in more recent years, when the Coast Guard operated the light, less than five people lived on the island. They could get ashore in the station powerboat whenever the need arose, but some members of the crew got no shore leave — the dogs.

In a May 1985 letter from Great Duck Island's officer-in-charge, D. W. Grant, the talents of the station's two dogs were comically but proudly outlined. Shannon, a male golden retriever mix, amused himself by digging up garter snakes, which his keen nose could smell holed up underground. He also made vertical jumps at low tree limbs and was often seen hanging from a limb by his mouth. From this strange behavior we might suppose that, like humans, not all dogs could deal with the demands of lighthouse living, particularly on a secluded, offshore island. Some became eccentrics!

In fairness to Shannon it should be mentioned that his canine comrade, Boats, probably gave him the idea of climbing trees. Boats was, according to Keeper Grant, "a social reject" sent out to the lighthouse for rehabilitation after biting another keeper's friend. The dog apparently spent much of his time trying to get into the trees for a better view of the mainland. "He climbs anywhere from six to twelve to fourteen feet off the ground," said Grant. "At times he climbs so high he cannot get down, and someone has to climb up and get him. But if he can find a limb that just supports his weight, he worms his way out to the end until the limb dips down, and then he simply slides off onto the ground." It seems Boats was no more thrilled with his sequestered island life than some of Duck Island's human inhabitants. He was always looking to get back on the mainland.

Lighthouse Livestock

According to lighthouse historian Ralph Shanks, the keepers of California's Punta Gorda Lighthouse had a stubborn station horse

The station horse at Old Point Loma Lighthouse, San Diego, stands ready to take the keeper's family for a buggy ride about 1880. The faithful service of lighthouse horses also included such tasks as hauling coal trams, packing supplies over rough roads, taking children to school, and even providing power for operating fog signal machinery. (National Park Service)

named Old Bill. A hard worker and devoted buggy and saddle horse, Bill spent his entire life at various lighthouses on the West Coast. Early in his career he was transferred aboard the district lighthouse tender from Point Reyes Light, north of San Francisco, to Punta Gorda Light — an ocean journey of some 150 miles. He suffered from seasickness en route to his new assignment and had to be lifted off the deck of the tender in a sling.

The keepers comically noted that Bill disliked walking through water and preferred to jump a puddle rather than wet his hooves. One particular leg of the seven-mile trek from the lighthouse to the nearest town necessitated a patient wait for a lull in the surf, followed by a wild gallop around Windy Point before the waves swept in again. There was no persuading Bill to walk through the surf, so keepers always planned their trips to town at low tide.

Ralph Shanks noted that Old Bill served a longer tenure at Punta Gorda than any lighthouse keeper. His career spanned 30 years; hence he lived a long and useful life, all of it devoted to the Lighthouse Service. But James Gibbs, in his Lighthouses of the

The keeper's horse waits patiently harnessed to a cart at Cape Cod's Race Point Light about 1865. The long, sandy access road to this station meant a good beach horse was needed, but grass for the loyal animal was sparse. It would have hauled the keeper's supplies and family, along with its own feed. (National Archives)

Pacific, reports that in 1851 the Punta Gorda Lighthouse was discontinued and shut down due to the fact that it was no longer crucial for navigation. The fate of Old Bill remains uncertain. Shanks reports that he was sold to a farm south of Humboldt Bay and spent his twilight years in a heavenly green pasture far from the surf, which he certainly deserved. Gibbs, on the other hand, says Old Bill was probably too ancient and lame to be of use on a farm and was sold "for horsemeat."

A more certain and meritorious end came for Jerry, a mule that served years ago at precipitous Farallon Lighthouse. Shortly after construction of the lighthouse was begun in 1852, workers requested that a mule be sent out to the island, 23 miles off San Francisco, to help carry materials up the 300 foot cliff to the site of the tower. After the project was completed, it was decided the mule should remain at the station, especially to haul coal up to the summit for the fog signal boilers.

Over the years, a number of mules served at Farallon Light, but Jerry was the first and the most remembered. In 1892, newspaper journalist Charles Greene visited the station and was given a detailed tour. One of the stops he made was at a simple grave marked "Jerry." Greene wrote of the mule's importance for the keepers:

"His duties were to act as locomotive on a little railroad that connected the North Landing with the keepers' houses and the siren. Other tasks were to pack the oil up the hill to the light, two five-gallon cans on each side of his pack saddle, and to walk around the windlass that hauled coal and heavy articles up on the platform of the North Landing."

Apparently, Jerry died of old age and was given a solemn burial on the station grounds. It was said that one of the keepers who had been at the station almost as long as Jerry wept miserably at the mule's death, as if he had lost a loyal colleague and friend.

Hardy, and as valuable as the horses and mules, were cows. They were not only a necessity at many stations — for the milk they provided and the dung for fertilizer in the impoverished, sandy soil — but comrades as well. Many lighthouse diaries and logbooks mention them, and almost always with fond sentiments. Cora Isabel Owens' recollections of living at several California

Elson Small and his cow, Blossom, appear contented in a Coast Guard publicity photo taken at St. Croix River Light in Maine about 1940. Coast Guard officials hoped this image of the pastoral lighthouse life would boost enlistments. (Courtesy of Connie Small)

lighthouses included the lighthouse "moos." At Point Sur Light, the head keeper, who owned the station cow, had built a platform extending out over the rocks from one of the buildings and housed the cow in this makeshift barn and yard. She provided milk for four families. Later, when the Owens family was transferred north to Point Arena Light, they bought a Jersey cow named Bessie. Owens said Bessie gave "lots of good rich milk," of which half was used for drinking and cooking and the rest for butter and cheese.

Cora Owens did most of the milking, assisted occasionally by one of her daughters. One morning she went to the barn to milk Bessie and found the cow missing. It was pouring rain, and Owens feared the cow had fallen over the cliff into the sea, as often happened to livestock at lighthouses. She searched along the cliff and found Bessie marooned on a ledge some eight feet down the precipice. Seeing Owens, the cow tried to climb out of her predicament but could find no solid footing in the soft, rain-soaked dirt of the cliff. The Point Arena crew, including Owens' husband, Bill, decided to hoist Bessie with a block and tackle pulled by one of the station cars. Within a short time Bessie was back on top

Karyn Terry visits with her pets in the backyard at Cape Neddick Lighthouse off York, Maine, in 1984. Red Dog, Tiny, and Tuffy provided much-needed companionship for Karyn and her husband during their stay as lightkeepers. (Courtesy John Terry)

again, acting as if nothing had happened. She ambled off, munching the sweet grass with an air of bovine hauteur, as if her rescue were simply part of the everyday routine at Point Arena Lighthouse.

Gustav Kobbe's visit to Matinicus Rock Twin Lights in the 1890s focused mainly on the keepers and their families, but it also included a somewhat lengthy and florid tribute to the station cow, Daisy. In Kobbe's own words:

The keeper owns the only quadruped on the rock – a cow. This valuable beast is named Daisy. Like the chickens and ducks, Daisy is sensibly affected by her environment. The very method of her landing upon the rocks was enough to cause her to lose faith in human nature during the rest of her existence. She was brought over from Matinicus Island in a small boat, and when within a short distance of the rock the boat was tipped over so far to one side that Daisy lost her balance and fell into water, where she was left to swim ashore. Although she is an object of affectionate regard to the little community on Matinicus Rock, she does not seem to have forgotten her involuntary plunge. Often I have seen her standing upon that mass of barren granite, the only living thing in view, the wind furrowing up her hide. She would gaze out upon the wild waste of waters with a driven, lonely look, the pathos of which was almost human. The patches of soil on the island yield about grass enough to last her during the summer. In winter the sear aspect of these patches adds to the desolate appearance of this treeless, shrubless ocean home. Often she looks across the reach in the direction of Matinicus Island, and moos pathethically, as if longing to wander over the distant pastures. She formerly found some companionship in a rabbit, with which she was accustomed to play at dusk; but the rabbit died. The cow's existence was again brightened by the birth of a calf. It became necessary, however, to kill the cow's little baby, and the mother's grief over the taking of her offspring was so intense that she refused food for three days.

All Manner of Beasts

The lighthouse menagerie included unusual pets too, such as the tamed Key deer that amused the children of 1880s keeper Henry Shanahan at Sanibel Island Lighthouse in Florida; or the albino frog that lived in the cistern at San Francisco's East Brother Island Light. Livestock often earned mentions in logbooks as well. Teen-aged Abbie Burgess rescued her pet hens during a gale at Matinicus Rock Light in the 1850s, and were it not for the eggs given by the hens in the days that followed the storm, the family might have gone hungry. Fanny Salter, widowed keeper at Maryland's Turkey Point Lighthouse during the Depression, had great affection for her flock of prize egglayers and was photographed with them on several occasions.

Keepers who served on the Reef Lights in the Florida Keys during World War II had carrier pigeons which were used to secretly communicate with the mainland when an enemy ship was sighted. Equally helpful were the sled dog teams that hauled supplies to remote outposts in heavy winter weather. Alaskan lighthouse keepers were grateful for the dogs' service, but so were those in certain Great Lakes regions where families were sometimes stranded on the lights at the end of the shipping season because winter ice had prematurely clogged the waterways. Many a sled dog team set off across the ice to take medicine to a sick child or to carry in food.

Perhaps the most amusing member of the exotic lighthouse zoo was Billy, an African parrot that belonged to Zebadiah Prout of Portland Head Light in Maine. Billy's character was deftly revealed in a little book by Arthur Cameron, *The Lighthouse at Portland Head*, in which a youngster named Don Campbell gave a firsthand account of growing up at the lighthouse. His father, John Campbell, served as assistant keeper in the years during and after World War I.

Don fondly recalled Billy's many colorful speeches and the bird's habit of sitting on the shoulder of the head keeper's wife. Not only did Billy chatter endlessly and meddle in everyone's business, he was also a careful observer and an excellent weather forecaster. He often admonished keeper Prout: "Zeb, turn on the horn; it's foggy." Billy had a voluminous vocabulary, some of it quite objectionable to sensitive ears; but mostly, his banter kept everyone entertained. "All ashore that's goin' ashore," was typical, along with "Down Bosun; down!" — meant for the rambunctious station dog.

On one occasion, Billy alerted the keepers to an emergency situation when young Don Campbell fell into the water and nearly drowned while trying to retrieve a toy boat. Billy's loud squawks and entreaties to "turn on the whistle" brought everyone running, and Don was rescued. When Zebadiah Prout retired, Billy retired with him and took up a quieter life away from shore. He outlived his owner and died in 1942 at the age of 90.

> *And exiles, lone, a loyal band...*
> *Made their abode on this lonely strand...*
> *—Milton Ray*
> *Farallon Light*

CHAPTER 10

Spectral Keepers

*Nothing moves the imagination like a
lighthouse.*
—Samuel Adams Drake

No book about lighthouses and their keepers would be complete
without a chapter on ghosts. Hardly a lighthouse exists that does
not have some supernatural being associated with it; some have
several, and lightkeepers have always entertained themselves and
their guests with stories of these peculiar spirits. This is still true
at many lighthouses, including Battery Point Light in Crescent
City, California, where the current civilian caretakers, Nadine and
Jerry Tugel, share their lighthouse home with a half dozen ghosts.
Battery Point Light is separated from the mainland by a narrow
and shallow tidal passage that can be safely traversed only at low
water. Bent, twisted cypress trees line the path up to the rugged,
old sentry, and driftwood in a variety of odd shapes and poses is
strewn about, making the whole compound look rather eerie.

The Tugels have written a small pamphlet about their spectral
companions and enthusiastically relate their uncanny experiences
with them to visitors who trek across the sandspit when the tide is
out. There's a rocking chair in one room that rocks by itself, an
unseen hand at the base of the stairs that taps people lightly, and
something invisible that upsets the Tugels' cats. Even with myriad
spirits inhabiting their home, and an uncompromising schedule
of the tides regulating their lives and dictating their comings and
goings, the Tugels seem to have adjusted well.

But not everyone who has lived in Battery Point Lighthouse
has been as content as the Tugels. One keeper in the last century
lost his senses while in the lighthouse, perhaps due to the daily
ordeal of ebb and flow. He claimed tiny mermaids came to visit
him, with pearls for eyes, delicate little webbed hands, and lovely
green seaweed tresses. He claimed that he had turned the tables

227

on the age-old tale of Odysseus and the sirens, by enticing the Nereids ashore and taming them. But it was really he who was taken ashore, far from the torment of the tides in a mainland hospital.

According to Nadine Tugel, "Some people just aren't cut out for this life." She and her husband, Jerry, have never seen mermaids, but they firmly believe a few benign spirits reside with them.

Perhaps because lighthouses often stand watch in remote and dangerous places and are sometimes the sites of tragedy, we think of them as ideal haunts. Of course, there are also physical aspects of a lighthouse that make it incredibly eerie: its sheer height, the spiral staircase and staccato echo, the probing eye of its beacon, the fickle sea at its base. In addition, history has left indelible marks on lighthouses by way of storms, shipwrecks, wars, and events in the lives of the keepers. Now that America's lightkeepers are gone, those empty sentinels have become all the more mysterious to us, and unquestionably more vulnerable to unexplained happenings.

Hundreds of lighthouse ghosts have been reported around the nation, certainly enough to warrant their own story in a separate book, but for the purposes here, a sampling of some of the more intriguing ones will suffice. As retired Coast Guard officer Kenneth Black suggests: "If you've seen one lighthouse ghost, you've seen them all." It could probably also be said, if you've heard about one lighthouse ghost you've heard about them all, for accounts of them are strikingly similar. Yet, we cannot resist a good hair-raising story. . . .

A Wraith Named Ernie

"Lots of people come out here and laugh about old Ernie. But then crazy things start happening; stuff gets mysteriously moved, tools disappear, and there's a presence, like someone is watching you all the time. I know he's real. All these strange things couldn't be my imagination."

This Coast Guard keeper, one of four men stationed on New London Ledge Lighthouse in December 1985, preferred not to be named because "people will just think I'm nuts." He wasn't alone in his belief about Ledge Light being haunted. Dozens of

Home to the mercurial "Ernie," New London Ledge Lighthouse has never out-
shone its mischievous ghost. New London Harbor Lighthouse, in the background,
is much older but lacks the haunted reputation of its companion sentinel. (Elinor
De Wire)

people, from lightkeepers to local fishermen to casual visitors,
have met the famous ghost of this handsome brick sentinel, which
sits on a concrete caisson in the Thames River Estuary about a
mile off New London, Connecticut. Some years back, the spectre
was given the name Ernie, although in a seance in 1981 he revealed his true identity as John Randolph.

Records for Ledge Light are threadbare, with few details on
the personnel assigned to the station. Though an important lighthouse for the ferry traffic in and out of New London Harbor, and
also for the nearby Naval Submarine Base, its career has been
short — less than a century — and there is little about its history to
intrigue us: No notable shipwrecks or rescues; no scandals or he-
roics; not even a good storm story from the infamous 1938 hurricane. There is, however, the ghost nicknamed Ernie, alias John
Randolph. Most local residents know about Ernie; his legend outshines the "light" in Ledge Light.

Lighthouse records make no mention of anyone named John
Randolph at Ledge Light, either as a keeper or keeper's family

member. He could have been a temporary relief keeper, or someone from a work crew sent to the lighthouse to do maintenance
or repairs. However, nothing of this nature is indicated in the
logbooks, and there is no record of a suicide either, which was the
popular explanation for the ghost when rumors about it first began to circulate in the 1940s.

According to those rumors, John Randolph lived on the light
in the 1920s with his wife, who was very unhappy with her lonely
confinement on a dismal hunk of concrete within sight of the
pleasures of city life, yet hemmed in by a mile of unpredictable
water. Bored and resentful, she began flirting with the harbor
pilots and fishermen who traveled in and out of New London
Harbor. Before the keeper realized what had happened, his wife
was gone, glad to have escaped the dreadful loneliness of Ledge
Lighthouse. Unable to bear the loss and the shame, the keeper
climbed out onto the lantern gallery, cut his throat, and fell from
the 65-foot lighthouse.

Legend says the suicide was hastily covered up by the government and a replacement for the keeper was sent to the lighthouse.
Almost immediately, the new man noticed strange things about
Ledge Light: A sudden waft of cold air would blow out a kerosene
lamp; a fishy smell could not be washed away from a room upstairs; doors would slowly open and close; items in a locked desk
drawer would be rearranged. At first no one thought to blame a
ghost, but by the time the Coast Guard took over the lighthouse
in 1940, its wraith was well-known. Keepers began calling the harmless spectre Ernie, for lack of a better name.

Ernie seemed to delight in moving things around, especially
in the room where he had supposedly slept during his time on the
light. Occasionally, his footsteps were heard, but he was mostly a
quiet ghost, surreptitiously drifting about and playing harmless
tricks on the mortals around him. Only when someone expressed
doubt about his existence did Ernie become vexed. Once, some
fishermen stopped by the lighthouse for coffee and told the keepers they thought the ghost was a hoax. When they were ready to
leave they found that their boat had been set adrift. Since all the
keepers had been inside having coffee with the fishermen, it was
decided Ernie was to blame. He had been insulted by the

fishermen's insistence that he was not real and had set their boat adrift for spite.

A curious fact about this ghost is that only women and children have actually seen him. A keeper's wife in the 1940s claimed to have awakened one night to find a rather tall, bearded man in a rain hat and slicker standing at the end of her bed. He lingered a moment, then seemed to dissolve. Her children also mentioned the man in their room. One Coast Guard keeper believes he saw Ernie's ghostly reflection in a mirror one morning as he was shaving, but when he turned to look behind him the image vanished.

In 1981, a psychic came to the lighthouse to help Ernie give up his duty at Ledge Light and find his way to the other side. During a seance held in the lighthouse, Ernie supposedly spoke through a trance medium, giving his name and claiming that he had once been a keeper at the station. He agreed to leave the lighthouse and was assisted in his departure by those present at the seance. Unfortunately, Ernie was not sincere. Reports of his impish behavior resurfaced with the next keeper to arrive. As late as 1987, when the lighthouse was automated and closed up, Ernie was still active, receiving considerable coverage on local TV and in newspapers.

Barbara Beebe Gaspar, whose father kept Ledge Light in the 1930s, denied Ernie's existence, believing he was a legend that keepers perpetuated out of boredom. Gaspar said her father served on the lighthouse for several years but never once encountered the ghost. She visited the lighthouse on many occasions, often fishing from the very spot where Ernie was thought to have died. During an interview in 1991, Gaspar said: "I just don't believe in him. You can talk yourself into anything, you know. I think somebody had an awful big imagination!"

The Ghost Who Plays Piano
From the beach at Fort Popham on sunny days, the Sequin Lighthouse almost looks like a white tusk rising from the nose of some huge leviathan, perhaps a south-wandering narwhale. The beacon shines 180 feet above water on an island at the mouth of Maine's Kennebec River. Serene as the isle may seem on a clear day, it is a desolate place, battered by wind and rough seas and often cloaked

Life on a lonely isle often took its toll. One of the early keepers of Sequin Lighthouse, at the mouth of Maine's Kennebec River, supposedly murdered his wife because she could play only one song on the piano. The haunting tinkle of piano keys is still heard around the island. Photo is circa 1885. (National Archives)

in fog. Living upon it a century ago was somewhat like living on a great ship that remained forever anchored in the same place. Fittingly, its name translates from the Abenaki as "spit in the sea."

Constance Scovill Small, whose husband kept the lighthouse from 1926 to 1930, recalled that the island was infested with snakes, fat from the huge rats that lived in the buildings, around the dock, and in a labyrinth of burrows coursing the rocky soil. The fog signal droned about three days out of ten, consuming its share of the precious coal that was so desperately needed in the bitter winter cold. Small remembered that during her first winter on the island, the coal supply was exhausted before spring, and she was forced to dig up the sand by the dock in search of any pieces that might have fallen out of the bags that had been delivered in the autumn. Her link to the mainland was a radio and an occasional ride ashore with her husband, if he could spare the room in the boat and her deft hands were not needed to tend the station.

A tale related by a couple in Bath in 1985 captures a dreadful segment in the history of Sequin Lighthouse. It tells of one of the early keepers, who came to the island sometime in the middle of the last century with his wife, a woman with a frail constitution and no experience as a lighthouse keeper's spouse. The near-perpetual fog at Sequin depressed her; when it cleared, she would gaze across at the mainland for hours on end, thinking of the delights to be had in the little village of Bath a few miles upriver. At night the warm, beckoning glow of lamplight from the windows of the shore homes mesmerized her, as she recalled wonderful evenings of talk, laughter, food and drink, songs by the piano, and dancing.

It was music she missed most — evenings of singing with friends, choir rehearsals at the tiny Methodist Church in Brunswick, lighthearted piano concerts delivered at family gatherings or with a favorite beau. It was music that had introduced her to her husband, at a dance in a carriage barn in nearby Arrowsic. She had been swept away by his great size, eyes that sparkled sky blue, and his waggish grin. Within the year, they were married and incarcerated, she thought, on the lighthouse at Sequin Island.

To assuage her torment, the keeper went ashore one day, purchased an old upright piano, and had it brought out to the lighthouse by boat. Only after much effort and many unkind oaths was the heavy piece safely stowed in the keeper's house and the delivery crew back in their boat and headed for shore, happy to be rid of both their cargo and its loquacious recipient. The keeper's wife had been hysterically excited to see faces other than her husband's, and her suffocating hospitality had alarmed the captive guests.

She began playing the old piano at once, but to her dismay only one sheet of music had made the trip across the water, and she could not improvise well. So, she played that one song repeatedly, sometimes singing in accompaniment. Even when her husband brought new music out to the island, she continued to play that one song, over and over again, at all hours. The keeper realized his wife was slowly losing her senses, and he blamed himself for her pitiful condition. She had become a near-skeleton of a figure bent over the piano, wild-eyed and unkempt, playing her song as if her fingers were drawn to the keys by some fiendish force.

As weeks passed, residents along the shore could not help

hearing the piano out on Sequin Island. When the wind was right, the haunting melody crept across the water in a never-ending serenade. And then one night . . . it stopped. The cessation of song was so abrupt and unexpected, it almost frightened the shore listeners. And with good reason: The keeper, himself driven to madness by the infernal song, had strangled his wife and taken an axe to the piano.

Little was said about the horrid event afterwards, even to the new keeper, a bachelor and a reclusive gentleman who appeared well-suited to life in such an isolated place. He kept the wicks trimmed and the brass polished and diligently wrote in his journal about the fog, the good fishing, the seabirds, the shipping that passed . . . and the occasional echo of a piano playing a haunting melody somewhere in the darkness.

A Dog and a Poltergeist

St. Simons Lighthouse, on the scenic Georgia island where Eugenia Price set several of her stories, is a museum today, capturing the tenor of post Civil War life at one of the South's most beautiful sentinels. The keeper's house has been lovingly restored with period furnishings from its lavish Victorian Era. Beside it, the 104-foot tower of glistening white still operates as an official navigational aid. Though the museum has plenty of factual history to interest visitors, the lighthouse ghost, rumored to walk the tower stairs from time to time, never fails to steal the show.

The ghost was first reported in the 1880s after an assistant keeper murdered the head keeper. Footsteps were heard in the tower, and doors opened and closed by themselves. Everyone assumed the spirit of the murdered man had returned to haunt the lighthouse. A true poltergeist, this ghost never materialized in figure form, but its noisy peregrinations have been heard by countless residents and visitors.

Of the many occupants of the lighthouse since the ghost's first appearance, only one was truly frightened by it. Around the turn of the century, the Svendsen family came to tend the beacon and brought with them a friendly dog named Jinx. Not long after their arrival, Jinx met the tower's restless spirit and immediately showed his dislike for it. Parapsychologists claim animals can sense much

Phantom footsteps haunt the tower staircase of Georgia's St. Simons Lighthouse. They are said to be those of a keeper who was murdered here early in the sentinel's history. (Coastal Georgia Historical Society)

Carl Svendsen, dapper in civilian attire, was keeper of the handsome St. Simons Lighthouse in 1907 when the famous phantom footsteps were first heard on the tower stairs. His dog Jinx was greatly tormented by the noisy ghost. (Nautical Research Center)

more about a ghost than people can, and Jinx may have known something about this one that his human companions did not.

Mrs. Svendsen customarily set supper on the table each evening when she heard her husband's footsteps coming down the tower stairs. On the evening of the ghost's first appearance, the footfall was heard as usual, and the meal was set out on the table; but when the kitchen door swung open slowly, the keeper was nowhere in sight. Mrs. Svendsen peered through the empty doorway and felt a cold draft pass by her and into the room. Jinx, who had been dozing on the floor by the stove, rose and bristled. His eyes seemed to follow something invisible crossing the kitchen, and when it neared his spot he backed into a corner, growling a low-throated warning.

Mrs. Svendsen hurried up the lighthouse stairs and found her husband still at work in the lantern. She told him about the mysterious footsteps and Jinx's unfriendly reaction. It was agreed the famous St. Simons Lighthouse ghost had introduced itself. The incident was repeated many times during the Svendsen's tenure at the station, and though they considered the footsteps harmless, Jinx never warmed up to the ghost. Whenever it moved about the tower or house, he withdrew with the same savage response as on that memorable evening when phantom and animal had first met. At times it seemed as if the ghost preferred the dog's company. Was it a dislike for Jinx and delight in tormenting him, or was there a fondness for the dog and a simple desire for his company? Either way, Jinx wanted nothing to do with the rogue spirit.

The Gray Lady of Heceta Head
On the grounds of Heceta Head Lighthouse, high on a protruding brow of Oregon coast, is an abandoned grave of a baby girl thought to have been the daughter of one of the sentinel's early keepers. Children died at lighthouses for many of the same reasons children died everywhere a century ago — smallpox, diphtheria, pneumonia, accidents. No one knows what took this lighthouse child, but certainly her loss was mourned, and for a time at least, someone tenderly cared for her grave.

The plot is overgrown now and difficult to find, but not long ago it became the focus of a series of strange events at the lighthouse. Nearly all the residents of the station since the 1950s have reported unexplainable things. One family heard screams in the house and, on several occasions, found things moved or missing. Rat poison left in the attic disappeared, box and all, and an 1890s silk stocking was left in its place. Cupboards that were left closed in the night were found open in the morning. Tools thought to be lost mysteriously reappeared elsewhere.

A worker who came to the lighthouse in the 1970s was in the attic of the keeper's house one day cleaning windows when he noticed a strange reflection on the glass. He turned quickly and found himself face to face with the ethereal visage of a silver-haired woman in a long, dark dress. She seemed to float over the floor, and the expression on her wrinkled face was one of supplication, as if pleading with the man to help her. The worker was so terrified by the ancient apparition, he bolted from the attic without speaking to her.

It took considerable persuasion to get him back to work, and only then with the promise that he would not have to return to the attic. However, while working on the outside of the house, he accidentally pushed in one of the attic windows, and it crashed on the floor. He repaired it quickly from the outside but left the broken glass on the attic floor, having no desire to enter that haunted space again. That night the couple living in the house heard scraping sounds on the ceiling above their bedroom. The next day they went to the attic to investigate and discovered the shards of glass had been neatly swept into a pile near the new attic window.

The Gray Lady, as the ghost has come to be called because of her smoky appearance, has been sighted many times. She lurks about the house or ascends the stairs; often she is seen peering out an upstairs window as if imprisoned. She walks the compound as well, always as if searching for something. Some years ago, a message spelled out on an Ouija Board gave the ghost's name as Rue. This, along with her imploring countenance, has led some people to believe she is the mother of the unidentified child in the small grave. Her domestic behavior suggests she is still keeping house, while her sorrowful face may be that of a mother who has lost a child.

Old Captain Johnson

In October of 1770, the 20-gun frigate HMS *Carrysford* wrecked on the Florida Reef some six miles off Key Largo. It was not the first vessel to go down there, nor would it be the last. Early on, the waters around the Florida Keys had earned the nickname "Grave-

yard of the Atlantic," and many fine southbound ships went to the
bottom after being slashed by the dragon's teeth coral as they
hugged the coastline to avoid the Gulf Stream's powerful resistance.

In 1824 the government tried to anchor a lightship on the site
of the HMS *Carrysford's* demise. The spot was then called Carysfort
Reef, a corruption of the name Carrysford. As the lightship headed
for duty out on the reef, a cyclone roared up Hurricane Alley and
disabled it. It returned to its station after being repaired, but ended
up running aground on the very reef it was sent to mark. A second lightship dropped anchor on the treacherous spot, but in
1848 a better solution was found. A huge iron lighthouse was
built on the reef with its legs screwed firmly into the coral bed.

It was the first of many screwpile lighthouses that would be
built in the United States. Though lacking the comely appearance
of traditional masonry lighthouses, the iron giants, a fitting nickname for these towering hulks of metal, were ideally suited to
unstable sites where wind and water were a constant menace.
Carysfort Reef Lighthouse flashed on in March 1852, and only a
few weeks later, when hot weather arrived, its keepers were horri-
fied to discover something unexplainable inhabited the tower.

The eerie intruder made its presence known on a routine April
evening, with the hot sun slipping down behind the reef to the
west and the silhouettes of shrimp boats heading back toward
shore. The keepers, weary from the day's oppressive heat, lit the
lamps for the night and assumed their duties: One took his turn
in the watchroom, just below the lantern, while the other two went
to bed until the time came for their watches. As darkness closed
in over the reef, and cool air began to snake its way through the
iron legs of the lighthouse, a low groan echoed up the stair cylin-
der, grew louder, then culminated in a high-pitched screech.

The noise jarred the sleeping men awake and sent the keeper
on watch scurrying about in a frenzy, unable to believe his ears.
The three men assembled quickly and compared notes on what
they had heard. To all three it seemed as if the prince of darkness
— old Lucifer himself — had joined them in the lighthouse for a
night of terror. There was no sleep for anyone the rest of that
night, as the devilish groans and screams continued until well past

All of the iron screwpile lighthouses on the Florida Reef, including this one at Fowey Rocks off Miami, experienced expansion and contraction sounds in their metal legs on hot summer days. These screeches and groans were thought to be ghosts of former keepers. (U.S. Coast Guard)

midnight, sending vibrations up and down the tower's iron braces. A few nights later the same ordeal was repeated, and it happened again and again throughout the summer months. When autumn arrived, the torment gradually subsided, but not before several keepers had come and gone. Only the toughest souls stayed on, for though the ghost caused no physical harm, it took a man with nerves as strong as the lighthouse itself to endure the noise. Over time, some grew accustomed to it, always knowing it would cease when cooler weather arrived.

The ghost was blamed on Captain Johnson, who had died at the lighthouse shortly after its construction. He was said to have been a great sinner, unable to secure a place in heaven and doomed to roam the reef and haunt the tower where he died. Everyone accepted this explanation until 1927, when a young man came to visit the lighthouse and encountered its noisy poltergeist.

Charles Brookfield had been fishing near Carysfort Light and had been invited to dinner by its keepers. He ended up staying the night after the head keeper decided Brookfield's boat engine sounded sick, too sick to risk a return to shore in the dark. He was given the second assistant keeper's bed, since the man was on leave at the time, and as he prepared to turn in, the first assistant keeper discovered that the recently installed phone line was down. The crew of the lighthouse did not seem overly concerned about this, but Brookfield, who was not accustomed to life on a sea-swept lighthouse, was somewhat disturbed. A short time later, his worries were confirmed when a low moan issued from the base of the tower and traveled up the structure, becoming an ear-splitting shriek near the top.

Brookfield bolted from his bed and tried to rouse the first assistant, but the man was a heavy sleeper and gave Brookfield little more than a few incoherent mumbles about someone named Johnson. Up the stairs Brookfield ran to the watchroom where the head keeper was on duty. He, too, seemed unruffled by the noise and looked up from his book in surprise to see Brookfield standing before him in only his underwear. Embarrassed, Brookfield made idle conversation for a moment, then asked if the keeper had heard any strange sounds.

The head keeper closed his book with a chuckle and recounted the entire tale of Captain Johnson and his eternal damnation as a lighthouse ghost. Even as he spoke the tower shuddered a second time, resonant with the voice of its unrepenting spirit. Brookfield was not one to believe in supernatural beings, but he had to admit the sounds were remarkably human. After several hours of discussion with the head keeper, and reassurances that Captain Johnson was a benign spirit, Brookfield returned to bed and attempted to sleep.

The ghost tale preoccupied him for days on end, and being a true skeptic, he sought out every possible explanation. The fact that Captain Johnson was in residence only during hot weather intrigued Brookfield, for no one had a reasonable answer for this. It wasn't long before Brookfield pieced together the puzzle of the Carysfort ghost:

On hot summer days, the metal tower expanded with the extreme heat, but as evening temperatures dropped, the metal plates and braces began to contract, and the joints moved to accommodate them. This expansion and contraction phenomenon produced the groans and screeches that reverberated through the lighthouse. In winter, when the temperature differential between day and night was less pronounced, the phenomenon disappeared. Brookfield was jubilant, but he had a difficult time convincing the keepers that his theory was correct. They preferred to believe in Captain Johnson and kept the Holy Bible in plain view on the kitchen table to assure the powers above that they were not following in the footsteps of a sinner.

The Most Haunted Lighthouse
The old lighthouse at Point Lookout, Maryland, is among some 30 sentinels that still stand in and around the Chesapeake Bay, a mere third of the hundred-strong legion that once lit the great "Mother of Waters." During its active years, Point Lookout Light served as a beacon guiding traffic in and out of the Potomac River, but today it serves only as a daymark whose walls show signs of age and neglect. No one tends the light anymore, and it has become somewhat of an eyesore.

In 1987 the 150-year-old beacon gained unique public recognition when a team of renowned psychic researchers arrived to give it a thorough examination. The lighthouse was said to be the most haunted in the nation, and a number of reputable individuals were willing to share their experiences with the research team. Point Lookout Light became the first lighthouse in the United States to have its ghosts formally investigated using scientific means.

Several other Chesapeake lighthouses are said to have ghosts, including Cape Henry and Seven Foot Knoll, but Point Lookout is, without question, the most haunted on the bay. Persistent reports in the 1960s and 1970s of unexplainable incidents in and around the tower led the state to enlist the help of the Maryland Committee for Psychic Research. Composed of a parapsychologist, several noted mediums, and a photographer specializing in supernatural phenomena, the committee conducted an intensive study of the old sentinel. Dr. Hans Holtzer, who is well-known for his thorough shakedown of the house at Amityville, led the team at Point Lookout. Though Hollywood has yet to express an interest in this bizarre old beacon, Holtzer has dubbed it quite haunted.

Among Point Lookout's spectral residents is a woman dressed in a long blue skirt and white blouse. Her misty form is most often seen standing at the top of the lighthouse stairs. Rangers at Point Lookout State Park believe her to be Ann Davis, the wife of the first keeper and keeper herself for 30 years after her husband's death. A feminine voice the research team taped on the tower stairway is also believed to be Ann. She tells visitors the lighthouse is "my home." Her sighs are heard from time to time, especially during the evening hours when the lighthouse would be lit were it not abandoned as a navigational aid. Park rangers believe Ann is grieving because the beacon no longer functions.

In December 1977, a resident park ranger met another of the lighthouse's many ghosts — Joseph Haney. Second officer aboard the steamer *Express*, Haney drowned in an 1878 storm and his body washed up near Point Lookout. The ranger saw Haney's ghost peering in the lighthouse's back door one evening as a storm approached. He wore the same clothes he had on the day of his death. When the ranger opened the door, the apparition drifted backwards and seemed to disintegrate in the porch screen. Psychics believe Haney's ghost was seeking refuge from the coming storm — a squall much like the one in which he died.

Numerous invisible ghosts inhabit the lighthouse as well. These noisy poltergeists move things around, open and shut doors, walk loudly, talk, and even snore. The same park ranger who met Joseph Haney's ghost recalled sitting in the kitchen one evening when several invisible people walked by him. Their footfall was heard, and the floor vibrated as they passed; even the air moved, and their clothing rustled. These unseen visitors walked calmly to another room and were not heard from again.

Many other invisible presences have been reported again and again in all parts of the lighthouse, especially the cellar and one particular room upstairs. Point Lookout was the site of a hospital during the Civil War and also a prison camp. Some 4000 soldiers are buried here. In addition, there have been several shipwrecks off the point. It's not surprising to find a few unsettled spirits still clinging to these shores.

One room in the lighthouse — the smallest upstairs bedroom — once had a distinct foul odor, but only at night. Several residents attempted, unsuccessfully, to scrub away the revolting smell, which has been described as "rotten." Holtzer's team of psychics felt the room had been used to incarcerate prisoners during the Civil War, women accused of spying or aiding the enemy in particular. According to Holtzer, the smell could have meant death or discord — someone wrongfully held against her will until she died. Amazingly, the putrid odor disappeared after Holtzer offered his explanation.

Perhaps the most extraordinary supernatural event at this lighthouse occurred when a woman who worked for the state of Maryland lived in the abandoned sentinel. She claimed to have been at ease with the ghosts and felt liked by them. One night after she had gone to bed, she was awakened by a ring of small lights whirling around on the ceiling over her. A moment later she smelled smoke, ran downstairs, and found a heater on fire. She never saw the ghost lights again, but believed they appeared intentionally to protect her and to keep the lighthouse from burning.

Point Lookout Lighthouse hasn't shone a beacon since 1965, and no one has lived in it now for a number of years. In fact, the Navy had plans to raze the structure and build a helicopter pad in its place until a group formed to rescue the historic tower. Spared the wrecking ball, the lighthouse still stands. Without a beacon it's often mistaken for an old deserted house, and it looks as haunted as the Maryland Committee for Psychic research claims it is.

There are plenty of doubters, though; folks who don't accept the ghost stories no matter how many scientific researchers confirm them. Perhaps the unbelieving should anchor off the light-house some night when bilious clouds are scudding across the sky and the wind has kicked up over the bay, whispering through the dry brush and snatching dead leaves from the trees. Possibly they'll experience a change of heart when the moon slides out from be-hind a cloud and its macabre reflection begins a wild dance on the lantern windows of Point Lookout Lighthouse . . . that is, if they're still around to watch.

What Happened to Muriel?

In August of 1985, during the author's visit to the Yaquina Bay Lighthouse Museum in Newport, Oregon, another spirit was added to the already lengthy list of reported lighthouse ghosts. At one time, the charming old sentinel at Yaquina Bay, which consists of a house with a tower rising from the backside of its roof, lit the way into the local harbor, but it was discontinued only three years after it was built, and it changed hands many times before it was opened as a museum in the 1970s.

Yaquina Bay Lighthouse has its legendary ghost of a lost girl named Muriel Travennard, but Yaquina Head Light, pictured here on an old postcard, actually looks haunted. In the 1980s this sentinel's ghostly interior was draped in fake cobwebs and used as the setting for a Hollywood horror movie. (U.S. Coast Guard Archives)

The museum docent enthusiastically provided details about everything in the downstairs of the restored lighthouse, but when it came time to tour the upstairs, she graciously declined: "There was a death upstairs many years ago, and I don't like to go up there. You'll find a dark bloodstain on the floor just at the foot of the stairs leading up into the tower. That's where Muriel died. A few people believe she haunts the lantern. We keep the tower itself cordoned off, but occasionally she's been known to come down to the second level." Her smile was less than reassuring as she offered a pamphlet on the history of the lighthouse, including the tale of its gloomy ghost. "Enjoy your visit," she added, "but don't stay too long. We close at five."

Muriel is quite a legend in Lincoln County. Her story is often told to scare the wits out of local teenagers who might be considering some bold venture or prank. It's a tale not unlike those turn-of-the-century "whodunits," only no one has ever unraveled the mystery of who the murderer was at Yaquina Bay Light. And if a suspect had ever been charged, the writ of habeas corpus would have applied, because the body of Muriel Travennard was never found.

Travennard was born to a sea captain and his wife toward the end of the 19th century. Her mother died when she was young, and for a time she sailed with her father in his sloop. When she grew into a pretty teenager, however, the captain became concerned for her safety. On one particular trip up to Coos Bay, he decided to leave his daughter with a friend in Newport rather than subject her to the coarse and cavalier crew he had temporarily signed. He promised to return for her in a few weeks when the short trip was completed.

At first Miss Travennard was very happy in Newport, but as weeks stretched into months, and her father did not return, she became despondent. A group of local youths sought to cheer her up by inviting her out for picnics, beachcombing, and other activities. The busy social life did ease her grief somewhat, and when the group decided one day to explore the abandoned lighthouse at Yaquina Bay, young Muriel was glad to accompany them, for the lighthouse was a pleasant reminder of her travels at sea and her father, whom she truly believed would return.

The lighthouse proved a disappointment. It was a shambles and contained little to interest a group of adventurous young people. They did find a strange iron plate in the floor on the second level, which they discovered was a door to a compartment in which a deep hole had been cut. They left the iron door open and went on to investigate the rest of the lighthouse. By late afternoon, their curiosity had been satisfied, and they decided to head for home. Just as the group stepped off the lighthouse porch, Travennard remembered she had left her scarf inside. She excused herself and rushed back inside to retrieve it.

While the others waited, the minutes ticked away. An amethyst glow of Pacific twilight began to descend over the bay, casting a sinister shadow over the dark lighthouse. The group began calling out to Travennard, and when she did not answer, several youths went back into the lighthouse to find her. After a few desperate minutes of searching without success, someone noticed a pool of blood on the floor at the foot of the stairs leading to the tower. A trail of droplets led to the upstairs and to the edge of the iron door, which had been mysteriously replaced over its secret compartment. The teenagers tried to open the door, to no avail. Terrified, they ran for help.

A complete search was made of the lighthouse — every corner and shelf, nook and cranny, but not the compartment covered by the iron door: No one could get it open. Not even a crowbar could budge it. Rumor began to circulate that someone, perhaps a vagabond, was living in the hole inside the floor and had murdered Muriel Travennard and hidden her body. Her remains were never found, and the puzzle of her disappearance was never solved. To this day, a dark stain marks the spot where her blood was found. Some people insist they've seen her ghost, peering out from the dark lantern or walking the shadowy path behind the lighthouse. Perhaps she's still looking for her father, for he never returned for her, and no one knows what became of him either.

Like spectral hounds across the sky
The white clouds scud before the storm,
And naked in the howling night
The red-eyed lighthouse lifts its form.

The waves with slippery fingers clutch
The massive tower, and climb and fall,
And, muttering, growl with baffled rage
Their curses on the sturdy wall.
Up in the lonely tower he sits,
The keeper of the crimson light –
Silent and awestruck does he hear
The imprecations of the night.
The white spray beats against the panes
Like some wet ghost that down the air
Is hunted by a troop of fiends,
And seeks a shelter any where.

Fitz James O'Brien
From "Minot's Ledge"
Harper's New Monthly Magazine,
April   1861

The Ghosts of Minots Light
In the New England seaside towns of Scituate and Cohasset, Massachusetts, there are numerous legends about the Minots Ledge Lighthouse. Tall, gray, and bleak, the seaswept tower stands on a rock outcropping a little over a mile offshore. At low tide, the granite beneath it is exposed, resembling the back of a great, sleeping sea serpent. As the tide rises, the monster slowly submerges, leaving the lighthouse looking as if it floats upon the sea.

Young people from nearby coastal towns dare each other to row out to the lighthouse and climb to its lantern, 114 feet above the ocean. Only on very calm days can this be accomplished, and only the strongest and bravest succeed. Part of the problem is the fact that Minots Light has been empty and padlocked since 1947; the other difficulty, perhaps more troublesome than locked doors, is that the tower is haunted inside and out.

Before the tall stone lighthouse was built in 1860, an old screwpile tower was anchored to the ledge with nine iron legs supporting a small house for the keepers. The idea was to build a

The first Minots Ledge Lighthouse looked a giant spider standing in the murky sea off Cohasset, Massachusetts. Though built to provide minimal resistance to wind and water, it toppled in an 1851 nor'easter. The two keepers aboard were killed. (National Archives)

structure on the perilous site that offered little resistance to winds and waves yet could comfortably house its attendants and show an adequate beacon for shipping headed in and out of Boston.

On New Year's Day of 1850, the strange lighthouse was lit for the first time by Isaac Dunham, its premier keeper. Only a few weeks into the job, Dunham realized his work was going to require enormous faith and fortitude. The tower shuddered with each wave that passed through its iron legs, and in gale winds it rocked slowly to and fro. In April, Dunham experienced "an ugly sea which makes the lighthouse reel like a drunken man." He wrote to the Lighthouse Service asking that the structure be strengthened and was paid a visit by the district inspector: "Higgins came onto the lighthouse. Very rough and had to swing from the lighthouse on a rope and drop on the boat. It would have frightened Daniel Webster," wrote Dunham in his logbook. Despite the inspector's harrowing visit, nothing was done to fortify the lighthouse.

Dunham endured the rocking and reeling until October, then resigned. His successor was a retired English sailor named John Bennett, who was assisted by John Wilson, also English, and a Portuguese seaman named Joseph Antoine. Bennett had 25 years of experience at sea and had weathered the worst of storms, yet only a few days after assuming charge of the lighthouse, he advised the district that its iron legs needed more braces, since some of the crosspieces had begun to bend. Subsequent rough nights on the Minots Ledge Light turned suggestion into agitated entreaty. Bennett expressed his concern for the lives of his assistants and himself, but no one seemed worried, least of all the tower's architect, Captain William H. Smith. He assured the lighthouse crew that the tower could withstand the worst seas. But to allay their fears, he ordered a repair crew to straighten a number of the bent cross braces.

In early April, after a difficult winter, Bennett went ashore for supplies. As he rowed to Cohasset, the wind began freshening and an unusually high tide pushed him toward shore. Being a seasoned mariner, he probably suspected some rough weather ahead. Had he known one of the greatest New England storms on record was bearing down on Minots Ledge and about to claim the lives of his assistants, he might have ignored Captain Smith's assurances and abandoned the lighthouse altogether.

Unable to return to the lighthouse later that day, Bennett watched from shore as monster waves began to build and assault the flimsy structure where Wilson and Antoine were marooned without a boat. When night came, they dutifully lit the lamps, but when the tower began to rock back and forth, to screech and groan with every crash of the sea, the men ran to the fogbell and began to pound it frantically, as if sounding their own death knell. Bennett could see the light glimmering through the driving rain and sleet, and the desperate toll of the bell tore through the howling wind and reached his ears with its fateful message. Shortly after midnight, the light went out and the bell was heard no more.

At dawn, only a stubble of iron pilings was seen out on Minots Ledge. Debris from the lighthouse had already begun washing ashore; sadly it included the body of Joseph Antoine, which came in with the surf at Nantasket Beach. John Wilson was a strong swimmer, however, and had found refuge on a wave-swept rock near Scituate. Unfortunately, the cold air accomplished what the sea could not: He died of exposure before help could reach him.

Undaunted, the Lighthouse Service made plans for a new tower on Minots Ledge, built of masonry this time and anchored into the ledge in the manner of Britain's great wave-swept towers at Eddystone, Skerryvore, Dhu Heartach, and the notorious Bell Rock. The new lighthouse — the one that still stands today — was completed in five years and ceremoniously lit for the first time on the night of November 15, 1860. Almost immediately, there were problems, but not with the structure or its beacon. This time it was the inhabitants of the lighthouse, both mortal and spectral, who gave the government grief.

In fairness to the men who served in this gloomy tower, it should be mentioned that Minots Ledge Lighthouse was, and remains, a dreadful place. The distance from shore, the dangers

Even before construction was completed on the second Minots Ledge Lighthouse in 1860, the restless spirits of the first tower's drowned keepers began haunting the new structure. A spectral figure was seen clinging to the base of the ladder, calling out a warning to "stay away from Minots Ledge." (National Archives)

encountered in getting on and off the tower, the cold and damp, the incessant whine of wind and crash of sea — only the most stalwart of mind and body could endure such tests of sanity. Perhaps the most unnerving experience was being inside the new masonry lighthouse when a big wave hit. The 100-foot tower would shiver and vibrate as the wave crawled up the walls and probed the lantern windows with its salty fingers. The withdrawal of the wave was equally incredible, for it sometimes created a backdraught of air through the tower that sounded remarkably like a long, painful sigh. To feel that cold, clammy breath of sea being sucked up the hollow stairwell and then hear its aching, salty sigh echo through the tower surely pushed men to the edge of madness. At least one succumbed. He left the tower in the usual way, dropped down to a waiting boat in a chair on a rope, but babbling and complaining that the lighthouse had no corners in its rooms and that his favorite framed picture would not hang flat on the round walls.

Not long after the new lighthouse went into service, ghost stories began to circulate. Ships passing near the lighthouse when the seas were running reported a man clinging to the exterior ladder on the lower part of the tower. His clothes were dripping wet, and he waved frantically and cried out undecipherable words. Portuguese sailors understood him though; his cries were both a warning to stay away from Minots Ledge and a plea for help. He was reported so often that no other explanation than a ghost would suffice — the ghost of Joseph Antoine.

Then, too, there were the tapping sounds inside the tower. They were heard only at night when one keeper was up in the watchroom and the other down below in the kitchen area. The taps were irregular, like a code, and resonated up and down the tower with no particular affinity for the iron stairs or other metal parts of the interior. Repeated attempts to find the source of the sounds met with failure, for they seemed to come from everywhere and nowhere. The keepers began to suspect each was playing some amusing game with the other.

One evening, just prior to "lighting up," as the men sat at the kitchen table eating, something happened that made them sure they were not alone in the lighthouse. It had been a cloudy day, with the wind steadily strengthening out of the southeast and the sea picking up. As the keepers ate in silence, a low gasp of air crept through the tower, sending a damp draft across their legs and exhaling a soft whistle as it departed up the stairs. The sea was already rumbling against the base of the tower, and the men looked at each other knowingly. It was going to be a rough night.

Then the tapping began, urgent and louder than the men had ever heard it before, seeming to fill the entire tower. They jumped up from the table and raced up the stairs, one behind the other, stumbling and shouting and cursing at the horrible commotion. But even before they reached the second landing in the stairwell they could hear the wind howling in the lantern above. The gallery door was open and swinging wildly on its hinges, inviting the night wind to invade every part of the light room. Quickly, they closed the door and secured the latch, then examined the lens and lamps for damage; fortunately, there was none. No one could explain how the door had come open, but in the quiet moments that followed, the keepers realized the tapping had been meant to alert them.

Its dreadful past nearly forgotten, Minots Ledge Lighthouse still looks ghostly on foggy days when viewed from the craggy shore at Cohasset, Massachusetts. Local youngsters consider a visit to the lighthouse by boat the ultimate dare. (Elinor De Wire)

Some weeks later, when one of the keepers was ashore picking up supplies, he met an elderly man who had worked on the
construction crew for the new tower. The workman was eager to
talk, and both men soon found their way to a smoke-filled tap-
room with a pitcher of ale in front of them and a plate of fried
fish. As inhibitions weakened, the keeper confessed that not all
was well on Minots Ledge. The strange events were related of that
windy evening with the gallery door mysteriously open and the
insistent tapping in the tower walls. Hearing this, the old workman's
eyes widened in terror. Gathering his wits, he leaned close to the
anxious keeper and in low whispers told of the hours he had spent
listening to the delirious ranting of Captain John Bennett.

Bennett, nearly driven to madness after the death of his two
assistants in the 1851 storm, had taken to spending too much
time in the mainland bars, brooding about the tragic affair. At
times he swore he could hear a fogbell violently tolling out on
Minots Ledge, or the men's voices calling for help. Storms disturbed him as never before, but most unsettling for Bennett was
any kind of rapping sound —a visitor at a door, the clink of a pipe
being emptied into an ashtray, a loose shutter banging against a

Washington's Willapa Bay Lighthouse was not reported to be haunted in its
active years, but after it was abandoned to erosion and collapsed into the sea,
local residents reported seeing an unexplainable glow where the old 1858 lighthouse had once stood watch. This photo was taken a short time before the lighthouse toppled. (Courtesy of Jack Hettinger)

window. All of these reminded him of the friendly game Antoine and Wilson had played in the tower, signaling to each other through a long stovepipe that ran from the lantern down to the living quarters. At times the game had even proven useful, especially in an emergency when one man needed to summon the other's help quickly.

Today the Minots Ledge Light has a much friendlier reputation. It's still a favorite dare with local youngsters, but the terrible memories of the 1851 storm have faded. The tower has a new lantern cap, and its 1-4-3 signal delights lovers along the shore: "I LOVE YOU . . . I LOVE YOU . . . I LOVE YOU . . ." If the ghosts still inhabit the tower, there's no one to scare. These days, Minot's Light has only spiders for keepers.

A Winsome Apparition

The most curious and certainly the most beguiling lighthouse ghost among those uncovered for this chapter was a small puff of gray inhabiting the second floor of the old keeper's house at the Fairport Lighthouse in Ohio. The beacon was long ago discontinued and the tower and keeper's house turned into a maritime museum, the oldest one on Lake Erie. It's a place where visitors can browse through a unique collection of Lake Erie memorabilia, which includes the history of the lake's navigational aids and the most magnificent relic of all, the Fairport Light.

In 1989, Pamela Brent was the resident curator of the museum. She lived on the second floor of the keeper's house, which had been converted into a small apartment. It was a cozy place, especially in the winter, when the museum was closed and icy blasts of wind and snow were howling in off the lake. Warm and undisturbed in her apartment, Brent could catch up on paperwork and devote important hours to the ever-expanding collection of marine and maritime artifacts. Cold, snowy days were spent with notebooks and coffee, and it was on one of these relaxed days the first winter after her arrival at the museum that she encountered the strange little ghost.

Brent had gone to her kitchen to prepare supper. It was twilight, and since the last bit of evening glow was still seeping in through the windows, she had not turned on the lights. As she quietly peeled potatoes and hummed a tune, something small and dark flitted by the kitchen door and disappeared down the hallway leading to the living room. Brent was startled, rubbed her forehead, then returned to the potatoes, thinking that in the faint light her weary eyes were playing tricks on her. Minutes passed, and Brent could not get the image out of her mind. She discarded the peelings and stepped to the kitchen doorway, looking expectantly down the hallway. Nothing was there.

With a shrug she turned back to the kitchen and the potatoes, but not a second later something caught her eye again. Leaning carefully around the doorway, she saw what it was, very clearly this time: A little gray cat, almost like a puff of smoke, was scuttering around the floor. Its eyes were small iridescent gold marbles, and its fur was thick and feathery. But strangely, the elfin cat had no feet. It moved about the floor at the opposite end of the hallway as if propelled by invisible wheels. It seemed to chase something, then scooted into the living room and disappeared.

Brent encountered the diminutive spirit several more times that winter and even played with it by tossing a balled-up sock into the hallway, which it scampered after with kitten-like joy. She never felt afraid or threatened by it; rather, it was a friendly little ghost that seemed only to be looking for companionship. When Brent decided to investigate the origin of the phantom cat, she uncovered a most heartwarming story centering on the Babcock family, who had tended the light for more than 50 years.

Captain Joseph Babcock had come to the lighthouse in 1871, a veteran of the Civil War. He would serve as keeper of the light for 48 years, with his son Daniel as assistant keeper from 1901-1912, then with Daniel Babcock stepping into his father's shoes until 1925. Besides Daniel, there were two other children, a daughter named Hattie and a son named Robbie who was born in the lighthouse and died there at about the age of five.

At some point during the Babcock's tenure at Fairport Lighthouse, possibly after the death of their little son, Mrs. Babcock became very ill and had to be confined to bed for several months. During this time, one of her delights was a gray kitten that frolicked about the upstairs rooms and provided hours of amusement for the bedridden woman. Her favorite game with the kitten was to toss a small, soft ball from her bed through the doorway. The ball would roll down the hallway, and the kitten would chase it merrily, returning with the ball in its mouth.

Brent knew that her apartment living room had once been an upstairs bedroom in the old keeper's house, probably the one in which Mrs. Babcock recuperated. But Brent was unable to find out the name of the kitten or what happened to it, for Mrs. Babcock was an ardent cat-lover and had many felines at the lighthouse, too many to identify individually. If the little cat ghost Brent saw was indeed the gray kitten who brightened Mrs. Babcock's convalescence, it may have died before reaching maturity. If so, it is eternally caught in the antics of kittenhood, still chasing an invisible ball and bringing delight to anyone who meets it.

The light still shone palely down the stairs;
we saw nothing coming; we only heard the steps.
—James Thurber
The Night the Ghost Got In

CHAPTER 11

A LIGHT LESS BRIGHT

Not all of them were saints.
–Grace Humes
Granddaughter of a Fire Island
Lightkeeper

Bird Island Lighthouse looks charming and serene today, a tiny stone tower marking the entrance to Sippican Harbor at Marion, Massachusetts. The island, almost two acres in size, was named for the many birds that have always come there. For years, it has been a favorite spot of duck hunters and their dogs. Long ago, the son of one of the lightkeepers accidentally shot himself with a hunting gun and, though badly injured, he survived.

The circumstances surrounding another mishap on the island are less clear. Though the lighthouse has long been empty, local residents still talk about its sordid past and the pirate who tended it when it first went into service two centuries ago. His name was William S. Moore, and he arrived at Bird Island to take up the duties of lightkeeper shortly after the War of 1812. With him came his wife, a faded beauty from Boston who had eloped with her swashbuckling husband many years before, when both he and his fortune were more desirable.

As Moore's riches had dwindled, and the excesses of life he and his wife so enjoyed became more difficult to obtain, his morals took an unexpected (some say calculated) turn for the better, and he was able to secure the job of lighthouse keeper at Bird Island. Rumors accompanied him to the light, however, and the townspeople took great pity on Mrs. Moore, whose raucous, pirate-wife lifestyle had left her with tuberculosis and a strong addiction to tobacco. The persistent dampness of the island aggravated her condition, and since her husband would not allow her to leave the place — fearing that she might desert him for a better life ashore — her illness and craving for tobacco intensified.

Her despairing cries were heard across the water, and to quiet her, the townsfolk smuggled bags of tobacco to the lighthouse, careful not let Moore find out. The local doctor entreated Moore to let him ease the tormented woman's pain, but to no avail. Moore seemed to have some unexplained power over his wife, and she refused all offers of medicine or care ashore. When she died, Moore raised the distress flag to summon help with her burial. A minister from Sippican was able to walk across the ice over the harbor to the lighthouse. His service was simple, followed by several backbreaking hours helping Moore dig a grave on the frozen island.

Almost immediately rumors began circulating that Moore had murdered his wife. He had shunned the community socially, and his background was checkered enough to fuel serious suspicion. His response to his accusers was cleverly condemning, the kind of tactic that no doubt got him a lightkeeper's job in the first place.

A pirate-turned-lightkeeper, with a wife addicted to tobacco, was the focus of a soap opera tale at Bird Island Lighthouse in the early 1800s. This little sentinel sat on a tiny island off Marion, Massachusetts. Photo date unknown. (U.S. Coast Guard Archives)

In a letter dated October 10, 1833, he ingeniously turned the tables by blaming the townspeople for the loss of his wife: "This bag contains tobacco, found among the clothes of my wife after her decease. It was furnished by certain individuals in and about Sippican. May the curses of High Heaven rest upon the heads of those who destroyed the peace of my family, and the health and happiness of a wife whom I Dearly Loved."

No one knows if the Bird Island lightkeeper murdered his wife. Some say his insistence that she not be allowed the care of a doctor indirectly caused her death — murder by neglect; others believe she was killed outright and the circumstances surrounding her death were hastily covered up and buried with her. Unfortunately, there are no records to confirm or deny the rumors.

Less Than Model Government Servants
While much of this story of the lighthouse establishment has been devoted to the courage and devotion displayed by lightkeepers and their families, it should be noted that not everyone who signed into the service was a model citizen. Keepers got drunk, operated illegal businesses, stole government property, fell asleep on watch, let the lights go out, had extramarital affairs, fought with their co-workers, and even tried to murder each other. Their spouses and children were occasionally disposed to bad behavior as well.

In his candid tale of a year spent on Harbor of Refuge Lighthouse in Delaware Bay in the 1950s, author Stephen Jones dispelled many nostalgic myths about lighthouse keepers. The steadfast watch with a book in one hand and a coffee cup in the other became the struggle to remain awake, a siege aided by a chair carefully positioned so as to jar a man wide-eyed if he slumped and dozed. The wholesome meals and friendly table conversation emerged as greasy slop eaten in glaring silence, punctuated by bouts of depressing talk and profanity. The titian sunsets and opaline seas so aptly described by lightkeepers of old were eclipsed by a menacing crack in the lighthouse caisson that grew wider every day, and the fetid smells and tastes of stagnant water from the cistern.

Returning from shore leave one afternoon, Stephen Jones spied brightly colored specks scattered on the rocks below the tower. At first he thought these might be shards of glass from broken bottles, but upon closer examination he found they were songbirds, dozens of them lying crumpled and twisted and blood-spattered. In a fit of boredom, one of his cohabitants had had a sadistic round of target practice with the birds.

Bar Colby, columnist for the *New London Day*, recalled his friendship with the Coast Guard keepers of the Ledge Lighthouse. Though confined in a waterbound lighthouse much like the Harbor of Refuge keepers, these men dealt with their boredom differently: They simply stole away to shore illegally. As a teenager in the 1950s, Bar Colby often went to the light by boat and sometimes looked after the station while the keepers went ashore to visit their girlfriends. On one such occasion, an officer from the Coast Guard Academy came by the lighthouse in a sailboat and paused at its base, waiting for a wind to take him back up the river. Colby was alone on the light, and when the officer hailed him for some conversation, he pretended to be one of the keepers, knowing full well what the consequences would be for his friends if their hiatus ashore with the ladies were divulged. The talk went well, since Colby knew enough about the lighthouse to put up a convincing front, and he was perched just far enough above the officer so that his too-youthful appearance was not obvious. Colby quaked with fear as the idle talk wore on and the lull in the wind refused to end. Finally, a breeze wafted in and the officer waved good-bye and departed.

Years later, in an interview shortly after the Ledge Lighthouse was automated in 1987, its last Coast Guard keepers talked frankly about their jobs and life on the offshore sentinel. It was not a glamorous occupation, in their opinion, nor was it the calling we all imagine lightkeepers hear — the voice that bids them tend the lamps in the late hours of the night with the tempest raging outside and a ship desperately seeking their light. Nor were they the stereotypical keepers whom we believe look much like the Gorton's fisherman.

Out on Ledge Light in the mid-1980s, rock music was playing, frozen pizzas sat in the freezer ready to be popped in the microwave, adult magazines and erotic books lined the top of the TV set, and every window had a set of binoculars laying on the sill,

the most powerful ones on a tripod aimed at the bikini-clad denizens of Ocean Beach. The four men were honest about lighthouse
duty:

"This place is worse than a prison."

"All we do out here is sit around and wish we weren't here."

"You get up and eat, then paint all morning, then eat lunch
and paint all afternoon, then eat supper and listen to the bos'un
telling you what you got to paint tomorrow."

"To keep from going crazy, I type letters to myself."

"If we didn't have a TV out here, we'd kill each other."

"I don't ever want to be a lighthouse keeper again."

"Pardon me, lady, but I got to tell you this place stinks!"

When asked what was good about duty on Ledge Lighthouse,
one man replied: "What's good is it's being decommissioned soon
and we can get the hell out of here!"

Some keepers, it appears, were always thinking of ways to get
off the lighthouses. Out on desolate Southeast Farallon Island in

"This place stinks" was the feeling of one unhappy keeper who lived on Ledge
Light. The Coast Guard men assigned here weren't always model lightkeepers.
Some took unauthorized trips to shore to visit girlfriends; others kept the light-
house bookshelf stocked with adult magazines and erotic paperbacks. (U.S. Coast
Guard)

1859, keeper Amos Clift was not only unimpressed with duty as a lightkeeper, but scheming to make big money on the side so that he could resign from his job a rich man. Farallon had long been the site of an Egg War, a battle between private business and the government over who should harvest the bounty in seabird eggs on the island. Collecting the eggs was no simple task, since the birds, above all others, took exception to the practice; but there was an enormous market for the exotic eggs, particularly in Chinatown, and hauling them to San Francisco was worth bloody hands and a soiled head.

Amos Clift, in a letter to his brother in Connecticut, tells of his predecessor's graft, then goes on to scheme for his own illegal departure as a wealthy man:

Before I came here this Egg Co. used to have things all their own way, as the former light keeper was a very ignorant man, and besides was a stockholder in the company and as long as he received his dividend, that was all he cared for, and the government knew nothing of the actual state of affairs, but since I have been here things have taken a turn, and they [the Egg Co.] have ascertained that I am not so easily bluffed as was Mr. Wines. They have always claimed that the island was their property and that they had exclusive rights to the eggs. . . .

They tried their best this past spring to have me removed . . . but I shall not abate my efforts in the least. . .if I succeed I may reap the benefits. The egg season is in May and June, and the profits from the company after all expenses are paid is every year from five to six thousand dollars, quite an item, and if this island is government property, I have a right to these eggs and am bound to try and gain it.

If I could have the privilege of this egg business for one season, it is all I would ask, and the Govt. might kiss my foot and so up along.'

Clift's scheme ran afoul of a perceptive and thorough government inspector, however, and he was dismissed on the grounds that his self-interests overshadowed his attention to duty at the lighthouse.

At stations with only one keeper, there was no one to watchdog behavior except the local customs collector or the inspector, and these men came to visit infrequently. Unauthorized activities could happen easily, and for a solo keeper whose salary was grossly inadequate, illegal money-making operations were sometimes

tempting. At stations where two or more keepers served, one had
to be in charge and the other subordinate; at these stations, there
was less temptation to travel a wayward path for fear of being
discovered.

Moonlighting at other jobs — or "daylighting," in the case of
lighthouse keepers — was a common practice during the early years
of the lighthouse service, due in part to the low wages paid to
keepers but also to a lack of regulation by the government. Inspections were rare, and there were no clear guidelines about
operating a profitable business on the side or working at other
jobs to earn desperately needed income.

In his 1890 book, *The Modern Lighthouse Service*, Arnold Burgess Johnson, who was Chief Clerk of the U.S. Lighthouse Board,
outlined the board's policy on second jobs:

*Keepers are forbidden to engage in any business which can interfere
with their presence at their stations, or with the proper and timely performance of their light-house duties; but it is no unusual thing to find a
keeper working at his station as a shoe-maker, tailor, or in some similar
capacity, and there are still light-keepers who fill a neighboring pulpit,
who hold commissions as justices of the peace, and there are still others
who do duty as school teachers without resigning their light-houses.*

Johnson's words were rather lofty, but understandable given
his position at the time. Ministers? Justices of the peace? School
teachers? There were probably a few of these, but more likely
keepers had second occupations as fisherman and harbor pilots,
farmers, and ferrymen. Some painted or made decorative arts to
sell, such as the unusual shell pictures done by the Israel family of
Old Point Loma Light in San Diego. Frank Jo Raymond of Long
Island Sound's Latimer Reef Light rowed ashore on Saturday nights
back in the 1920s to play saxophone in a local jazz band. He also
sold photographs he took during the 1938 hurricane for picture
postcards; they sold at 25 cents each and he made a profit of $150.

Others were less noble in their efforts to supplement the family income. Distilling and selling booze during Prohibition was a
business with some lighthouse keepers; so was mooncussing — the
scandalous practice of luring ships onto shoals with false lights,
then plundering the wrecks. A keeper at Cape Cod's Chatham
Lighthouse was accused of extinguishing his light to cause ship-

The urge to take advantage of their unusual situations infected some keepers. An early keeper at Chatham Twin Lights was accused of extinguishing his light to cause shipwrecks, then joining the Cape Cod wreckers to claim the spoils. Another indulged in slander in an attempt to regain his job as keeper after it was given to a woman. Photo circa 1880. (National Archives)

wrecks, then splitting the spoils with the wreckers. The same complaint was made about a Key West lighthouse keeper shortly after the first lighthouse was built in the Florida Keys. In this case it may have been a ploy to have the keeper run out of town, for his lighthouse interfered with the profits from wrecked ships.

A Boston lightkeeper named Tobias Cook set up a cigar factory on Little Brewster Island in the 1840s and brought young women out to the island to manufacture what he called "Spanish Cigars." These were profitably sold in Boston under the guise of being imported from Spain. Working conditions in the factory were miserable, and the women were poorly paid and housed in squalor. When Tobias' fraud was found out, the factory was quickly shut down and he was advised to resign, which he did in 1849.

A letter written in 1863 by R.J. Marshall, keeper of Maryland's Piney Point Lighthouse, challenged the government's decision to shut down a profitable wartime venture – a general store whose primary customers were soldiers. Marshall opened the store on a nearby government-owned island meant as a place to cultivate a garden. Indeed, the garden went in and grew well, supplying food for the hungry forces marching by Piney Point and lining Marshall's pockets with coins. It's probable the government became suspicious that Marshall was siding with Rebel forces, or perhaps the sharp division in political allegiance in and around the Chesapeake resulted in a desire to have Marshall removed and a more sympathetic keeper appointed.

A local inspector pronounced the station in "poor condition" with its light often out. It was suggested Marshall be dismissed and the store dismantled. The government saw it as a clear case of running a business that interfered with the proper keeping of the light. Since 1852 there had been specific regulations forbidding the operation of profit-making businesses on lighthouse stations. Charges of neglect and failure to comply with regulations were brought against the keeper.

Marshall's letter of reply was an impassioned plea that he be retained as keeper and also be allowed to continue to aid the Union forces by offering goods at his store. Several pages long, it cleverly portrayed him as a "loyal public servant" and the "only Union man in the area," whose services were sorely needed in order to hold Rebel activities in check, including those possibly perpetrated by the local inspector, whose credibility Marshall challenged. He pledged that all profits from his store would go to pay an assistant at the lighthouse and that without the store many Union soldiers would likely go hungry and freeze. In spite of his convincing arguments, he was removed and the store was shut down.

After the establishment of the Lighthouse Board in 1852, keepers were required to meticulously measure out and record quantities of oil used. This regulation was instituted in part due to the illegal practice of selling off government oil for personal profit. Inspectors examined the records closely and determined if there were any discrepancies in amounts delivered and amounts used or still in storage. If the figures did not agree, a keeper was penalized, usually by docking pay for the missing oil or cutting off pay until an investigation was completed. Penalties appear often in

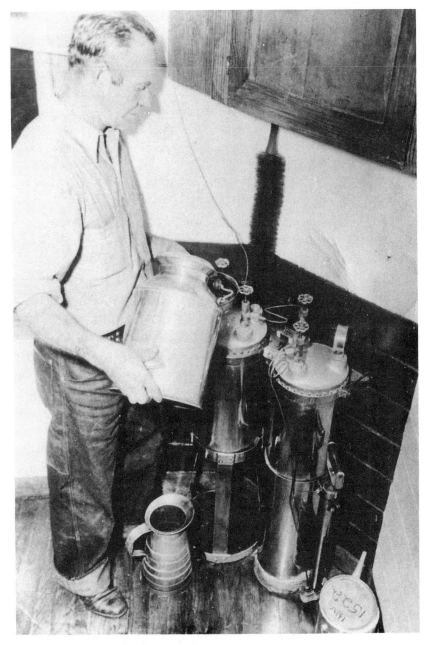

Block Island lightkeeper Howard Beebe carefully pours kerosene for the lamps. Lighthouse keepers were required to meticulously measure and record the quantities of oil used in the lamps and report the figures to the government inspector. Records were scrutinized carefully to be sure the oil was not being squandered or sold on the side for profit. (Courtesy of Barbara Beebe Gaspar)

government records for the years immediately after the establishment of this policy. It took some time for lightkeepers to get into
the habit of keeping detailed records and also to learn to be frugal
with oil supplies. An excerpt from a letter from A.M. Pennock,
Lighthouse Inspector for Chesapeake Bay, dated August 22, 1853,
is somewhat typical of that period:

*The pay of the keeper of Turkey Point L.House has been suspended
for the reason of her not rendering a proper account of the oil she should
have on hand.*

Elizabeth Lusby, the Turkey Point lightkeeper, responded with
this excuse for being derelict in duty:

*I have been frequently indisposed and not able to attend to measur-
ing the oil myself, and those I have to assist me may have carelessly given
a lesser quantity than they should.*

Lusby might have gotten herself out of this jam by juggling
the figures in her logbook, but she probably knew falsifying lighthouse record books was an even more serious offense for which
keepers paid dearly, usually by a loss of pay and sometimes by the
loss of a job. Even as late as 1916, the Lighthouse Service Bulletin
was circulating warnings to keepers about tampering with the truth:

*Several cases have occurred recently where it was found that keepers
were absenting themselves from the station without proper authority, and
had made false entries in the station records in an attempt to conceal
shore liberty taken and not reported. Three keepers have been dismissed
from the service and two other keepers were severely reprimanded and
charged with 30 days' leave each. One assistant keeper resigned under
charges, one was reprimanded and had his salary reduced, and another
assistant keeper received a reprimand and was charged with 30 days'
leave. It is believed that the shore liberty granted under the regulations is
ample, and the regulations in regard thereto must be observed.*

The coffers of the iniquitous were illicitly augmented in a variety of ways, and few methods were more contemptuous than those
of Nathaniel Fadden at Lake Superior's Manitou Island Lighthouse
in the 1880s. The trouble centered on keeper Fadden's sale of
liquor to the local Indians, liquor that he was illegally making at
the lighthouse. Animosity over price, quantity, and availability no
doubt culminated in an Indian attack on the lighthouse in 1886.
When the government surmised that Fadden was at the heart of

the problem, with his distilling operation and sale of cheap guzzle at an outrageous price to a vulnerable clientele, he was dismissed and jailed.

Booze was simply not tolerated by the Lighthouse Service, not the making of it, the selling of it, nor the consuming of it, and especially not the use of it to exploit those who were susceptible to its evil influence. Yet many people who lived at lighthouses considered liquor making, selling, and consumption a deserved bonus. One lighthouse daughter mirthfully recalled that during Prohibition, her father delighted in hiding the family's forbidden booze under a loose floorboard and watching the district inspector tread unaware over the cache, all the while praising the keeper's work.

Grace Humes, whose grandfather tended Fire Island Lighthouse in the 1920s, remembered: "My grandmother used to go up in the tower and keep watch over the light when my grandfather was away. It was because the assistant keeper was no good, not cut out for that kind of a job. As soon as my grandfather left, he'd get a bottle and drink like a fish, and there he'd be, flat out on the floor up in the lighthouse, drunk. Mother told me about going up in the tower on those nights; she remembered stepping over him, drunk on the floor. Not all of them were saints."

Drunkenness was cause for dismissal, but on at least one occasion a keeper was so well-liked by the district superintendent, an attempt was made to save him from the depravity of liquor. Ralph Shanks, in his *Guardians of the Golden Gate*, tells how this man (who remains unidentified) could not resist the San Francisco bars whenever he went ashore from Southampton Shoal Light. Often, he wound up in a fight and headed back across the bay in his power boat with his eyes nearly swollen shut and thoroughly intoxicated, barely making it home without a serious mishap. After several close calls with bay shipping, the district superintendent decided to transfer the keeper to a station far from the taverns.

Southeast Farallon Lighthouse was the secluded spot chosen, some 23 miles out to sea from San Francisco. The superintendent felt certain the keeper would remain sober and alert on Farallon; but he didn't. A clever plan was quickly contrived to quench his thirst: He arranged with his friends at the Lighthouse Depot to

A San Francisco newspaper article in 1887 reported drinking problems at Point Reyes Light. Other reports concerned fighting, marital discontent, abusive language, and even mental illness. This was one of the most difficult stations in the country, owing to its location on a wind-scoured, rocky cliff with a fog signal that seemed to groan incessantly. (U.S. Coast Guard)

have booze sent out to the island in crates labeled "oranges." The superintendent was pleased to see so much fresh fruit being shipped out to Farallon, but very puzzled by the crew's lack of sobriety!

Liquor was the tonic of many a keeper, and not without reason. The solitary nature of the work, the monotonous routine punctuated with bouts of stress, usually related to weather and lack of human contact, exacted a physical and emotional price. It was worse at certain stations. Throughout its career as an attended station, lonely Point Reyes Lighthouse and its wretched crew kept the *San Francisco Chronicle* in news, not always of the flattering kind. In 1887 the newspaper ran this embarrassing report concerning the habits of a keeper alumnus:

Another local celebrity, in his way, was a late (and now happily deposed) keeper, notorious for his love of the flowing bowl. It is said that he even regaled himself, when out of whiskey, with the alcohol furnished for cleaning lamps, and a familiar sight to the ranchman was the genial gentleman lying dead drunk by the roadside, while his horse, attached to the lighthouse wagon, grazed at will over the country. It is no unusual thing for him to be drunk for days at his station.

In addition to drinking, there were frequent arguments among the families at Point Reyes, induced partly by the misery of life there but also by the lack of inhibitions due to inebriation. Slapping one another, cursing, and throwing things was not uncommon. One keeper was reprimanded by the District Inspector because his wife used foul language toward the head keeper; another keeper cursed at the inspector himself. Anger was heaped upon anger, and woe upon woe, until someone snapped: A logbook entry dated January 30, 1889, matter-of-factly read: "The second assistant went crazy and was handed over to the Constable in Olema." In defense of such behavior, it should be said that Point Reyes was an exceptionally difficult station, what with the smelly and raucous foghorns blowing more than one-third of the year, the wind scouring the station constantly, and the access road barely more than a cow path full of ruts and potholes. Even the station horses rebelled.

Especially vulnerable to misconduct were the crews of lighthouses on remote capes and headlands, and the offshore island and rock stations. Living together in cramped quarters with water in every direction and little chance for relief from the daily routine demanded considerable fortitude. Disagreements and personality conflicts were most often the trouble at these stations, as the following excerpts from the logbook of Keeper William H. Prior at Minnesota's Big Bay Point Lighthouse illustrates:

November 18, 1897: "Keeper returned from Marquette at 2 p.m. yesterday and kept watch last night. Fire banked in signal [fog signal] to keep pipes from freezing. I cannot see that Asst. has done any work around the station since I left, he has not energy enough to carry him down the hill, and if I speak to him about it he makes no answer, but goes on just the same as if he did not hear me. He is so much under the control of his wife that he has not the heart to do anything. She has annoyed me during the season by hanging around him and hindering him from working, and she is altogether a person totally unfit to be in a place like this, as she is

In 1892 an assistant keeper at Sandy Hook Lighthouse complained to district headquarters about the foul language of the head keeper. But worse things undoubtedly happened at this New Jersey station. In 1850 a skeleton was found sitting at a table in a secret underground compartment under the keepers' house. Almost a century later the Army Corps of Engineers discovered the bodies of four men and one woman buried at the base of the lighthouse. Photo taken about 1890. (National Archives)

discontented and jealous, and has succeeded in making life miserable for everyone at the station.
December 27, 1897: *"As my assistant objects to working during the closed season [usually December 1 to March 31], I have written to the inspector to get his opinion on the matter. . . ."*
January 1, 1898: *"My assistant claims now that he is unable to work as he has a lame back. . . ."*
February 14, 1898: *"Mr. Heater arrived from Marquette at 6 p.m. and walked the entire distance 33 miles in 12 hours including two rest stops of over an hour each . . . pretty good gait for a lame man."*
February 27, 1898: *"Mr. Heater gone across the ice to the other side of Big Bay with his wife. It is Sunday so his back is not lame today."*
March 5, 1898: *"Arrived station at 3:30 PM today and found that Mr. Heater had not finished the ladders, but had been fishing again."*

March 8, 1898: "*Received a letter from the Office informing me that my Asst. would be transferred to Granite Island. For which I have every reason to be thankful.*"

September 10, 1898: "*Asst. Beamer [Heater's replacement] does not take hold of his work as he should. He evidently expects me to work with him whenever he is at work, and if I do not . . . he leaves the work and does nothing until I go back to him.*"

(Author's Note: We would think, with a name like "Beamer," this man would take to lighthouse keeping in a flash! Such was not the case, according to Head Keeper Prior. His criticisms of Beamer riddle the pages of the Big Bay Point logbook for 1898.)

October 1, 1898: "*As Mr. Beamer always objects to my questions and resents my interference, and I have passed over his dereliction before and not caring to be constantly making reports unfavorable to him, I have written this for future reference when the Inspector arrives.*"

October 27, 1898: "*Asst. Beamer complains of being sick and talks of leaving the station to go home to Detroit. . . . He is too high strung for a light keeper's asst., between himself and his wife this season I imagine that I am keeping a Home for the Helpless Poor instead of a U.S. Light House. I and my family having to do the greater part of the work while they receive the pay.*"

November 1, 1898: "*This Beamer is the last straw on the camel's back. He is without exception the most ungrateful and the meanest man I ever met.*"

April 23, 1899: "*Sunday, Mr. William B. Crisp [new assistant] arrived at the station at noon today.*"

July 11, 1899: "*He [Assistant Crisp] has decided to resign and wished to leave at once. . .*"

At Sombrero Key Lighthouse, a few miles off the Florida Keys, the heat and confinement in an area only a few square feet in size caused many confrontations. Personalities contributed to the disagreements, too, particularly in the 1870s when taskmaster K.J. Buckley was in charge of the light and recorded the monotonous routine in his station journal:

August 4, 1874: "*The Assistant, Josiah Butts, went with the keeper on board a schooner from Havana loaded with sugar and bound for New Orleans, to buy some sugar from the Captain. While on board the assis-*

tant got several drinks of gin so that he could hardly keep his watch in the light. He growled at me and insulted my wife. "

October 8, 1874: *"De Coury [an assistant keeper] had left oil leaking from the drum; it filled the overflow bucket and leaked two gallons on the floor. When I accused him of it he quit. "*

October 28, 1874: *"I took the first watch and called Asst. Butts at twelve midnight to relieve the watch; I went to bed. I awoke at half past four and went to look at the light, and it was very dim. I went up to see what was the matter. Asst. Butts was laying in the chair in the watchroom asleep, his stool on the trap door to prevent me from taking him by surprise for when I opened the door the stool fell over making a racket which awakened him. Besides he left the oil carrier on the stairs with two gallons of oil in it hoping I would fall over it. "*

November 4, 1874: *"Butts went to Key West and got drunk and came back to the station with two stone jugs of whiskey. He argued with me and quit. "*

January 24, 1876: *"Thomas Cassity [DeCoury's replacement] left this station for good after kicking up a row with me because I would not let him go to Key West. . . . "*

January 27, 1877: *"C.W. Ridlen [another assistant] when spoken to*

Stag stations, like St. George Reef Lighthouse, 6 miles off Northern California, were miserable assignments for men. Tempers could erupt over the most trivial things — bad coffee, a dropped dish, a sideways glance — and often such spats resulted in the men not speaking to one another for days, even weeks. In 1952 one man went mad. (U.S. Coast Guard)

about the cleaning of his glass kicked up a row with me and accused me of trying to run him out of the Lighthouse Service and swore he would have satisfaction if he could."

May 13, 1877: "I asked Mr. Ridlen to scrub the watch room . . . he cursed and . . . hurried to his room and began to play on the flute. . . ."

The entries continued like this, with each new assistant unable to work for Keeper Buckley. We have to wonder who was at fault here, for it appears no one could please Buckley. Perhaps he was among the few people who enjoyed the prolonged isolation of life on the Florida Reef and the anguish it caused his assistants. Most of the disagreements appeared to have centered on trips ashore, which Buckley obviously felt little need to take.

A letter from the assistant keeper of Sandy Hook Lighthouse, New Jersey, in December 1892 to the Third Lighthouse District Inspector addressed a problem that might today be labeled harassment:

I am sorry that I have to call on you, but I am tired of the profane abuse of the keeper. I have taken it for over two years without saying anything before. He is the most profane man at times that I ever heard talk; he has cursed me and called me very vile names a great many times for no good cause whatever, and if there is any way of stopping it I would like to have it done. I don't want you to injure the man in any way for he has a large family to support, and nice family too. I only want his abuse stopped.

I think he will tell you that I am not able to do the work here, but I do more than my share of the regular work and have done it all the time. Captain if you can give me one of the small lights to tend I would feel very grateful to you for I would like to be by myself and away from this man. Should there a vacancy occur on Staten Island or the N. Jersey Shore I would consider it a great favor if you would give it to me. I am the man Mr. West spoke to you about who lost a leg at the Battle of Coal Harbor."

Violence seldom erupted as a result of disagreements, but there were a few isolated cases. When tempers flared in far-off places, with no one around to police those involved, the consequences could be grisly, everything from child abuse to murder. At Currituck Beach Lighthouse, North Carolina Keeper W.G. Burris recorded a deplorable series of events in the 1890s:

May 11, 1895: "2nd Assistant cussed and abused the Keeper."
May 10, 1896: "Keeper went to Long Point for supplies and returned at
3:30 and found his boy 10 years old brutally beaten by one L.N. Simmons,
former keeper at this station, who is now teaching in a public school here
on this island."
June 1, 1896: "L.N. Simmons stopped in front of the station this morn-
ing and abused keeper and made threats. . . .Keeper requests a transfer to
some other lighthouse."

A letter in 1859 from Peter White, a port officer at Marquette, Michigan and directed to Thornton Jenkins of the Lighthouse Board, reveals the abusive behavior of the town's lighthouse keeper:

"Great complaint is made about the Keeper of the "Light" at this place. He is a habitual drunkard – frequently thrashes his wife and throws her out of doors. He has several times failed to "light-up" until near morning."

Even murder appears in Lighthouse Service records; newspapers and radio gave such ghastly events thorough and colorful airings. Tabloids of the day indulged readers' imaginations with journalistic hyperbola. When assistant keeper Charles Bjorling of Tillamook Light was suddenly removed from his job, local newspapers hustled to print the most outrageous explanations. It seemed Bjorling was not at all content with his second-rate position, and so passionate about his call to the lightkeeping profession that he stopped at nothing to gain a promotion. He was dismissed when it was determined that he had attempted to murder the head keeper at Tillamook Light by putting finely ground glass in the man's food.

The Associated Press released the following headline which ran in newspapers across the nation on November 21, 1958: "Keeper of Lighthouse Slain; Colleague Held. Men Quarrel During Fog Inside Quarters Alone; Domestic Triangle Blamed."

The place was Coney Island Lighthouse on Staten Island, New York. Keeper Jacob Hughes came to the lighthouse in 1957 with his wife Marion. Thomas Somogyi, also married and the father of three children, served as assistant keeper. According to Army personnel who took Jacob Hughes into custody, the men were at odds over flirtations with each others' spouses. When Somogyi began paying too much attention to Mrs. Hughes, a fight erupted in which Somogyi wielded a hammer and Hughes a knife. "A thick fog held the harbor in its grip Tuesday night," wrote a reporter for a Virginia newspaper that carried the story, "when the two keepers acted out their savage drama in their quarters inside the semicylindrical tower." The argument ended in tragedy when Hughes slashed Somogyi's throat. He bled to death before help could arrive.

Administrative Ailments

Certainly, serious problems at lighthouses were few, and most of the men and women who tended the beacons were a credit to the service. The troublesome situations surely had something to do with the nature of the job, but also with the disposition of the people who served at lighthouses. What little corruption existed — the illegal sideline businesses, the illicit sale of government property, the bungling of paperwork — might easily be blamed on the government itself. Had keepers been properly instructed, paid, and supervised, many of the enticements to err might have been avoided. Indeed, when the Lighthouse Service finally took stock of itself in the 1850s, many of the chronic problems disappeared.

The systematic lighting of the American coast had begun in colonial days with the Boston Light in 1716 and eleven more lighthouses before the Revolution. In 1789 this fledgling effort to make our shores safe was handed over to the new Federal Government under the auspices of the Treasury Department and Alexander Hamilton. Perhaps it grew too quickly for its own good, for mismanagement, graft, and a general lack of regulation left the Lighthouse Service in a deplorable state by the middle of the 19th century.

So many and so grave were the problems, a massive government investigation was launched in the 1840s and as a result of the findings, the service underwent drastic reorganization. In 1852 the newly created, nine-member Lighthouse Board gathered to make its report on the condition of the nation's sentinels. The following excerpts from that report reflect the state of misery into which lighthouse keeping had fallen:

Robbins Reef Lighthouse, New York Harbor:
    Richard Cary, keeper, took charge July 1, 1849. Absent; found a small boy in charge, sixteen years of age. Light in very bad order – dirty; and lamps not trimmed at 1 p.m. Lamps and burners out of adjustment.

Bodkin Point Lighthouse, Patapsco River, Maryland:
    Keeper's son and little daughter commenced taking down the lamps and reflectors [to clean them] so soon as the keeper saw the collector with us.

Navesink Lights, New Jersey:
    James D. Hubbard, principal keeper. No vocation; was a farmer when made keeper; four assistants; only one of the four found there when he took charge remains; the three others were dismissed by him without the authority or sanction of any one; no report made to the collector of the changes; took charge of the light August 28, 1849. . . . .The keeper keeps no daily account of expenditure, or journal of any kind. . . . . Never trims during the night, except when bad oil is used. . . . Principal keeper does not keep watch; goes to bed at 9 p.m.

C. J. Norton, assistant keeper at Maine's rock-island Saddleback Ledge Lighthouse in 1859, appears to have been a bit of a visionary concerning the problems at lighthouses: ". . . it is by changing keepers too often [that problems arise]. . . those [who are] inexperienced can do better on land." Norton may have realized that the government's practice of making political appointments at lighthouses, which required a change of the watch every few years, did not garner the kind of stability, routine, and pride in work needed to create a superior force of keepers. The old saying was: Whenever the watch changes at the White House, the watch changes at the lighthouse.

Not all troubles could be blamed on bureaucracy, though. Some keepers just didn't take to their work. It had a lot to do with character. Said Grace Humes: "Not everybody can be a lighthouse keeper. It takes a special kind of person to live a life like that, someone who's willing to work hard, make sacrifices, live tough."

BRASSWORK

Oh, what is the bane of the lightkeeper's life
That causes him worry, struggle, and strife,
That makes him use cusswords and beat up his wife?
    It's brasswork.
What makes him look ghastly consumptive and thin,
What robs him of health, of vigor, and vim,
And causes despair and drives him to sin?
    It's brasswork.
The devil himself could never invent,
A material causing more worldwide lament,
And in Uncle Sam's service about ninety percent
    Is brasswork.
The lamp in the tower, reflector and shade,
The tools and reflectors pass in parade
As a matter of fact, the whole outfit is made
    Of brasswork.
The oil containers I polish until
My poor back is broken, aching, and still
Each gallon and quart, each pint and gill
    Is brasswork.
I lay down to slumber all weary and sore,
I walk in my sleep, I awake with a snore
And I'm shining the knob on my bedchamber door
    That's brasswork.
From pillar to post, rags and polish I tote,
I'm never without them, for you will please note
That even the buttons I wear on my coat
    Are brasswork.
The machinery, clockwork, and fog signal bell,
The coal hods, the dustpans, the pump in the well,
Now I'll leave it to you mates, if this isn't, well,
    Brasswork.
I dig, scrub and polish, and work with a might,
And just when I get it all shining and bright,
In comes the fog like a thief in the night;
    Good-bye brasswork.

I start the next day, and when noontime draws near,
A boatload of summer visitors appear,
For no other purpose than to smooth and besmear
    My brasswork.
So it goes all the summer, and along in the fall
Comes the district machinist to overhaul
And rub dirty and greasy paws over all
    My brasswork.
And again in the spring, if perchance it may be,
An efficiency star is awarded to me,
I open the package and what do I see?
    More brasswork.
Oh, why should the spirit of mortal be proud,
In the short span of life that he is allowed,
If all the lining in every dark cloud
    Is brasswork.
And when I have polished until I am cold,
And I'm taken aloft to the Heavenly Fold,
Will my harp and my crown be made of pure gold?
    No, brasswork.
                        —Fred Morong
                Maine Lightkeeper, circa 1920

According to Lighthouse Service machinist and amateur poet Fred Morong, the never-ending task of polishing brass caused myriad problems at lighthouses. This keeper at Cape Flattery, Washington, in 1940 might have agreed. (U.S. Coast Guard Archives)

CHAPTER 12

IN THE FOOTSTEPS

OF THE KEEPER

*If I had a nickel for every trip up and down
those stairs. . .*
–Gladys Meyer Davis
Lightkeeper's Daughter
Ponce Inlet, Florida

"Lighthouses are an endangered species," according to Wayne Wheeler, founder and president of the U.S. Lighthouse Society, the nation's largest nonprofit group devoted to the preservation of lighthouses and their history and lore. Wheeler points out that the occupation of lighthouse keeping has already become obsolete and that the need for visible lights is rapidly being eclipsed by modern technology. Lighthouses are no longer being built, and the ones still operating have undergone drastic changes to make them self-sufficient and inexpensive to operate. There may come a time when lighthouses, in the traditional sense, are not needed at all.

As early as the 1920s, the government devised ways to operate lighthouses without keepers, but it took time for the idea of automatic lighthouses to catch on. There was something cold and uncaring about such conveniences; they made the mariner wary, and nostalgics could not abide lighthouses without human hands tending them every night. But economics prevailed. Thrift has always characterized the Lighthouse Service, but especially so after 1910, when the Bureau of Lighthouses was formed and a parsimonious chief of operations named George Putnam took over.

Putnam's emphasis on frugality was carried almost to extreme. Lightkeepers lived by the rule "use it up and wear it out" — paintbrushes were worn down to their handles before being replaced, brooms continued to sweep long after they had been reduced to stubble, even rags had to prove themselves generously shot with holes before new ones were issued. In addition, Putnam scrutinized the entire service to find those excesses that seriously hampered tightening of the budget. It quickly became apparent to Putnam that much fat could be trimmed by eliminating what he termed "overlighting" of the coasts and using automation technology to reduce the number of lightkeepers.

One of the first areas he addressed was multiple lights — old stations that had twin and triple towers. These were originally built before the development of a technology to differentiate lighthouses at night by means of light characteristics. After 1850, when flashing and occulting optics became available to U.S. lighthouse engineers, the need for multiple lights ended, but these stations continued in service for sentimental reasons. Putnam was not motivated by sentimentality, however, and he quickly curbed spending by reducing the multiple light stations to single beacons.

The termination of the "Three Sisters of Nauset" was typical of Putnam's economic moves. Built in 1838, these three petite sentinels had served the inshore traffic of small vessels along the backside of Cape Cod, each a white conical tower about 30 feet tall with a black lantern cap. From a distance at sea the three lighthouses resembled ladies in white dresses and black bonnets — sisters. An investigation in the 1840s reported that there was need for only one beacon on this site, but nothing was done to remedy the situation until 1911, when George Putnam ordered two of the towers extinguished.

Their beacons were removed and they were sold as government surplus to a family who moved them to another site about a mile away and, with a little clever carpentry work, converted them into summer cottages. The third "Sister" served until 1923, when it also was replaced and sold. It sat forlornly dark on the bluff and saw various types of employ, the least flattering of which was a brief career as a summer food stand. When the Cape Cod National Seashore was established in the 1960s, park service personnel quickly recognized the exceptional historic value of the "Three Sisters" lighthouses and expressed an interest in recovering them

Their former keepers would have despaired to see the Nauset Triple Lights in such dilapidated condition as they appeared in the early 1980s (top). These unique beacons, the nation's only set of triple lights, were established in the 1830s and quickly nicknamed the "Three Sisters" because of their diminutive stature (bottom). After decommissioning in the 1920s, these little sentinels spent years as beach cottages and a hamburger stand before being rescued by the National Park Service. Now restored and on display in a wooded area near their original sites, they greet thousands of visitors annually. (top - Elinor De Wire, bottom - National Archives)

for display. All three were eventually purchased from their private owners and restored. Today, they stand in a wooded park not far from the beach.

Many lighthouses were similarly discontinued in the first half of this century. A few, such as the sentinels at Old Point Loma in Southern California, at Stonington in Connecticut, and at Fairport, Ohio, were purchased by government and municipal agencies and opened to the public as historic landmarks. But most were either razed or transferred into private hands, where they underwent unseemly conversions to restaurants, gift shops, and vacation homes. In the 1960s, when the Coast Guard launched LAMP (Lighthouse Automation and Modernization Project), the number of abandoned and unattended lighthouses burgeoned and with them concern about the imprudent uses to which they were being put. People like Wayne Wheeler, then on active duty with the Coast Guard, expressed dismay over the loss of these important relics. Many were either demolished or excessively altered in appearance to accomodate new optics and other automatic machinery. In addition, 1966 Congressional legislation relating to historic preservation mandated that lighthouses nominated to or included on such grand lists as the National Register of Historic Places

Lighthouse guru Wayne Wheeler became interested in lighthouse preservation while working in the Coast Guard Aids to Navigation Office in San Francisco. He launched the U.S. Lighthouse Society in 1984 from his dining room table. It has since grown to almost 7000 members, has its own slick publication, and operates out of an archive-rich office in San Francisco's financial district with Wheeler as president. His motto? "Shine on!" (Courtesy of U.S. Lighthouse Society)

Standing on the lantern deck of the obsolete Old Point Loma Light years ago, a man seemed to salute, as if to say good-bye to the venerable old sentry. Fortunately for this lighthouse, restoration followed, and it was returned to its former glory as part of Cabrillo National Monument. (National Park Service)

could not be indiscriminately discarded as surplus real estate.

A decade later, while working in San Francisco for the Coast Guard's Twelfth District, Wheeler and his heritage-conscious staff came up with a number of creative options that offered a compromise between historic preservation and the Coast Guard's need to cut costs. Wheeler's work resulted in the transfer of several California lighthouses to groups and agencies that would preserve the unique character of the sentinels while making them available to the public. The charming little East Brother Island Light Station was carefully restored and converted to a bed and breakfast inn, with the knowledgeable counsel of Walter Fanning, who had lived at the station as a child. American Youth Hostels acquired the defunct keeper's quarters at Pigeon Point and Point Montara lighthouses, both of which had suffered deterioration and vandalism after being automated. The still-active but automated lighthouses at Big Sur, Point Bonita, and Point Reyes became showpieces in public parks and were periodically opened and interpreted for visitors.

During these same years in Maine, Coast Guard officer Ken Black was scrambling to save the historic mementos of New England lighthouses. He began with a small collection at the Coast Guard station in Rockland and eventually moved it into the town's Shore Village Museum where, in his retirement, he now serves as director. "Wheeler was saving the lighthouses," recalls Black, "and I was saving the stuff in them. We caught up to each other and realized we had common goals." With the energetic help of Black and many other enthused lighthouse buffs, Wheeler launched the U.S. Lighthouse Society in 1984. A number of satellite groups formed, each with its own particular focus. The Great Lakes Lighthouse Keepers Association set its sights on preserving the history and lore of several hundred lighthouses on the Great Lakes; the Lighthouse Preservation Society concentrated its efforts mostly on New England lighthouses. And scores of smaller organizations, mainly historical societies, took matters into their own hands by adopting individual lighthouses.

The Rose Island Foundation was typical. It formed in the 1980s to save the abandoned Rose Island Lighthouse in Narragansett Bay, Rhode Island. The sentinel was a shambles when a local resi-

As the traditional lighthouse keeper fades into the pages of history, replaced by modern technology and remembered only in journals and photographs, a new kind of keeper is emerging, one who assures that the winds of time and change do not erase the memory of what it was like to be a lighthouse keeper. This image from a 19th-century magazine preserves the ideal of "the keeper of the light." (*Harper's New Monthly Magazine*)

dent, Charlotte Johnson, decided to rescue it. As a child, she had been captivated by the quaint little house and beacon with its sturdy family, and she could not bear to see it lost. Realizing that a community effort was the lighthouse's last hope, she spearheaded the fundraising that ultimately put a gleam back in its lantern. The most creative part of the campaign was the slogan "own a piece of the lighthouse." Donors were permitted to buy parts of the lighthouse — shingles, bricks, windows, doors, etc. — on the condition that the pieces be left in place. The entire structure was refurbished to its former splendor.

Block Islanders fought fiercely to save their two historic sentinels. The North Light Commission formed in the late 1970s to raise funds to repair and relight "Old Granitesides," the lighthouse on Sandy Point at the north end of Block Island. A tireless devotee to the cause was the late John McPherson who, shortly before his death, was attempting to repair the tower's exquisite Fresnel lens. The English and French lens companies that manufactured

"Old Granitesides," the North Light on Block Island, Rhode Island, was saved by a group of tireless island residents in the 1980s. Today it is open as a museum. (Courtesy of Barbara Beebe Gaspar)

these huge optics years ago took the secrets of molding with them, leaving designers like McPherson experimenting in the dark. At the opposite end of Block Island, the Gothic-looking Southeast Light stood perilously near the edge of the erosive Mohegan Bluff in the 1980s. Nothing could be done to shore up the clay bluffs. The sea was relentless in its assault, stealing sand from the eastern shore of Block Island and carrying it to the other side. Local residents knew one powerful storm could send the lighthouse tumbling into the surf. It had happened to historic Great Point Light on Nantucket in April 1984; it could happen to Southeast Light. Block Islanders resolutely set about raising funds to move their lighthouse back from the cliff's edge. The project was a logistical nightmare and very expensive, but not impossible. The lighthouse could be moved by jacking it up and placing rollers beneath it. Storm after storm tore away more of the cliff behind the lighthouse as the fund raising campaign struggled to find some $2 million. The project became reality in August 1993, when the International Chimney Company of Buffalo, New York, and the Maryland-based Expert House Movers relocated the 4-million-pound Southeast Lighthouse 245-feet inland.

A hundred similar stories could be told about other lighthouses around the nation, accounts of individuals and communities holding fund raisers to save their beloved sentinels — selling T-shirts and coffee mugs, holding car washes and clambakes and raffles, and passing out bumper stickers with slogans like "Keep the Light Burning" and "I Brake for Lighthouses." Not every lighthouse needs to be moved, as Southeast Light did, but many require extensive repairs and a human presence to keep them in good shape. These are structures that were built to be lived in, to be someone's home. They are vestiges of an era when human hands were needed to do all the work, not robotics. They need our care if they are to remain the handsome old relics we want them to be. Many people are willing to keep the keeper alive through a kind of stewardship. These are the new guardians of the lights.

The final chapter in the story of lighthouse keeping in America seems to have a happy ending. The era of the lightkeeper has surely ended, but a new kind of keeper has emerged, one who not so much follows in the footsteps of yesterday's keeper as assures that the winds of time and change do not erase them. The new keepers dust and polish, scrape and paint, and tread up and down the spiral stairs, all to keep the legacy alive so that future generations will know what is was like to be a lighthouse keeper.

> *Oh, to be able to go back and live it all over*
> *again. . . . It was such a good life; I was so happy.*
> *–Marie Carr*
> *Lightkeeper's Wife*

The Harbor Light

The ancient lighthouse stands along the shore,
But it has not a keeper anymore.
Skilled hands that kept the lenses bright;
A guide for some lost seaman in the night;
The tender who turned upon the sea his watchful eye,
And, sleepless listened for the searching sailor's cry,
Has taken his last ride back to the shore.
The spiral stairway hears his steps no more,
And no more will his keen eye, or ear
See signals of distress, or hear
Cries of despair above the wind-flung sea.
Technology now switches on the light,
And times the beam that penetrates the night.
We've gained a long-sought economic goal;
Retained the Harbor light, but lost its soul.

Lawrence Anderson

An old engraving of the harbor beacon at Erie, Pennsylvania, sketches a romantic portrait of a lifestyle gone by. (U.S. Coast Guard Archives)

CHAPTER 13

THE BEST PLACES
TO WALK IN THE FOOTSTEPS
OF THE KEEPERS

As lighthouses became automated or abandoned as navigational aids, many were transferred to other agencies and new uses were found for them. The following list is a sampling of lighthouses that now operate as inns, hostels, vacation rentals, museums, and parks, along with museums and organizations that preserve lighthouse history. Not all lighthouses accessible for viewing or open to the public are included. Such a listing would be quite large and could easily warrant its own guidebook. Those listed here are among the author's favorites because of their architectural beauty and historical significance, or because they accurately portray the life of the lighthouse keeper through exhibits or other interpretive means. A few "pseudo-lighthouses" (replicas of real lighthouses) also appear on the list, each worth visiting because its builder/owner took special care to recreate a little of yesterday's lightkeeping in a modern setting.

When visiting lighthouses, keep in mind that many are open seasonally and operate with volunteer staff. Some are open on a limited basis or only on special occasions. A few are privately owned and not open to the public. It's best to call or write in advance to find out "what" is open and "when." Remember to respect private property and to obey "No Trespassing" signs and park rules.

Happy lighthouse hunting!

Key:
★ Tower Open to Public
✿ Museum / Exhibits
✪ Overnight Accomodations

Alaska
Rockwell Lighthouse ✪
Replica of Alaskan lighthouse
Box 277, Sitka, AK 99835
(907) 747-3056

California
Pigeon Point Lighthouse ★ ✿ ✪
AYH - Hostel
Pescadero, CA 94060
(415) 879-0633

Point Montara Lighthouse ★ ✿ ✪
AYH - Hostel
Box 737, Montara, CA 94037
(415) 728-7177

East Brother Light Station, Inc.
★ ✿ ✪
117 Park Place
Point Richmond, CA 94801
(415) 233-2385

Point Arena Lighthouse ★ ✿ ✪
Box 11, Point Arena, CA 95468
(707) 882-2777

Old Point Loma Lighthouse ★ ✿
Cabrillo National Monument
Cabrillo Historical Association
Box 6670
San Diego, CA 92106-0670

Point Fermin Lighthouse
Dept. of Recreation and Parks
Los Angeles, CA 90012
(213) 485-4880

Anacapa Island Lighthouse
Channel Islands National Park
1901 Spinnaker Dr.
Ventura, CA 93001

Point Pinos Lighthouse ★ ✿
Monterey History & Art
  Association
Box 805, Monterey, CA 93940
(408) 375-2553

Point Sur Lighthouse ★ ✿
Box 189, Big Sur, CA 93920

U.S. Lighthouse Society
244 Kearny St., 5th Floor
San Francisco, CA 94108
(415) 362-7255

Point Reyes Lighthouse ★ ✿
Point Reyes National Seashore
Point Reyes Station, CA 94956
(415) 663-8016

Point Cabrillo Lighthouse
California State Coastal
  Conservancy
1330 Broadway, Suite 1100
Oakland, CA 94612-2530

Battery Point Lighthouse ★ ✿
Lighthouse Caretakers
Box 396, Crescent City, CA 95531
(707) 464-3089

Connecticut
Stonington Point Lighthouse ★ ✿
Stonington Historical Society
Box 103, Stonington, CT 06378

Project Oceanology
(Educational tours of Long Island
  Sound lighthouses)
Avery Point, Groton, CT 06340

New Haven Harbor Lighthouse
Lighthouse Point Park
East Haven, CT 06512

Sheffield Island Lighthouse
Cruise with Norwalk Seaport
    Association
132 Water St.
S. Norwalk, CT 06854
(203) 838-9444

Delaware
Fenwick Island Lighthouse
Box 6, Selbyville, MD 19975

Florida
Amelia Island Lighthouse (replica) ✿
Amelia Island Lodging Systems
584 S. Fletcher
Amelia Island, FL 32034
(904) 261-4148

St. Augustine Lighthouse ★ ✿
81 Lighthouse Ave.
St. Augustine, FL 32084
(904) 829-0745

Key West Lighthouse Museum ★ ✿
938 Whitehead St.
Key West, FL 33040
(305) 294-0012

Jupiter Inlet Lighthouse ★
Loxahatchee Historical Society
805 N. Route 1, Jupiter, FL 33477
(407) 747-6639

Ponce de Leon Inlet Lighthouse
    Museum ★ ✿
4931 S. Peninsula Dr.
Ponce Inlet, FL 32019
(904) 761-1821

Cape Florida Lighthouse ✿
Bill Baggs State Recreational Area
1200 S. Crandon Blvd.
Key Biscayne, FL 33149

Garden Key Lighthouse ★ ✿
Take boat from Key West
Fort Jefferson National Monument
Box 279, Homestead, FL 33030

Old Port Boca Grande Lighthouse
    ★ ✿
Gasparilla Island Conservation &
    Improvement Association
Box 446, Boca Grande, FL 33921
(813) 964-2667

St. Marks Lighthouse
St. Marks National Wildlife Refuge
Box 68, St. Marks, FL 32355

Pensacola Lighthouse ★
(Periodic Open House)
Naval Air Station Pensacola
(904) 476-4314 or (904) 932-8965

Georgia
Tybee Island Lighthouse ★ ✿
Tybee Island Historical Society
Box 366, Tybee Island, GA 31328
(912) 786-5801

St. Simons Island Lighthouse ✿
Coastal Georgia Historical Society
Box 1136
St. Simons Island, GA 31522

Hawaii
Hawaii Maritime Center
(Aloha Tower and displays on
    island lights)
Pier 7, Honolulu Harbor
Honolulu, HI 96813
(808) 523-6151

Kilauea Lighthouse ✿
Fish & Wildlife Service
Box 87, Kilauea, HI 96754

Illinois
Grosse Point Lighthouse Park ★
Evanston Lighthouse Park
    Commission
Evanston, IL 60201
(312) 328-6961

Indiana
Michigan City Lighthouse ★ ✿
Washington Park
Box 512, Michigan City, IN 46360
(219) 872-6133

Maine
Isle au Haut Lighthouse ✿ ○
The Keeper's House
Box 26, Isle au Haut, ME 04645
(207) 367-2261

Lighthouse Motel & Cottage Court
✿ ○
Exhibit in Coffee Shop
Rt.1, Belfast Road
Camden, ME 04843

Bass Harbor Head Lighthouse
Acadia National Park
Box 177, Bar Harbor, ME 04609
(207) 288-3338

Fort Point Lighthouse
Fort Point State Park
Stockton Springs, ME 04981

Pemaquid Point Lighthouse ✿
Fisherman's Museum
New Harbor, ME 04554
(207) 677-2494

Marshall Point Lighthouse ★ ✿
Box 247, Port Clyde, ME 04855

Shore Village Museum ✿
Extensive displays and archives
104 Limerock St.
Rockland, ME 04841
(207) 594-0311

Maine Maritime Museum ✿
Exhibits on Maine lighthouses
Cruises to area lighthouses ★ ✿
Washington St., Bath, ME 04530

Seguin Lighthouse ★ ✿
Box 348, Georgetown, ME 04548

Portland Head Lighthouse ✿
1000 Shore Rd.
Cape Elizabeth, ME 04107
(207) 799-2661

"Lighthouse Digest"
(Hobbyist Publication)
Box 1690, Wells, ME 04090
(800) 758-1444

Maryland
Hooper Strait Lighthouse ★ ✿ ○
Chesapeake Bay Maritime Museum
Box 636, St. Michaels, MD 21663
(410) 745-2916

Chesapeake Bay B & B ○
(Replica of a screwpile light)
1423 Sharps Point Road
Anapolis, MD 21401
(410) 757-0248

Concord Point Lighthouse ★
Friends of the Lighthouse
Box 212
Havre de Grace, MD 21078

Drum Point Lighthouse ★ ✿
Calvert Marine Museum
Box 97, Solomons, MD 20688
(410) 326-2042

Massachusetts
Bass River Lighthouse ✿
The Lighthouse Inn
West Dennis, MA 02670
(508) 398-2244

Boston Lighthouse ★ ✿
Friends of the Boston Harbor
  Islands
P.O. Box 9025, Boston, MA 02114
(617) 523-8386

Flying Lighthouse Santa Project
Hull Lifesaving Museum
Hull, MA 02045

Lighthouse Preservation Society
Box 736, Rockport, MA 01966

Scituate Lighthouse ★ ✿
Scituate Historical Society
Scituate, MA 02066

Thachers Island Twin Lights
Thachers Island Association
Box 73, Rockport, MA 01966

Three Sisters Lighthouses
Nauset Beach Lighthouse
Highland Lighthouse
Cape Cod National Seashore
Wellfleet, MA 02667
(508) 349-3785

Plymouth Maritime Museum
Exhibits on area lighthouses
Ocean Spray Complex
225 Water St.
Plymouth, MA 02360
(508) 830-0688

Gay Head Lighthouse ★ ✿
Take ferry to Martha's Vineyard
Dukes County Historical Society
Box 827, Edgartown, MA   02539

Michigan
Big Bay Point Lighthouse ★ ✿
3 Lighthouse Road
Big Bay, MI 49808
(906) 345-9957

St. Helena Lighthouse ✿
Overnight Educational Workshops
Great Lakes Lighthouse Keepers
  Association
(313) 287-6318

Grand Traverse Lighthouse ★ ✿
Leelanau State Park
Grand Traverse Lighthouse
Foundation
Box 43, Northport, MI 49670

Old Presque Isle Lighthouse and
  Museum ✿
5295 Grand Lake Rd.
Presque Isle, MI 49777

Peninsula Point Lighthouse
  Picnic Area ★
Rapid River Ranger District
Hiawatha National Forest
Box 316, Escanaba, MI 49829

Rock Harbor Lighthouse ★
Isle Royale National Park
87 N. Ripley St.
Houghton, MI 49931-1895
(906) 482-0984

Seul Choix Lighthouse and Museum
✿
Gulliver, MI 49840

Sand Point Lighthouse ★ ✿
Box 1776, Escanaba, MI 49829
(906) 786-3763

Point Iroquois Lighthouse ★ ✿
Hiawatha National Forest
Box 273, Brimley, MI 49715
(906) 437-5272

White River Lighthouse ★ ✿
6199 Murray Rd.
Whitehall, MI 49461

Tawas Point Lighthouse ★
Tawas Point State Park
Tawas Beach Rd., Tawas, MI 48763
(517) 362-4429

*Point Aux Barques Lighthouse
   Museum* ★ ✿
Huron City Museum
Huron City, MI 48467
(517) 428-4123

Fort Gratiot Lighthouse ★
Omar & Garfield St.
Port Huron, MI 48060
U.S. Coast Guard Auxillary
(313)982-0891

Whitefish Point Lighthouse ✿
Great Lakes Shipwreck
   Historical Society
Whitefish Point
Paradise, MI 49649

South Manitou Island Lighthouse
★ ✿
Ferry from Leland
Sleeping Bear Dunes National
Lakeshore
Empire, MI 49630

Eagle Harbor Lighthouse ★ ✿
Keweenaw County Historical
   Society
Eagle Harbor, MI 49950

Big Sable Lighthouse ★
Pictured Rocks National Lakeshore
Big Sable Lighthouse Keepers
   Association
Box 673, Ludington, MI 49431

Sturgeon Point Lighthouse ★ ✿
Alcona Historical Society
Harrisville, MI 48740
(517) 724-6297

Old Mackinac Point Lighthouse ★ ✿
Fort Michilimackinac
Mackinaw City, MI 49701

*Great Lakes Lighthouse Keepers
   Association*
Box 580, Allen Park, MI 48101

Minnesota
Split Rock Lighthouse ★ ✿
2010 Highway 61 East
Two Harbors, MN 55616

New Hampshire
White Island Lighthouse
Isles of Shoals Steamship Company
Box 311
Portsmouth, NH 03802-0311
(603) 431-5500

New Jersey
New Jersey Lighthouse Society, Inc.
P.O. Box 4228
Brick, NJ 08723

Navesink Twin Lights ★ ✿
Twin Lights Historic Site
Lighthouse Road
Highlands, NJ 07732
(908) 872-1814

Sandy Hook Lighthouse
Exhibits at Visitor Center
Gateway National Recreational
    Area
Box 437, Highlands, NJ 07732
(908) 872-0115

Barnegat Lighthouse ★ ✿
Museum on 5th & Central
(609) 494-2016
Barnegat Light State Park
Box 167, Barnegat Light, NJ 08006

Sea Girt Lighthouse ★ ✿
Beacon Blvd. & Ocean Avenue
Sea Girt, NJ 08750
(908) 449-9337

Hereford Inlet Lighthouse ★ ✿
1st & Central Avenues
North Wildwood, NJ 08260
(609) 522-4520

Cape May Lighthouse ★ ✿
Box 164, Cape May, NJ 08204
(609) 884-5404

New York
Tibbetts Point Lighthouse ✿
AYH - Hostel
RR 1, Box 330
Cape Vincent, NY 13618
(315) 654-3450

Saugerties Lighthouse Conservancy
★ ✿ ✿
Box 654, Saugerties, NY 12477
B & B Reservations (914)246-9170

Selkirk Lighthouse Vacation Rental ✿
Box 228, Pulaski, NY 13142
(315) 298-6688

Horton Point Lighthouse ✿
Southold Historical Society
Box 1, Southold, NY 11971
(516) 765-5500

Fire Island Lighthouse ★ ✿
Fire Island National Seashore
Take ferry from Bayshore
Fire Island Lighthouse Preservation
    Society
Captree Island, Box C-8
Babylon, NY 11702
(516) 661-2556

Roundout Lighthouse ★ ✿
Launch from Hudson River
    Maritime Museum
Kingston, NY 12401
(914) 338-0071

Old Sodus Point Lighthouse ★ ✿
Sodus Bay Historical Society
Allen Rd., Sodus, NY 14551

Buffalo Lighthouse
Buffalo Lighthouse Association
1 Fuhrmann Blvd.
Buffalo, NY 14203

Fort Niagara Lighthouse ★ ✿
Old Fort Niagara Association
Youngstown, NY 14174

Genessee Lighthouse ★ ✿
70 Lighthouse Street
Rochester, NY 14617

Dunkirk Lighthouse ★ ✿
(716) 366-5050

Montauk Point Lighthouse ★ ✿
RFD Box 112, Montauk, NY 11954
(516) 668-2544

North Carolina
Currituck Lighthouse ✿
Outer Banks Conservationists
Box 1891, Manteo, NC 27954
(919) 453-4939

Bodie Island Lighthouse ★ ✿
Cape Hatteras Lighthouse ★ ✿
Cape Hatteras National Seashore
Box 675, Manteo, NC 27954
(919) 473-2111

Cape Lookout Lighthouse ✿
Take boat from Harkers Island
Cape Lookout National Seashore
131 Charles St.
Harkers Island, NC 28531
(919) 728-2250

Bald Head Lighthouse ★
Take ferry from Southport
Old Baldy Foundation
Box 3007
Bald Head Island, NC 28416

Ohio
Fairport Lighthouse ★ ✿
Fairport Marine Museum
129 Second Ave.
Fairport, OH 44077

Marblehead Lighthouse
State Road 163
Marblehead, OH 43440

Lorain Lighthouse
Lorain, OH 44052
(216) 288-8940

Oregon
Heceta Head Lighthouse ✿
Devils Elbow State Park
Siuslaw National Forest
Box 1148, Corvallis, OR 97339

Cape Meares Lighthouse
Cape Meares State Park
Tillamook, OR 97141

Yaquina Bay Lighthouse ★ ✿
846 Government St.
Newport, OR 97365

Rhode Island
Rose Island Lighthouse ★ ✿ ○
Take boat from Jamestown
Box 1419, Newport, RI 02840
(401) 847-4242

Southeast Lighthouse ★ ✿
North Lighthouse ★ ✿
Block Island Historical Society
Block Island, RI 02807
(401) 466-2982

Beavertail Lighthouse Museum ✿
Conanicut Island
Jamestown, RI 02835
(401) 423-3484

Watch Hill Lighthouse ✿
14 Lighthouse Rd.
Watch Hill, RI 02891
(401) 596-8757

South Carolina
Hunting Island Lighthouse ★ ✿
Hunting Island State Park
Box 668, Frogmore, SC 29920
(803) 838-2011

Hilton Head Lighthouse (new light) ★
Sea Pines Plantation
Hilton Head Island, SC 29925

Texas

Point Isabel Lighthouse ★
Point Isabel Lighthouse State Park
Port Isabel, TX 78578

Friendswood Lighthouse
Pseudo-Light
3502 FM 528
Friendswood, TX 77546

Vermont

Colchester Reef Lighthouse ★ ✿
Shelburne Museum,
   Lake Champlain
Shelburne, VT 05482
(802) 985-3344

Virginia

Assateague Island Lighthouse ✿
Exhibits in Visitor Center
Chincoteague National Wildlife
   Refuge
P.O. Box 62
Chincoteague, VA 23336
(804) 336-6122

Mariners Museum ✿
Exhibits on Chesapeake
   Lighthouses
Museum Drive
Newport News, VA 23606
(804) 595-0368

Cape Henry Lighthouse ★
City of Virginia Beach
Box 89, Virginia Beach, VA 23458

Lighthouses of the Virginian Sea
Preservation Society
27 Dalgren Rd.
Richmond, VA 23233
(804) 784-4060

Washington

North Head Lighthouse
Ft. Canby State Park
(206) 642-4184

Admiralty Head Lighthouse ★ ✿
Ft. Casey State Park
1280 S. Ft. Casey Rd.
Coupeville, WA 98239
(206) 678-4519

Mukilteo Lighthouse ★
Mukilteo Historical Society
Mukilteo, WA 98275

Coast Guard Museum
Exhibits on lighthouses
1519 Alaskan Way South
Seattle, WA 98134
(206) 286-9608

Wisconsin

Apostle Islands Lighthouses
Apostle Islands National Lakeshore
Box 4, Bayfield, WI 54814

Cana Island Lighthouse ★
Door County Maritime Museum
Baileys Harbor, WI 54202

Eagle Bluff Lighthouse ★ ✿
Peninsula State Park
Fish Creek, WI 54212

Bibliography

Chapter 1: Up the Spiral Stairs

Caldwell, Bill. *Lighthouses of Maine.* Portland, Maine: Gannet Books, 1986.

Davidson, Donald W. *Lighthouses of New England: From the Maritimes to Montauk.* Secaucus, N.J.: Wellfleet Press, 1990.

De Wire, Elinor. "Mainland Soil." *The Keeper's Log.* Spring, 1986.

Holland, Francis Ross. *America's Lighthouses.* Brattleboro, Vt: Stephen Greene, 1972.

Snow, E.R. *Famous Lighthouses of New England.* Boston: Yankee, 1945.

Snow, E.R. *Lighthouses of New England.* New York: Dodd Mead, 1973.

Chapter 2: All In A Day's Work

Adamson, Hans Christian. *Keepers of the Lights.* New York: Greenburg, 1955.

Carr, Marie. Interview. Beavertail Lighthouse, Rhode Island, June 1989.

Gibbs, James. *Lighthouses of the Pacific.* West Chester, Pa.: Schiffer Publishing, 1986.

Gleason, Sarah. *Kindly Lights.* Boston: Beacon Press, 1991.

Glunt, Ruth. *Lighthouses and Legends of the Hudson.* Monroe, N.Y.: Library Research Associates, 1975.

Holland, F.R. *America's Lighthouses.* Brattleboro, Vt.: Stephen Greene, 1972.

Hyde, Charles K. *The Northern Lights.* Lansing, Mich.: Two Peninsula Press, 1986.

Instructions to Light-Keepers & Masters of Light-House Vessels. Washington, D.C.: GPO, 1902.

Johnson, Arnold Burgess. *The Modern Lighthouse Service.* Washington, D.C.: GPO, 1890.

Jones, Stephen. *Harbor of Refuge.* New York: W.W. Norton, 1981.

Kobbe, Gustav. "Life in a Lighthouse." *Century Magazine,* January 1894.

Lighthouse Service Bulletin: (various monthly issues in the collection the National Archives, Washington, D.C.)

Living at a Lighthouse. Edited by LuAnne Gaykowski Kozma. Allen Park, Mich.: Great Lakes Lighthouse Keepers Association, 1987.

McCurdy, James. "Cape Flattery & Its Lights." *Overland Journal*, April 1898.

National Archives, Washington, D.C.; Record Group 26 (Various Letters and Correspondence).

Nordoff, Charles. "The Lighthouses of the United States." *Harper's New Monthly Magazine*, March 1874.

Putnam, George R. *Lighthouses and Lightships of the United States*. Cambridge, Mass.: Riverside Press, 1933.

Putnam, George R. *Sentinel of the Coasts*. New York: W.W. Norton, 1937.

Rattray, Jeannette Edwards. *The Perils of the Port of New York*. New York: Dodd Mead, 1973.

Snow, E.R. *The Lighthouses of New England*. New York: Dodd Mead, 1973.

Talbot, F.A. *Lightships and Lighthouses*. Philadelphia, Pa.: J.B. Lippincott, 1913.

The Keeper's Log, San Francisco, Calif.: U.S. Lighthouse Society, Fall 1989 & Spring 1990.

U.S. Coast Guard Crew, Oak Island, South Carolina. Interview. August 1983.

Wass, Philmore. *Lighthouse in My Life*. Camden, Maine: Down East Books, 1987.

"Welcome to Point Pinos Light Station." (Pamphlet distributed through the Monterey History & Art Association, Monterey, California).

Wheeler, Wayne. "The Keeper's New Clothes." *The Keeper's Log*, Summer 1985.

Willoughby, Malcolm F. *Lighthouses of New England*. Boston: T.O. Metcalf, 1929.

Chapter 3: Chasing Away The Fog

Clark, Admont. *Lighthouses of Cape Cod – Martha's Vineyard – Nantucket*. East Orleans, Mass.: Parnassus Imprints, 1992.

De Wire, Elinor. "Fog Songs." *Sea Frontiers*, May/June 1987.
De Wire, Elinor. "Voices in the Fog." *Weatherwise*, October 1991.
De Wire, Elinor. "Whale Oil and Wicks." *Mariners Weather Log*, Spring 1988.
Gibbs, James. *Lighthouses of the Pacific*. West Chester, Pa.: Schiffer Publishing, 1986.
Hall, Pat. *The Point Reyes Light*. Point Reyes, Calif.: Coastal Parks Association, Inc., 1979.
Holland, Francis Ross, Jr. *America's Lighthouses*. Brattleboro, Vt.: Stephen Greene, 1972.
Nelson, Sharlene P. & Ted W. *Umbrella Guide to Washington Lighthouses*. Friday Harbor, Wash.: Umbrella Books, 1990.
Shanks, Ralph & Janetta Thompson Shanks. *Lighthouses and Lifeboats of the Redwood Coast*. San Anselmo, Calif.: Costano Books, 1978.
Shanks, Ralph & Lisa Woo Shanks, editor. *Guardians of the Golden Gate*. Petaluma, Calif.: Costano Books, 1978.
Snow, Edward Rowe. *The Lighthouses of New England*. New York: Dodd Mead, 1973.

Chapter 4: Next To Nature
Adamson, Hans Christian. *Keepers of the Lights*. New York: Greenburg, 1955.
Baker, T. Lindsay. *Lighthouses of Texas*. College Station, Texas: Texas A & M University Press, 1991.
Cameron, Arthur. *The Lighthouse at Portland Head*. Privately printed, 1982.
Dean, Love. *The Lighthouses of Hawaii*. Honolulu, Hawaii: University of Hawaii Press, 1991.
DeGast, Robert. *The Lighthouses of the Chesapeake*. Baltimore, Md.: Johns Hopkins University Press, 1973.
De Wire, Elinor. *Guide to Florida Lighthouses*. Sarasota, Fla.: Pineapple Press, 1987.
De Wire, Elinor. "Whale Oil & Wicks." *Mariners Weather Log*, Spring 1989.
Floherty, John J. *Sentries of the Sea*. New York: J.B. Lippincott, 1942.
Gaspar, Barbara Beebe. Interview. Montville, Conn., April 1991.

Holland, F. Ross. *America's Lighthouses.* Brattleboro, Vt.: Stephen Greene Press, 1972.

Jones, Stephen. *Harbor of Refuge.* New York: W.W. Norton, 1981.

Manning, Gordon P. *Life in the Colchester Reef Lighthouse.* Shelburne, Vt.: Shelburne Museum, 1958.

Putnam, George R. *Lighthouses & Lightships of the United States.* Cambridge, Mass.: Riverside Press, 1933.

Putnam, George R. *Sentinel of the Coasts.* New York: W.W. Norton, 1937.

Snow, E.R. *The Lighthouses of New England.* New York: Dodd Mead, 1973.

Sterling, Charles A. *Hog Island, Virginia.* Privately printed, 1903.

The Keeper's Log, U.S. Lighthouse Society, San Francisco. Fall 1989.

Chapter 5: Tempest and Tide

Allen, Everett S. *A Wind to Shake the World.* Boston: Little, Brown & Co., 1976.

Baker, T. Lindsay. *Lighthouses of Texas.* College Station, Texas: Texas A & M University, 1991.

Cipra, David L. *Lighthouses and Lightships of the Northern Gulf of Mexico.* Washington, D.C.: U.S. Coast Guard, 1976.

Dean, Love. *Reef Lights.* Key West, Fla.: Historical Key West Preservation Board, 1982.

De Wire, Elinor. *Guide to Florida Lighthouses.* Sarasota, Fla.: Pineapple Press, 1987.

De Wire, Elinor. "Memorable Lighthouse Storms." *Mariners Weather Log,* Spring, 1990.

Gibbs, James. *Lighthouses of the Pacific.* West Chester, Pa.: Shiffer Publishing, 1986.

Holland, Francis Ross. *America's Lighthouses.* Brattleboro, Vt.: Stephen Green, 1972.

Lowry, Shannon and Jeff Schultz. *Northern Lights: Tales of Alaska's Lighthouses and Their Keepers.* Harrisburg, Pa.: Stackpole Books, 1992.

Mooney, Michael. "Tragedy at Scotch Cap." *Sea Frontiers,* March 1975.

Shanks, Ralph. *Lighthouses and Lifeboats of the Redwood Coast.* San Anselmo, Calif.: Costano Books, 1978.

Snow, E.R. *The Lighthouses of New England.* New York: Dodd Mead, 1973.

Chapter 6: Conflagration
"Blast Wrecks Bloody Point Light Station." Unidentified clipping in the files of Mariners Museum, Newport News, Virginia.
DeGast, Robert. *The Lighthouses of the Chesapeake Bay.* Baltimore, Md.: Johns Hopkins University Press, 1973.
De Wire, Elinor. "The Bulging Eye of Makapu'u." *The Keeper's Log,* Fall 1986.
De Wire, Elinor. "The Lighthouse Pele Spared." Unpublished manuscript.
De Wire, Elinor. "The Loneliest Place in the World." *The Keeper's Log,* Fall 1986.
De Wire, Elinor. "The Paradise Lights." *Aloha,* October 1986.
Fenton, Frank J. "Schooner Crashes into Lighthouse." *Newport News Times Herald,* Nov. 16, 1979.
Holland, F. Ross. *America's Lighthouses.* Brattleboro, Vt.: Stephen Greene Press, 1972.
Lighthouse Service Bulletin, Washington, D.C. January 1919, June 1925, January 1939.
McCormick, W.H. *The Modern Book of Lighthouses.* London: A & C Black, Ltd., 1936.
"Probe Cause of Blast on Lonely Lighthouse." Unidentified clipping in the Van Hoey Collection, St. Helen, Michigan.
Rattray, Jeannette Edwards. *The Perils of the Port of New York.* New York: Dodd Mead, 1973.
Schreiner, Samuel A. *Mayday! Mayday!* New York: Donald I. Fine, 1990.
Shanks, Ralph & Lisa Woo Shanks. *Guardians of the Golden Gate.* Petaluma, Calif.: Costano Books, 1990.
Snow, E.R. *Famous Lighthouses of New England.* Boston: Yankee, 1945.
Snow, E.R. *The Lighthouses of New England.* New York: Dodd Mead, 1973.
Stevenson, Alan. *The World's Lighthouses Before 1820.* London: Oxford University Press, 1959.
The Keeper's Log, U.S. Lighthouse Society, San Francisco. Winter

1986, Summer 1991, Winter 1991.
Witney, Dudley. *The Lighthouse.* Boston, New York Graphic Society, 1975.

Chapter 7: Children of the Light

Cameron, Arthur H. *The Lighthouse at Portland Head.* Privately printed, 1982.

Davidson, Donald W. *Lighthouses of New England From the Maritimes to Montauk.* Secaucus, N.J.: Wellfleet Press, 1990.

Emerson, Willie. *First Light.* East Boothbay, Maine: Postscripts, 1986.

Engle, Norma. *Three Beams of Light.* San Diego, Calif.: Tecolote Press, 1986.

Gross, Ruth Carr. Interview. Beavertail Lighthouse, Rhode Island, June 1989.

Kobbe, Gustav. "Heroism in the Lighthouse Service." *Century Magazine,* 1897 (Reprinted 1981 by Outbooks, Golden, Colorado).

"Lighthouses of New England." Connecticut Public Television, 1988. Audio Visual Collection of Mystic Seaport Museum.

Migliaccio, Fran. "The Girl Who Grew Up At North Light." *Block Island Times,* Nov. 28, 1992.

Pendleton, Marjorie. Interview. Charlestown, Rhode Island, April 1992.

Shanks, Ralph. *Lighthouses & Lifeboats of the Redwood Coast.* San Anselmo, Calif.: Costano Books, 1978.

Sherman, Martha P. "The Lighthouse Keeper's Daughter." *Tidings,* September 1991.

Snow, E.R. *Famous Lighthouses of New England.* Boston: Yankee, 1945.

Snow, E.R. *The Lighthouses of New England.* New York: Dodd Mead, 1973.

Thaxter, Rosamond. *Sandpiper: The Life and Letters of Celia Thaxter.* Hampton, N.H.: Peter E. Randall, 1963.

The Keeper's Log, U.S. Lighthouse Society, San Francisco. Summer 1990.

Chapter 8: Keepers in Skirts

"A Heroine of the Pacific." *Woman's World*, August 1929.

Adamson, Hans Christian. *Keepers of the Lights*. New York: Greenburg, 1955.

Barrett, Luther. "A Successful Woman Lighthouse Keeper." *Delta County Historical Society Newsletter*, July 1985.

De Wire, Elinor. "Keepers in Skirts." *Sea Frontiers*, January 1983.

De Wire, Elinor. "Women of the Lights." *American History Illustrated*, February 1987.

Engel, Norma. *Three Beams of Light*. San Diego: Tecolote Publishing, 1986.

"Fifty Years' Work: Woman Lighthouse Keeper's Record of Half a Century." (Unidentified article in the Coast Guard Archives, Washington, D.C.).

Gallant, Clifford. "Emily Fish: Keeper of Point Pinos Lighthouse." *The Herald Weekend Magazine*, Sept. 3, 1978.

Harrington, Frances. "The Heroine of Lime Rock." *Oceans*, November 1985.

Hemingway, William. "The Woman of the Light." *Harper's Weekly*, August 4, 1900.

Hyde, Charles K. *The Northern Lights*. Lansing, Mich.: Two Peninsula Press, 1986.

McLean, Karen. Interview, Kennebec River Light Station, July 1986.

Nelson, Sharlene P. and Ted W. *Umbrella Guide to Washington Lighthouses*. Friday Harbor, Wash.: Umbrella Books, 1990.

Perry, Frank. "California's Lighthouse Keeper Naturalist." *Pacific Discovery*, September 1980.

Perry, Frank. *Lighthouse Point*. Soquel, Calif.: GBH Publishing, 1982.

Schreiner, Samuel A. *Mayday! Mayday!* New York: Donald I. Fine, 1990.

Snow. E.R. *The Lighthouses of New England*. New York: Dodd Mead, 1973.

Thompson, Sue Ellen. "The Light is My Child." *The Log of the Mystic Seaport*, Fall 1980.

Wass, Philmore. Letter to the author dated Sept. 17, 1993. Surry, Maine.

Chapter 9: Companions
Beston, Henry. *The Outermost House.* New York: Viking, 1923.
Booth, Sandy and Scott Gamble. Interview. Boston Lighthouse, Little Brewster Island, May 1991.
Cameron, Arthur. *The Lighthouse at Portland Head.* Privately printed, 1982.
De Wire, Elinor. "Dogs of the Lighthouses." *Dog Fancy,* December 1983.
De Wire, Elinor. "Lighthouse Cats." *Purrrr!* October 1986.
Gaspar, Barbara. Interview. Montville, Connecticut, April 1991.
Gibbs, James. *West Coast Lighthouses.* Seattle, Wash.: Superior Publishing, 1974.
Grant, D.W., Duck Island Lighthouse. Letter, May 1985.
Jennings, Harold. *A Lighthouse Family.* Orleans, Mass.: Lower Cape Publishing, 1989.
The Keeper's Log, U.S. Lighthouse Society, San Francisco, Fall 1989.
Kobbe, Gustav. "Heroism in the Lighthouse Service." *Century Magazine,* 1897 (Reprinted 1981 by Outbooks, Golden, Colorado).
Shanks, Ralph. *Lighthouses and Lifeboats of the Redwood Coast.* San Anselmo, Calif.: Costano Books, 1978.
Shattuck, Clifford. *The Nubble.* Freeport, Maine: Cumberland Press, 1979.
Small, Connie. Interview. Kittery, Maine, July 1986.
Snow, E.R. *The Lighthouses of New England.* New York: Dodd Mead, 1973.
Terry, Karyn. Cape Neddick Light Station, Maine. Letter, December 1983.
Villiers, Alan. *Joey Goes to Sea.* New York: Charles Scribners Sons, 1939.

Chapter 10: Spectral Keepers
Bilek, Babette. "The Ghosts of Point Lookout Light." (Unidentified article in the collection of Shore Village Museum, Rockland, Maine.)
Black, Ken. Interviews. Shore Village Museum, Rockland, Maine. October 1985, July 1986.
Brent, Pamela. Interview. Fairport Marine Museum, Fairport, Ohio.

October 1990.

Dean, Love. *Reef Lights*. Key West, Fla.: Historical Key West Preservation Board, 1982.

De Wire, Elinor. "Spectres on the Spiral Stairs." *The Keeper's Log*, Winter 1986.

Gaspar, Barbara. Interview. Montville, Connecticut. April 1991.

"Heceta House: A History and Architectural Survey." (Clipping from the Jack Hettinger Collection, Spokane, Washington).

Jones, Lance. "Crew Maintains Keeper's Tradition: Seguin." *First Word*, April 1985.

Miller, Lischen M. "The Haunted Lighthouse at Newport By the Sea." *Lincoln County Historical Society, Pub. No. 10*, 1973.

Myers, Arthur. *The Ghostly Register*. Chicago: Contemporary Books, 1986.

Scheina, Robert. "The Wave-Swept Lighthouse at Minots Ledge." (Clipping in the collection of the U.S. Coast Guard Archives, Washington, D.C.)

Schwabel, Peg Connolly. "The Lighthouse at Minots Ledge." *The Compass*, August 1981.

Small, Connie. Interview. Kittery, Maine. July 1986.

Tugel, Nadine. "Battery Point Lighthouse: Ghosts, Dragons, Mermaids." Privately printed booklet.

Tugel, Nadine. Phone Interview. Battery Point Lighthouse, Crescent City, California. January 1992.

U.S. Coast Guard Crew, Ledge Lighthouse. Interview, New London, Connecticut. December 1985.

Wanner, Cheryl D. "Legends of Lincoln County." *Oregon Coast*, December 1986 and January 1987.

Witney, Dudley. *The Lighthouse*. Boston: New York Graphic Society, 1975.

Chapter 11: Light Less Bright

Colby, Bob. "Becalmed Visitor Livens a Stint on Ledge Light." Article in the Ledge Light file in the collection of the Town of Groton, Connecticut.

"Historic Lighthouse Shrouded By Mystery." *Maine Sunday Telegram*, October 9, 1986.

Humes, Grace. Personal Interview. Fire Island, May 1986.

Hyde, Charles K. *The Northern Lights*. Lansing, Mich.: Two Peninsula Press, 1986.

Johnson, Arnold Burgess. *The Modern Lighthouse Service*. Washington, D.C.: GPO, 1890.

Jones, Stephen. *Harbor of Refuge*. New York: W.W. Norton, 1981.

"Keeper of Lighthouse Slain; Colleague Held." *The Virginian Pilot*, November 21, 1958.

Lighthouse Service Bulletin, October 1916. (National Archives, Record Group 26 Curator's Collection)

"Lighthouses of New England." Connecticut Public Television, 1988. Audio-visual collection of Mystic Seaport Museum.

Livingston, Dewey. "The Keepers of the Light." *The Keeper's Log*, Winter 1991.

National Archives Record Group 26, Washington, D.C. Various letters and correspondence.

Stories of Bird Island. Privately printed, 1911. Collection of John Somers, Mystic, Conn.

Shanks, Ralph. *Guardians of the Golden Gate*. Petaluma, Calif.: Costano Books, 1990.

Snow, E.R. *Famous Lighthouses of New England*. Boston: Yankee Publishing, 1945.

The Keeper's Log. Winter 1986, Summer 1989, Winter 1989, Fall 1990, Spring 1991.

U.S. Coast Guard. Personal Interviews with Lightkeepers, Ledge Lighthouse, December 1985.

INDEX